First to *Damascus*

First to Damascus

The Great Ride and Lawrence of Arabia

Jill, Duchess of Hamilton

Kangaroo Press

First published in Australia in 2002 by Kangaroo Press,
an imprint of Simon & Schuster (Australia) Pty Limited
20 Barcoo Street, East Roseville NSW 2069

A Viacom Company
Sydney New York London

Visit our website at www.simonsaysaustralia.com

© Jill, Duchess of Hamilton 2002

National Library of Australia
Cataloguing-in-Publication data

Hamilton, Jill, Duchess of
    First to Damascus: the Great Ride and Lawrence of Arabia.

    Bibliography.
    Includes index.
    ISBN 0 7318 1071 6.

    1. Australia. Army. Australian Light Horse. 2. World War,
    1914-1918 – Campaigns – Palestine. 3. World War, 1914-1918
    – Cavalry operations. 4. World War, 1914-1918 – Participation,
    Australian. I. Title.

940.434

Cover design: Gayna Murphy GREENDOT
Internal design: Avril Makula GRAVITY AAD
Typeset in Garamond 11.5 pt on 15 pt
Printed in Australia by Griffin Press

10 9 8 7 6 5 4 3 2

Dedication

—◦◦◦—

My father owned a horse in Egypt. It carried him from the shadow of the Pyramids, across the deserts to Palestine and to the fringes of one of the last great cavalry feats in the history of warfare. This book is dedicated to that horse – and to the 50,000 horses shipped from the Australian bush to Egypt, Palestine and Syria in the First World War, under the care of Banjo Paterson, never to return. Monuments, after all, can be in words as well as in stone.

For the bushmen love hard riding where the wild bush horses are,
And the stock-horse snuffs that battle with delight...
THE MAN FROM SNOWY RIVER – BANJO PATERSON

A percentage of the royalties of this book will go to the Brooke Hospital for Horses in Cairo – this charity was set up to care for some of the horses that never came home.

Contents

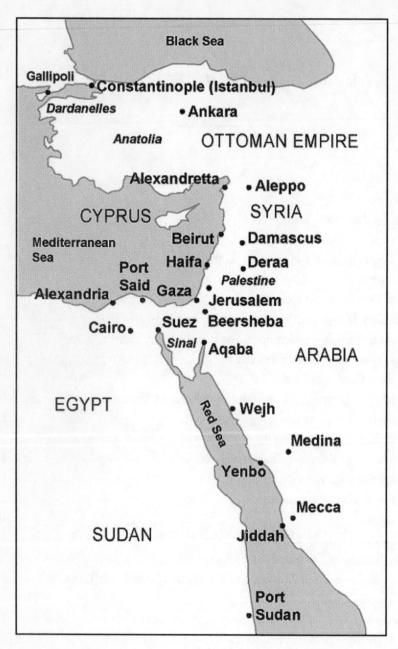

Map of the Middle East c.1914, when Palestine was still part of Syria.

Timeline – Middle East 1914–18

1914
4 August	Britain declares war on Germany.
November	Ottoman Empire enters World War I on side of Germany. Sultan proclaims a *jihad*.

1915
3 February	First Turkish attack on Suez Canal is repulsed.
18 March	Naval attempts to force the Dardanelles.
25 April	Landings at Gallipoli – Anzac Cove and Cape Helles.
6 August	Landing at Suvla Bay.
December	Evacuation of Anzac and Suvla.
14 July 1915 – 30 January 1916	
	Letters exchanged between Sherif Hussein of Mecca and Sir Henry MacMahon, British High Commissioner in Egypt.

1916
January	Evacuation of Cape Helles.
March	Formation of Egyptian Expeditionary Force.
April	Action at Katia; in Mesopotamia the British surrender at Kut.
May	Sir Mark Sykes (for Britain) and Charles Georges-Picot (for France) make a secret agreement dividing much of the Middle East between France and Britain into zones of influence, with Palestine internationalised.
June	Arab revolt against Turks in Hejaz begins.

August	Battle of Romani.
December	Action of Magdhaba. (In Britain D. Lloyd George succeeds H.H. Asquith as Prime Minister.)

1917

January	Action at Rafa.
26 March	First Battle of Gaza.
6 April	United States of America enters the war.
19 April	Second Battle of Gaza.
28 June	Allenby takes over command.
31 October	Capture of Beersheeb.a
7 November	Fall of Gaza.
November	Letter from British foreign secretary, Lord Balfour to Lord Rothschild: Britain 'views with favour the establishment in Palestine of a national home for the Jewish people...'
9 December	Capture of Jerusalem.

1918

21 February	Capture of Jericho.
March – May	First and second raids east of Jordan.
19 September	The Great Ride begins with decisive attack on Turks.
23 September	Capture of Haifa. (Six days later on the Western Front the Hindenburg Line broken.)
1 October	Capture of Damascus.
3 October	Prince Feisal, with British support, takes military control over Damascus.
8 October	Occupation of Beirut.
26 October	Occupation of Aleppo.
31 October	Armistice with Turkey signed at Mudros.
11 November	Armistice with Germany.

1919

February	Paris Peace Conference

Prologue

First light confirmed a scene of horror. During the night, horses and men had gone down together in hundreds and died in one tangled, bleeding mass. The ground was thick with the dead and the dying. Most of the fugitives in the Barada Gorge, the main escape route to Beirut, were Turkish and German soldiers who had refused to surrender and had been machine-gunned under orders from High Command.

Sealing all the exits of Damascus was urgent. The British wanted the Turkish and German military commanders, troops and officials to surrender, not to escape, but many, including Mustafa Kemal, had already raced ahead. At great speed, leading the remnants of his army, he had galloped out of range. Narrowly, he had escaped becoming one of the 40,000 prisoners taken in less than a fortnight. When the Allies had opened fire, the Turks in the front of the column had tried to turn back to the city, but the push of the people behind them was so strong that they were shoved forward into the zone of endless bullets pouring down from the cliff above.

After four centuries, the crescent moon and star flag of the sprawling Ottoman Empire, which had fluttered over Damascus since 1516, was soon to be hauled down. World War I had just entered its fifth year. The British were about to have a significant victory in the Middle East, a conquest that would give them a dominant role in the area.

Night and day since 19 September 1918, the Allies had relentlessly gone on in pursuit of the Turkish soldiers, whose stirring war cry of 'Allah! Allah! Allah!' was all too familiar. Now thousands were trying to flee before the British army finally seized the fabled city. Hundreds of dead men, horses and even a flock of dead sheep, lay in between broken-down vehicles, abandoned guns, machinery and disabled transport, blocking the path of the advancing horsemen. Some unlucky human survivors were heard, feebly calling for water. Those who were still conscious gazed with eyes that begged for a little mercy; mercy that they knew would not come from the Arabs. The air was heavy with the nauseating smell of unburied corpses of men and beasts. At dusk, the prowling jackals would close in to perform their funeral rites.

As the riders made their way through the dead and wounded, they took care that the horses' iron hooves would not trample and mangle the faces of the fallen. Corpses were strewn everywhere. Groans and screams echoed pitifully in the silent dawn. The animals waited either for rescue, the relief of a quick pistol shot or a bayonet stab.

In the half-light of early morning, a troop of scouts raced back. For nearly a mile ahead the road was almost impassable. Progress through the debris was slow – both the riders and their horses were showing signs of exhaustion. Most of the soldiers – from the Kimberleys, Geraldton, Perth, Kalgoorlie and the back of Broome – felt like old campaigners now. Thirteen days earlier, they had started at Jaffa (from where the famous orange had taken its name), then swept up the coast of Palestine on what they already referred to as the 'Great Ride'. Few mounted troops and horses could have endured such a journey. Feeding and watering 12,000 horses and their riders as they invaded new territory, let alone the 57,000 troops in the rear, together with the tens of thousands of camels, mules and donkeys, was such a formidable task that both man and beast often went without forage and water.

This was the largest group of cavalry ever used in an advance by the British army, and the largest deployed in modern times. It was on a par with the cavalry at Waterloo or at Omdurman with the Hussars against the Mahdi's Black Flags when Winston Churchill charged against the Dervishes.

Although the Australian mounted troops' mastery of horses set tham apart and they received the admiration and adulation now reserved for pop bands, film stars and footballers, few people are aware of their major role in the fall of Damascus. It was to be the culmination of a campaign that had started four years earlier in Gallipoli.

Usually, the disastrous nine months of the Gallipoli campaign are seen in isolation, not as part of the ongoing campaign between the British and the Turks in the western Mediterranean, but between 1915 and 1918, battles had endlessly dragged on between two empires: the shrinking Ottoman Empire and the expanding British Empire that encircled the globe. By chance, on the roads to Damascus, two of the main players on the Turkish side were the same commanders as had been at Gallipoli: Mustafa Kemal and Otto Liman von Sanders. For twelve days, the British Desert Mounted Corps had been pursuing them, from Nablus and Nazareth. But now on the steep and terrible hills above Damascus the wheel of fortune was turning full circle. Kemal, despite fighting desperately, was losing.

God, the Koran and the Germans were failing the Turks. The Germans, too, had overrated the effect of the Sultan announcing a *jihad* – a holy war. Strong though the Muslim faith was, it had not proved a unifying force. The Sherif (Governor of Mecca) and the British – with much help from Lawrence – defused the *jihad* so effectively that few people now associate the word with World War I.

Britain's Egyptian Expeditionary Forces, with headquarters in Cairo, had led the offensive around the Mediterranean coast and, right from the beginning, had defiantly used Muslim soldiers, pitting co-religionists against each other. (This was a separate operation from the British campaign run by the India office in Mesopotamia, which does not fall within the scope of this book.) The four-year operation can be divided into four distinct phases, each one with a different British commander.

The first, in February 1915, the initial Turkish–German offensive against the Suez Canal, was successfully repulsed by General Sir John Maxwell; second, Gallipoli, was where the Turks, under the German general, Otto Liman von Sanders, aided by Mustafa Kemal, later known as Ataturk, had defeated General Sir Ian Hamilton's forces; the third was the slow British advance across the Sinai Peninsula, led by Sir Archibald Murray between 1916 and 1917, which ended in disaster for the British when General Kress von Kressenstein had twice beaten them at Gaza. General Sir Edmund Allenby led the fourth and final phase. After breaking through Gaza at the end of 1917, he had captured Jerusalem. Merged into the last two phases of the Turkish–British conflict was the guerrilla warfare of the Arab Revolt, immortalised in the *Seven Pillars of Wisdom*, by T. E. Lawrence.

Capturing Damascus had seemed a wild dream when Lawrence, soon to be known as 'Lawrence of Arabia', had first proposed it to the Arabs in 1916. It was then one of the great cities of the Middle East, more central to the region than Cairo or Baghdad and, as Lawrence later wrote, 'the climax of our two years' uncertainty'. He again stressed its importance in his book's epilogue: 'Damascus had not seemed a sheath for my sword when I landed in Arabia; but its capture disclosed the exhaustion of my main springs of action'.

The Australians pummelled the road through the deep Barada Gorge, down the barren, steep hills. Lawrence, who had been part of the group that had bivouacked in their rough camp on the ridge above the gorge the previous night, was not, as planned, behind them. With his small stature arrayed in extravagant, flowing robes similar to those of a desert sheikh, complete with Bedouin headdress and dagger, standing beside his huge armoured Rolls Royce, the 'Blue Mist', he was more than noticeable. Below the minimum height for soldiers, Lawrence had not qualified for active service like his two brothers, who had both been killed in France. He had gone into the army through the intelligence department, and for two years had acted as British liaison officer to Prince Feisal and the Arab irregulars. He was already renowned for his daring guerrilla tactics, especially blowing up trains. With Prince Feisal, the small Arab regular army and the colourful rag-tag band of

Arab irregulars, he had rendezvoused with the Australians at the town of Deraa. Both groups had been progressing in a northerly direction for over a year, but the last few days had been the first time that the two forces had been in the same area. Now, having slept briefly beside his car, Lawrence was now nowhere to be seen.

In the distance, the Australian horsemen could see the indistinct outlines of the slender white minarets and the glittering domes of Damascus's mosques. They horsemen were still too far away to hear the holy chants of the Muslims in the mosques; still oblivious to the destruction, calls to prayer still rang out. Under the threat of sniping from the odd survivor in the dense undergrowth on either side of the Barada Gorge, the men of the 10th Light Horse Regiment flung themselves from their horses, and proceeded to clear a path through this shambles. When they pushed the dead to the side of the road, a quick count revealed 370 Turkish corpses. Wounded Turks – and they were in their hundreds – were carried to the grassy bank of the river. Arrangements were made for them to be picked up by ambulances later.

Once the men were past the bodies, the command to 'Push on!' was given. Short of water, short of food and short of sleep, their faces smeared with sweat and dirt, their lips dry and cracked, the Australians rode on. Engulfed in a thick cloud of dust, they galloped as fast as the steep descent and the stamina of their horses would allow. The weather was hotter than usual for early autumn. Spirits rose. The river in front was not a mirage. It was forbidden to drink straight from rivers but, as always, some men filled the crown of their felt hats with water and let their horses drink. Others also managed to splash their eyes. But the unofficial halt was short.

Damascus, reputedly the oldest city in the world to be continuously inhabited, had for centuries been a vital nerve centre of the sprawling Ottoman Empire and the key to Syria. Soon, though, this fabled city was to be taken over by the Allies. And soon the question would arise – who entered first? Was it the Australians? Was it the Arabs? Had Lawrence descended the hill by another route, met up with some Arabs and got there first? Was there really a sham entry staged by the British to deceive the French? Did the Australians unwittingly undermine the Arabs' quest for self-government in the ruins of the Ottoman Empire? What was the significance of the order to the Australians not to go into Damascus?

As political consequences would follow from the claim of who was first into Damascus, each side, each faction, was passionate about the honour of being the first who entered. Even war diaries differ in their answers. Historians have made the debate about who was first in to Damascus a bone of contention. The chaos and confusion at Damascus of different forces reaching the city at similar and/or overlapping times created a scenario where claims could be staked – and pushed aside by counter-claims. While some books present the 10th Light Horse as the first past the post, in others Lawrence and the Arabs are not only the winners, but are often depicted as the real victors of the campaign. The issue of who was first to Damascus went far beyond personal pride.

Professor Eliezer Tauber, of the Bar-Illan University in Israel, goes so far as to say, in his book *The Arab Movements in World War I*: 'One of the most controversial questions in the history of the First World War in the Middle East is the question of who conquered [Damascus], or to be more exact, who reached Damascus first.' Because of the Declaration to the Seven – a statement made by British officials in the Arab Bureau in Cairo in mid-1918 – the question of who arrived first in Damascus was critical. The Declaration stated that the British would recognise Arab independence in Arab areas that had been independent before the war, or that had been liberated by the Arabs themselves. Therefore the question of who got to Damascus first was significant enough for people to distort the truth. More importantly, the fate of this fabled city could affect the sharing of the lands in territories around it.

Could there really have been an error in the official reporting of the date and hour? The 1951 edition of *Encyclopaedia Britannica* says that Lawrence, '…after breaking up the enemy's trans-Jordan army, entered Damascus some hours ahead of the British. Lawrence took charge of the city till Allenby could reach it, and suppressed attempts at reaction'. The historian B. H. Liddell Hart wrote that Damascus was taken with the help of 'two comparatively novel tools – aircraft and Arabs'. Leon Uris's epic novel *The Haj* says that Feisal 'entered Damascus and had himself proclaimed King of Syria…'.

Respected historian Elie Kedourie was one of the earliest and strongest advocates of the theory that the Australians were first into Damascus. Tauber, too, thought they were first there. But then Professor Stephen Tabachnick, at Memphis University, joined in the debate to resolve the question (as far as it can be resolved) of whether or not Lawrence was truthful about who actually entered first. Qualifying his remarks with 'it may well be a matter of interpretation', he cautioned me to remember that city limits were not always clearly delineated.

David Lean's 1962 prize-winning film, *Lawrence of Arabia*, starring Peter O'Toole, gives the impression that Lawrence was first into the city. No Australian horsemen appear in it at all. Robert Bolt adapted the screenplay from Lawrence's classic history of the campaign, *Seven Pillars of Wisdom*. In this, Lawrence is the central figure and narrator, unfolding the campaign's grandeur, its epic proportions, its brutality, cruelty and gore. Both book and film omit to mention the Australian Light Horse galloping towards Damascus, let alone ever entering it, or the twelve-day cavalry offensive by the Australian horsemen and the pitched 'head-on' battles fought by British troops.

The jostling, politics and jealousies at the gates of Damascus were not reported at the time. My interest stems from my father, Robbie Robertson, who was a trooper with the 10th Light Horse in the last year of World War I. While writing a book on Napoleon and his horses, I became curious about my father and his warhorse.

I decided to write about the story of the Light Horse in the Middle East during the war; not a 'drums and trumpets' history with details of a long string of battles, but a story giving an overall view of its achievement. It lays no claim to historical completeness. At the same time as following the Light Horse from Gallipoli in 1915 to Syria in 1918, I decided to try to unravel the controversial and touchy question of 'Who was first to Damascus?' In searching for the answer to this question, I also found the reasons why details of the campaign have remained mostly in obscurity.

The fact that Field Marshall Earl Wavell, who had been Allenby's Chief-of-Staff in the Middle East, praised the advance as the largest body of cavalry employed in modern times under one commander is usually forgotten. He went so far as to say that it was 'the greatest exploit in history of horsed cavalry, and possibly their last success on a large scale...'. The cavalry historian, the Marquess of Anglesey, called it 'the last [campaign] in the history of the world in which the mobility conferred by men on horseback was successfully employed on a large scale. Never before in the annals of the British army had so numerous a mounted force been employed'.

No matter how he is described, Lawrence is usually mentioned in histories of the Middle East campaign, whereas the Australians are usually omitted. In the battle-filled fortnight that preceded the fall of Damascus, Lawrence and the Arabs usually overshadow all other participants, such as the Australian Light Horse, who formed the bulk of the cavalry, together with regiments from New Zealand, India, Britain and France. Another point usually omitted in descriptions of the campaign is the support given to the horses by the aircraft. This combination of cavalry and air power was unique in military history. In Europe, aircraft were restricted by bad weather and limited landing places, but in Palestine and Syria, pilots could take advantage of the clear skies and some of the immense treeless plains for landings and take-offs, although flamingoes, once they were inured to the noise, could be slow to move and got in the way.

To disentangle the mystery, I realised I would have to entwine the stories of the Australians in the Great Ride with the role of Lawrence in the Arab Revolt and as an intelligence officer. Did some of the ambiguity lie in the fact that 'Lawrence of Arabia' was a forerunner of cloak-and-dagger intelligence officers? Professor Tabachnick raised the possibility when he asked, 'Does he [Lawrence] see himself as a heroic knight or a cynical agent? Is he a dreamy arts graduate forced to participate in a brutal war that destroys him, or a willing sadomasochist who loves war too much?'

Wanting to extract the truth from the blurred falsehoods and extravagant claims that so often, and so casually, accompany war, I set off to Damascus, Deraa, Jaffa, Jerusalem, Amman and many other places touched on during the advance into Syria. No Hashemite royal archives opened their hitherto sealed doors, but the fascinating chain of events that led the Allied and the Arab forces to meet in Damascus still needed to be unresolved. The campaign, plotted in London, Syria, Cairo, Paris, Berlin, Constantinople (Istanbul) and Damascus, was shaped by many players, including the Arab irregulars with Lawrence, the German generals with the Turkish troops, the Egyptian Expeditionary Forces General Headquarters and, of course, the individual corps, divisions and regiments.

Despite writing the 1,188 pages of Lawrence's official biography, Jeremy Wilson, former chairman of the Lawrence Society, ignores the Australian entrance into Damascus. When answering my request for information on who was *first* into Damascus he said:

> *In the end, the problem for most researchers is simply logistical: the documents are split between London and Australia, and no-one has had the resources to study both sides...*

Wilson overlooks the hundreds of overseas researchers welcomed into the library of the Australian War Memorial in Canberra, some of whom have been given fellowships. Among them were Dr Yigal Sheffy of Tel Aviv University and Dr Matthew Hughes from Northampton University in England. Their theories, together with those of Tauber, and the papers delivered during the Israeli–Turkish International Colloquy held in Tel Aviv and Istanbul in 2000, have thrown new light on the Middle East during World War I – and the role of the Australians in it.

Wilson stressed, in his reply, that:

> *The capture of Damascus is a fuzzy area in Lawrence's life and could do with clarification. I don't see this as a question of Lawrence's version against the Australian version, because in their more moderate forms both versions are probably correct. But there are unanswered questions, and the documents must exist to establish exactly what happened. I am intrigued, for example, by [General Sir Harry] Chauvel's differing accounts, and by insinuations in the 1922 text of* Seven Pillars *that are toned down in the subscriber's abridgement.*

Wilson's allusion to 'differing accounts' by the corps commander was challenging. Were the Australian reports really contradictory? As with everything to do with special or undercover agents and espionage, it seemed shrouded in mystery. In 2001, when the British Foreign Office began lifting the embargo on certain old intelligence files, more contradictions emerged, but at the same time, paradoxically, more clarity. Research led me not just to files, but to one of the most exclusive clubs in the world, the Special Forces Club in Knightsbridge, in the heart of London. Although details of the intelligence organisation in Cairo that employed Lawrence were still not easy to come by (like much to do with the Secret Service), something filtered through, as will be seen at the end of this book, which made the story clearer.

The great-grandson of an Irish horse-breaker, my father was the proudest of riders. Through persistence and a little lying – he was only sixteen – he had been accepted into Western Australia's mounted infantry. With neither a bridle nor the crucial bit, he could turn a horse by tapping on its neck. Skilled though he was, the tough school of the Outback, where he had learnt to tame wild bush horses, did not produce riders who cared for the niceties of dressage, accoutrements, class distinctions – or rules.

Riding had given him a nonchalant sense of daring, and like his father, he was also a gambler. Risking arrest, he had briefly run a 'two-up' school both in the back streets of Cairo and twenty miles away in Heliopolis. Two shiny copper Australian coins, with the profile of George V on the front and the word 'penny' on the reverse, usually jingled in his pocket in expectation of a game. Whenever the cry 'Come in spinner!' was heard, he would flick and toss the lucky coins with dexterity from the tips of two outstretched fingers. Also always ready for a quick round of poker, he kept a well-thumbed pack of cards inside his khaki jacket with his cigarette papers, or if he was in luck, some Woodbines or Navy Cut.

There is a photograph of my father taken in the Middle East. He is astride his faithful steed, sitting deep in the saddle, wearing the uniform of the Australian Imperial Force (AIF). I have looked at this equestrian picture nearly every day of my life, yet I do not really know my father, or even his horse's name. Overcome with emotion at any mention of his horse, he rarely spoke of him. When a child, I mentally fused my father with his battle-scarred animal until they became a single entity, as they seemed to be in the photograph. If I gaze long enough at the picture, tears well up in my eyes. I see him on his horse galloping across those sandy and stony deserts, heading towards uncertainty and heartbreak.

Over two decades after the Great Ride, when I was born, my father was still proud of having once been in the Light Horse. But despite always wearing his Returned Soldiers' League badge on the lapel of his fine wool suits, he was one of a minority who did not attend ceremonies. We never went to Anzac Day services. He told his sister, Dorothy, that anything to do with the slaughter was too much for him. The one parade in which he did take part was traumatising. Years later, he said to our mother, 'I hate bringing back those times'. Like many young men, he had enlisted with enthusiasm, only to find himself dehumanised, disillusioned and exploited – appalled at the thought of what he was obliged to do with his sword and rifle in either self-defence or the heat of combat. The poet, Siegfried Sassoon, who tried 'to touch the hearts of men with poetry', described similar sentiments:

> *I stood with the Dead, so forsaken and still:*
> *When dawn was grey I stood with the Dead.*
> *And my slow heart said, 'You must kill, you must kill:*
> *'Soldier, soldier, morning is red'.*

My father's sister explained how my father was also forced to kill the one thing he loved. He never, she believed, recovered emotionally from having to shoot his beloved horse. Shooting his constant companion was the only way to save him from being sold as a beast of burden to join the overworked wretches in the streets of Cairo or in quarries or mines. (Many horses were so cruelly treated that in the 1930s, a charity, the Brooke Hospital for Horses, was set up to care for the survivors.)

Australian men in those days had no outlet for their grief other than rage or drink. My father shut part of himself down and bore the emotional scars for the rest of his living days. Remembering what his sister had told me, it is possible that he was suffering from post-traumatic stress disorder, but there was little help then available for the war-damaged soldier, except advice such as 'Go home; get on with a job; be a man!'

I lived with Robbie Robertson for fourteen years but can recall no closeness. We shared over 5000 days and nights in a respectable but dreary liver-coloured brick house on pale stone foundations near a golf course, three miles from Manly beach, Sydney. At the age of fifty-three, mumbling something about feeling unwell, he collapsed on the floor and died from a massive heart attack. He had not seemed the same since returning from a short business trip overseas four months earlier – even though he was, at last, able to talk in an easy manner about some of his experiences. The Italian ship sailing to Naples had gone via the Suez Canal, taking him briefly back to his old haunts from the war around Cairo. Heavier and not so agile, he again rode out to the Pyramids at Giza this time, not riding his own horse by moonlight but riding a tourist camel in daylight. Nor could he fulfil his youthful wish of striding through the heavy, double wooden doors of Shepheard's Hotel, which during the war had been off-limits to all but officers. He never saw its lotus-topped pillars or bought a gin and tonic at the Long Bar. All he found was a hole in the ground. The building, along with all its old snobbery and exclusivity, had gone up in flames two years earlier in the riots that had deposed King Farouk.

While I was writing this book, my sister said that our father comes to life for her 'only when I either turn the stiff cardboard pages of the old family photograph album or when I meet a pet cockatoo'. He was unusually animated when pointing out talking birds – a yellow-crested white cockatoo that screeched out his name had been a close companion of his youth. For me, though, my father exists solely in that photograph of him mounted on his beloved horse. With his brown eyes alert, his lean bronzed face stern, he is unsmiling beneath the distinctive Australian hat with its upturned brim and plume of emu feathers in the band. The weather was hot, yet he was wearing his serge khaki soldier's uniform with its coarse jacket with voluminous exterior pockets. Not so tall as powerful – he was still growing –

he had fine features, a fresh, clear skin, profuse brown hair, bushy eyebrows and prominent cheekbones. In the photograph, the head of the horse is as important as that of the rider. Take away the horse and the picture is nothing. The animal gives potency to the rider.

Little remains besides the photograph to tell of my father and his time in the war. Records simply list Private Noel Robertson, number 57192, who served with the AIF from 24 April 1918 until 10 July 1919 in the Great War and in the Egyptian Rebellion, religion Church of England. His campaign medals, the British War Medal and the Victory Medal, have gone, and his horse's bones lie in Syria.

Remembering the 12,000 horsemen, together with the 12,000 horses – the geldings from the Kimberleys, the bays from the Albany grass country and the bright chestnuts bred on the tawny plains behind Wagga – I set off to find out what was real, what was imaginary, and what had just been invented so that I could answer the much-repeated query – who was first to Damascus?

Chapter One

'We are the ANZAC army!'

━◦◦◦◦━

Men and horses started to develop a permanent squint. The fine flying sand, the white glare of the dusty roads and the ice-cold winter nights were a shock after the seventy-seven day voyage from Albany, Western Australia. Apart from a brief stop at Colombo to take on coal, the men had seen only blue seas and skies – and ships. It had taken thirty-six transports and three cruisers to convey the first contingent – 21,529 volunteers and 14,000 horses. While most of the men stepped onto Egyptian soil with eagerness, others were disappointed and furious. This land of deserts, mud huts, palm trees, minarets and mosques had not been their destination when they had boarded the ships in Australia, but years of patient work by Germany in Constantinople had been rewarded a few weeks earlier when the Turks had become allied to the Central Powers. By 11 November, while the Australian contingent was still at sea, Turkey entered the war against Russia, France and Britain. Most of the Australians had enlisted so they could go and fight the Germans in France. It was the Kaiser whom they intended to fight, not the Sultan Caliph.

Originally the Australian Imperial Force was to go to France via England, to be trained on a site reserved for colonial forces in transit at Salisbury Plain, near Stonehenge in Wiltshire. But soldiers already there were suffering from overcrowding and incomplete facilities made worse by snow. Since the Canadians, with thousands of horses, had arrived, the place had become a shambles. When alternative camps had to be found, the sands of Egypt seemed an ideal place – the Australians could train, protect the canal and act as a deterrent to Turkey.

The decision to disembark the Australians in Egypt was so sudden that the British army had not made adequate arrangements or sent enough equipment. Men were forced to spend ice-cold nights sleeping on groundsheets in the open until tents were issued. In England, recruits were also suffering because of deficiencies in guns, uniforms, leather boots, horses, metal horseshoes and blacksmiths, and volunteers often had to wear civilian clothes or old uniforms. Other improvisations included using broomsticks instead of rifles and latrines that were nothing but poles over communal pits.

The Australian battalions were sent to three sites around Cairo. Each Australian Light Horse regiment was commanded by a lieutenant colonel and each regiment was composed of three squadrons, each commanded by a major. The largest camp was near Mena; the second further out, at Moascar, with a fine view of lines of sand dunes; and the third was at Maadi, a pleasant English suburb on the banks of the Nile in an area busy with feluccas. Excellent water supplies and large areas easily fenced off into paddocks made these places ideal for the Light Horse – and the tens of thousands of horses soon to arrive. Danger and war seemed far away. Apart from the odd fox, jackal, unusual spider and scorpion, the men were disturbed only occasionally by the flocks of pink flamingoes soaring over the marshes at the mouth of the Nile. Route marches across the sands with packs on their backs weighing eighty pounds, trench digging (shovelling earth and rubble) and rifle practice were strenuous, so men sought fun during time off. Many spent their spare time playing two-up and all manner of card games.

Horses thrive in dry climates, and they adapted well to Egypt, despite the irritation of a particularly unpleasant horsefly, which collected underneath their tails. But after the long cramped voyage, packed so tightly into the holds of the boats, standing for over seven weeks, with no fresh food and limited water, the animals were not fit enough to be ridden. At first no mounted work was done, owing to the risk of serious leg breakdowns among the horses. In an article in the *Egyptian Gazette* of December 1914, one of the camps was described thus:

> *Large wood fires burn beneath and around oval iron pots of tea;*
> *toast, too, seems a great favourite, baked and sadly burned in the*
> *wood ashes…the many lines of beautiful and much-loved horses*
> *had practically constant attention day and night…There are wild*
> *and almost-wild horses amongst them, many of which were*
> *presented to the regiment before they left.*

It took a month for each horse to be acclimatised, and for their weakened and stiffened legs to be brought up to condition. Gentle exercise was increased until they were enjoying ten miles a day at a fast pace. Later they swam over the Nile at the Barrage on a rope. These healthy horses from Australia were the pride and the joy of the newly arrived soldiers. Men rode them to the Pyramids on starry nights, and also organised horse races and amateur horse carnivals.

More ships brought more horses and more men. During February 1915 two more brigades of Australians arrived. One was under the command of Colonel John Monash, a successful engineer from Melbourne, a former member of the part-time militia, who rose to become one of the great generals of World War I. The other brigade was under Colonel G Ryrie, a tough pastoralist, politician and one-time pugilist. Together with the New Zealand Brigade, the Australians were formed into the Australia–New Zealand Army Corps, commanded by the dapper fifty-year-old General Sir William Birdwood, often referred to as 'good old Birdie'. Although not himself an Australian or a New Zealander, the popularity of this former cavalry officer in the Indian army was higher than for the average World War I commander. Like the commanders of the Canadian, New Zealand and

South African forces, he had a dual responsibility: to safeguard the Australian troops while, at the same time, serving the 'Mother Country'.

The stories about the origin of the acronym ANZAC during those early months in Egypt are many. One story says that Birdwood saw the initials on a packing case addressed to 'the A(ustralia) N(ew) Z(ealand) A(rmy) C(orps)'. An alternative account says that he saw the letters used by a New Zealand signaller, Sergeant Keith Little. Yet another version says that the initials were used in a telegram. The name became well known and the basis of a song, sung vigorously to the tune of 'The Church's One Foundation':

> *We are the Anzac Army,*
> *The ANZAC,*
> *We cannot shoot, we don't salute,*
> *What bloody good are we?*
> *And when we get to Ber-lin*
> *The Kaiser he will say,*
> *'Hoch, hoch! Mein Gott, what a bloody odd lot*
> *To get six bob a day!'*

At times, life was tougher for the men than the horses. Days were filled with endless drills, shooting dummy targets and enduring fatigue duties – a similar routine for almost all soldiers from the time of Caesar's legions. With shoulders heavily laden with backpacks and bandoliers of bullets, with feet burning hot after hours of monotonous marching, men were habituated to going 'left, right, left, right, left' – 110 paces to the minute. The odd man collapsed into a ditch, unable to walk another step. Obedience and authority dominated everything. To bring troops up to their maximum stamina and to instil automatic unthinking obedience so that they would obey any order in battle, however strange it might seem, they were conditioned to mindless routine tasks. There were also, of course, familiar comforts such as concerts or sightseeing, but men, regardless of the exotic location and the unknown pleasures they had never tasted before, were homesick. In one letter, the censor was surprised to read the words: 'They call this the Promised Land.

I don't know who they promised it to, but whoever it is, I wish they'd give it to him and let us get back home.' The more timid soldiers sought solace in things familiar from home – steaming mugs of hot chocolate, tea and toast, writing or reading letters.

The tradition of communal singing on Outback stations and on drovers' camps was so strong that even without a mouth organ, piano, piano accordion or guitar, groups sang Christmas carols or bush ballads around their campfires with loud and hearty choruses. Instruments were improvised – a stick and beer bottle tops, a comb with paper, clapping spoons or a gum leaf, plucked from one of the groves of stately eucalyptus trees, the fastest growing hardwood trees in the world, which had spread around the Mediterranean a century earlier.

Most of the horses were 'Walers' – tough Arab crosses, with strong necks, short backs and the small hooves of desert-bred horses. A little bigger than Arab horses, they stood about fifteen to sixteen hands. Originally they were sired by an English thoroughbred from breeding mares, and were said to be part draughthorse. They had a well-deserved reputation for having similar endurance to the legendary Cossack ponies, and tens of thousands had been exported to India since the 1830s. Favoured as stock horses and cavalry remounts, they were named after the state in which they were originally sired and raised, New South Wales.

Colonel John Monash summed up the cleverness of this unique Australian breed. In a letter home, he said:

> My horse Tom is a real beauty. He is my favourite. He is a gentle
> and well-mannered horse, very strong, and very willing, and
> answers to the slightest hint, both as to pace and direction, stands
> perfectly still when told, still enough for me to write orders in the
> saddle, and trots or canters or gallops at a touch of the knee
> without spur or whip. In fact, I now carry neither. He never tires,
> and is as strong and sure-footed after a heavy day, without feed or
> water, as he is on starting out. He is still a little nervous of

camels, but his particular aversion is a donkey, and he can spot
them long before I do.

Cosmopolitan though Cairo was, the Australians often stood out, and not
just because of their size. Some were big spenders; others were high-spirited,
with an inclination to boisterous behaviour, even the odd bit of brawling.
When possible, most men jumped on the old trams, which plied backwards
and forwards to the centre of the city. The famous museum, with its
embalmed bodies, was a great attraction, as were the Blue Mosque, the
Citadel, the Kersaal Theatre (especially backstage) and other fleshpots. Music
and dance halls added to the feverish atmosphere. According to the British
administrator, Ronald Storrs, the Australians spent between three and four
thousand pounds a day in the city. The coins and notes were confusing, and
men often felt they were 'being had', saying that '…once or twice bitten and
you're ready for the next time…'. But money quickly slipped out of their
large khaki pockets. Diversions in the so-called 'undesirable quarters' were
exciting and bewildering – the noise, the smells of incense, cigarette smoke
and opium, the beggars, the fortune tellers, the mixture of Jews, Greeks,
Arabs, Lebanese, Sudanese, Turks and Europeans. There was also an open
display of sexuality in this cosmopolitan city. Soldiers haggled in the
labyrinths of tiny streets crammed with veiled women, men with turbans or
a fez who sat cross-legged beside piles of carpets, sandalwood, brass pots,
scent, a snake in a cage or the latest copy of *The Times* from London.

Some dives were half café, half brothel. Most cafés had a tinkling piano or
pianola. Whether drinking or eating in lively cafés or nightspots, shopping
for wire pipe cleaners at a penny each, buying sesame cakes or exploring
bazaars with balconies overhung with laundry, there were always hints of
hidden temptations. The sight of women resting their breasts on balcony
railings, belly dancing or what was nicknamed the 'can-can' suggested many
activities. Stage shows set out to shock. They were a far cry from Mata Hari's
sophisticated nude dancing at the Folies Bergères in Paris.

Prostitution, mainly operated by Europeans, was openly practised in the
red-light areas such as the Wasser district. An estimated 30,000 prostitutes

plied their trade in Cairo, including scantily clad women soliciting custom in doorways, on balconies and in alleyways. Nothing seemed to stop the men: neither warnings about venereal diseases (mostly syphilis and gonorrhoea), nor lectures on its dangers, nor lurid pictures of victims, nor even the discontinuation of pay during harsh treatment at strict hospitals. One in ten of the AIF reported sick with what was referred to as 'a self-inflicted wound' but the rate, for some unexplained reason, was lower among the Light Horsemen.

The treatment of Egyptian women and animals shocked the Australians. Especially distressing were the overburdened donkeys, mules and horses. Some had ribs protruding through shrunken scabby coats, covered in fly-infested sores, being urged on with the brutal goad of the whip. Seeing a man riding a donkey with his wife walking behind in a shapeless black tunic, her bright kohl-rimmed eyes peeping over the yashmak and an infant with a fly-ridden face in a sling over her back, did seem a bit strange. Comments such as 'the people are filthy and do nothing but lounge about and smoke...' were mild compared to Colonel John Monash's remarks about 'a yelling, screaming crowd of dirty, smelly Arabs and donkey boys...'.

A. B. Facey's reaction, in *A Fortunate Life*, was typical:

> *Cairo was a dirty city after what I was used to. The Egyptian people were ragged and poorly clothed...the living conditions of the poor were terrible. I saw a married couple with several children, eating and sleeping with the house goat, in one room...we had to keep a close watch on our clothes and equipment or it would be stolen. I had one of my tunics stolen...The Egyptian religion permitted a man to have as many wives as he could afford to keep...the sheiks had harems...*

Visiting archaeologists had recently unearthed hordes of treasures and sites. The army recruited many of these experts, as they had a thorough knowledge of the country, were used to working with Arabs and spoke Arabic. Among the most prominent were Leonard Woolley and T. E. Lawrence, who had worked in Palestine and Syria, and Howard Carter, who was in 1915, with the help of Lord Carnarvon, on the verge of discovering the tomb of Tutankhamen in the Valley of the Kings. Carnarvon's half-brother, who was to play such an active role at Gallipoli, was Aubrey Herbert, who, like Lawrence, was recruited into intelligence in Cairo. He became the model for John Buchan's hero in his spy story, *Greenmantle*. But Flinders Petrie (the grandson of the Australian explorer Matthew Flinders), who had surveyed the pyramids at Giza and is regarded as the founder of scientific archaeological methods, was considered too old, at sixty-one, for military service of any kind.

Earlier pioneers in archaeology had opened up the wonders of Egypt, the Holy Land and the ancient world to an ever-increasing stream of sightseers and tourists. After ships had begun plying the Suez Canal, Thomas Cook, a Baptist lay preacher, had launched his Eastern Tours. In the 19th century, close to a million European tourists visited Jerusalem alone. Due to the extreme heat and the mosquitoes, most tourism took place during the cooler months. Now, as six million men in uniform marched and fought in Europe, and British bases were formed in Egypt, the war was starting to fill Cairo all year round, including the sweltering summer months.

When the second convoy had departed from Port Phillip Bay, near Melbourne, with 10,500 troops and thousands of horses, in Egypt the Australians were preparing for Christmas in a Muslim country. But 25 December was a disappointment to many. According to Henry Bostock, one soldier later wrote complaining of newspapers reporting incorrectly that they had been served roast turkey. 'The officers might have been, but we had sardines and bread, and any amount of nuts, figs and oranges. I was on guard one day about the middle of January when they brought us pudding that came from England – Xmas pudding.'

Every month ships from Australia brought letters, comfort parcels, troops and horses. The men and horses of the 10th Light Horse arrived at Alexandria on 8 March. Within hours they were entrained to Cairo, arriving at midnight at Abu-el-Ela, where despite the blackness of night, the men were marched to Mena, leading the horses on foot. A halt was called at about two o'clock in the morning, just as the pyramids of Mena loomed up through the mist. The weary men set up a camp there and then on the edge of the already established area of tents of the First Infantry Division. No time was lost. From the very next day, 10 March, to 27 April, the regiment went into intensive training in the desert – troop, squadron and regimental tactical exercises proceeded without hindrance. The men of the 10th Light Horse were living up to their reputation. General Sir Ian Hamilton, when he had visited Australia before the war, had described them as 'the pick of the bunch…real thrusters who would be held up by no obstacle of ground, timber or water…'.

Although hundreds of thousands of Australians were willing to put their lives at risk, they often found it difficult to grasp the precise reasons for the war. Nor were many really sure of the causes for which they might die – or kill. But everyone knew that one assassin's revolver shot, killing the Archduke Ferdinand, heir-apparent to the Austrian throne, had sent the world spinning into war. The previous heir to the Austrian throne, Crown Prince Rudolf, the son of Emperor Franz Joseph, had shot himself in 1889, after killing his mistress at Mayerling. When the assassination on 28 June 1914 had first been announced, not much attention was given to what was seen as yet another incident in the dramas of Central Europe. There had recently been two Balkan wars, the latter of which had ended only a year earlier. Another unexpected death in the Imperial Austrian succession, in Sarajevo, the capital of the wild and remote mountain province of Bosnia-Herzegovina, was not immediately seen as the final straw in a bitter struggle between Austria and Serbia, a struggle in which Austria was determined to wipe Serbia off the map. The assassin was a member of the Black Hand, an underground nationalist movement aided and funded by the secret service of neighbouring Serbia, set to liberate Bosnia from Austria. For decades the Balkan states had seethed in conspiracies, jostling for power. Bosnia, like its neighbours, had for centuries been a possession of the Ottoman Empire. The former Turkish provinces comprising Albania, Bulgaria, Rumania, Greece, Serbia and Montenegro had nearly fallen to Russia in 1878, but had gained or maintained their independence thanks to British intervention. However, the lands of the Ottoman Empire still stretched in a vast arc from Turkey around the eastern Mediterranean to Syria, Palestine, Sinai and Egypt. Large numbers of Turks were garrisoned in Palestine and Syria, which was provisioned with guns, food and ammunition by the newly constructed German-built railway running from Constantinople.

British policy had always been to contain Russia and to hold her firmly back from gaining more land or provinces in southern Europe. In fifty years Turkey had lost almost all of her territories in Europe and also in North Africa – Tunisia, Morocco and Libya. Because Turkey had relied upon the support of Britain to retain its remaining Empire, Egypt was still officially part of the Ottoman Empire – but, only officially. In actual fact, it had become a showpiece of British imperialism. Now the old antagonists of the Crimean War, Russia and Britain, were uniting to drive the Turks out of Europe and the Middle East.

Nearly fifty years earlier, in 1869, the high-flying Khedive, the Viceroy of the Sultan of the Ottoman Empire, Ismail Pasha, had officially opened the prestigious Suez Canal with much ostentation. One extravagance included a lavish Opera House in which to stage the world première of *Aida*, by Giuseppe Verdi. Such was Ismail Pasha's flamboyance that he was forced to sell half his Suez Canal shares to British investors. European shareholders, or 'bondholders', of the canal soon controlled Egypt by collecting half of the country's revenue to service the liabilities. The unofficial British occupation of Egypt increased as Egypt's debt increased, as did anti-British feeling. Saad Zaghloul, the leader of the popular Egyptian Nationalist Party, made moves towards independence, but activity was mostly underground.

When Turkey entered the war, Britain annexed Cyprus; proclaimed a protectorate over Egypt to a border just east of the canal itself, in the Sinai Peninsula; invaded Mesopotamia; started negotiating with Paris and St Petersburg as to the disposal of the Sultan's dominions; and, in a bloodless coup, deposed the pro-Turkish Khedive of Egypt, Hussain Kemal, and replaced him with the pliable son of Ismail, Ahmed Fuadi (the grandfather of King Farouk).

In his palace at the Golden Horn on the Bosphorus, the Sultan's fury knew no bounds. He launched a *jihad*, a holy war, against the infidel, and in the name of the 'Servant of the two holy cities, the caliph of the Muslims and Commander of the Faithful', he prohibited all Muslims from joining any Allied armies. This was the trump card that Turkey held, which she then considered almost greater than her military strength. For Mehmet V, the old and weak Sultan of Turkey, was also the caliph of Islam, the spiritual leader of the tens of millions of Muslims in Egypt, India, Russia, Africa and the Arab countries. As commander of the faithful, he was well aware that Britain had over 100 million Muslims within her Empire. Since the late 18th century, the sultans in Constantinople had placed a lot of importance on their role as the titular heads of the Sunni Muslims and keepers of the insignia of the caliphate – the Prophet's mantle – in the royal palace, to which pious pilgrims continued to pay homage. The key to their holy position was as official guardians of the two Holy Places, Medina and Mecca in the Sinai Peninsula. Distant though these were from Constantinople, control was exercised through the Sultan's representative, the sherif of Hejaz.

In Constantinople, no effort was spared to give substance or publicity to the *jihad*. It was quickly reinforced by a similar declaration by the highest Muslim authority in the capital, Sheikh al-Islam. No less than five 'fatwas' (religious rulings) followed. These calls to holy war were read out in every mosque, printed in every newspaper throughout the Ottoman Empire and soon distributed throughout the Muslim world. Emphasis was placed on the wrongdoing of Muslims prepared to join in any attack on another Islam state, in alliance with the non-believer. Civil uprisings were also demanded.

The declaration of the *jihad* put Muslims outside the Ottoman Empire in a dilemma. Did they stay loyal to the King, also Emperor of India, the Tsar of all the Russias, the President of the French Republic and the French Empire, or to the injunction of the Sultan–Caliph? While many subjects, especially in India, became anxious about their now conflicting allegiances, governments, especially in London and Paris, feared civil strife in their colonies.

Proclaimed with much pomp and publicity, the *jihad* urged followers of Mohammed 'to struggle in the path of God'. According to the 1951 edition of *Encyclopaedia Britannica*, it threatened all Muslims 'with the punishment of hell if they supported his [the Sultan's] enemies'. The first *jihad* had been issued in Baghdad in about 825, when Muslim territory was attacked – a defensive measure, not an act of aggression. Over the centuries, whenever Islamic territory was under attack from infidels, a call for *jihad* had been issued.

Unlike *jihads* issued in previous centuries, the Sultan's call to holy war was supported by a Christian country, and Kaiser Wilhelm was presented as a champion of Islam. German-inspired rumours went so far as to suggest that he had been secretly converted and assumed the name Gulliam Haji. As soon as the *jihad* was announced in November, copies of it were rushed to Berlin from Constantinople. Once translated into languages such as Russian, Hindu and Arabic, it became the basis of thousands of leaflets secretly distributed to enemy armies.

So Germany, exploiting the propaganda angle of the *jihad*, used it as an extra weapon in their policy to spread unrest and rebellion through Allied countries. David Fromkin, in *A Peace to End All Peace*, said: 'The staff of the German Foreign Ministry predicted that the Sultan's actions would "awaken the fanaticism of Islam" and might lead to a large-scale revolution in India'.

Turkey attempted to ensure that she had the strategic initiative in the Middle East by launching a multi-front war, with offensives in the Caucasus and in the Sinai. Strategy was based on the belief that the Egyptians, seeing their fellow Muslims up in arms against the infidel, would immediately rush in and assist in the invasion. At the beginning of 1915, 20,000 conscripted Anatolian Turks, Armenians, Kurds, Syrians and Arabs, accompanied by 11,000 camels, marched in an ill-conceived offensive from Beersheba across the merciless sands of the Sinai Desert to cut off the Suez Canal from Egypt. Despite dragging steel punts, boats and field guns, the march took only ten days. But the British, just by changing the Khedive, had made a strong show of force. Neither the *jihad*, nor the propaganda leaflets, had much effect. There was no sign of the Muslims of Egypt joining their brothers-in-arms or aiding them against the British.

Ignoring the aeroplanes overhead, which began strafing them en route, on 3 February the Turks attacked the Suez Canal, the crossroads of the British Empire. Despite being quickly repulsed by Indians and the 6th Ghurkha Rifles from Nepal, the Turks launched a flotilla of pontoons. At this stage the Turks had expected that their arrival would be met with a huge local uprising – the purpose of the boats was to carry men with arms across the canal to link up with the anticipated Egyptian insurgents. But there were no takers. Even the rebellious Egyptians failed to rebel openly. Despite propaganda leaflets, Egypt's Muslims failed to rise up against either the new Khedive or the British. Without any local response from residents, the Turks stood no chance. Only about twenty-five Turks made it to the western bank of the canal, disappearing into the Egyptian crowds to harness the support of the locals. Once the officers realised that they had no backing, they limited themselves to damaging installations in the canal, trying to sink vessels and disrupt traffic. Reluctantly, by evening, having suffered 2,000 casualties, the Turks fled back to their line in the Sinai, leaving 700 prisoners.

Turkish forces had more success further south. From the Yemen, they entered the Aden protectorate and installed themselves both in the highlands and near Aden, the vital coaling station for British ships en route from the Suez Canal to India and Australia. Here, protected by inhospitable terrain, Turkey's threat was very real. If they got to the coast, they would threaten Britain's Red Sea route, and the Germans could deploy their submarine U-boats. But the British responded effectively, with a blockade of the Red Sea. This left two routes for the Turks to send goods to their bases at Mecca and Medina: overland from the Yemen or via the legendary Hejaz or Pilgrim railway. After running from Medina through the Maan desert to the big junction at Deraa, the trains went on to Damascus, to be loaded with military supplies and reinforcements for the Turkish garrison controlling the area.

Ironically, just as the Turks had planned to incite the population in Egypt to revolt, certain British strategists in Cairo dreamt of an Arab uprising against the Turks. Turning this area into a base friendly towards the British would diminish the threats to the Red Sea and bring the Muslim Holy Cities, Mecca and Medina, back into the realm of 100 million Muslim subjects in the British Empire. Since the outbreak of war, they had been in the grip of the enemy. Medina, the birthplace of the Prophet, was 300 miles from Mecca, so strategically it was not a formidable task. British authorities wanted to be able to reassure Muslims throughout the world that the Holy Cities were inviolate and that pilgrimages were secure. Ideally, the caliphate would be separated from the Ottoman dynasty; the Sacred Places would be put under an independent ruler, and the title of 'Keeper of the Holy Places' would be transferred from the distant Sultan to the local sherif of the Hejaz, Hussein Ibn Ali, who would become the caliph.

The problem of the conflict of loyalties for the Muslims was stressed by the Viceroy of India, who had tried to reassure Muslim subjects by explaining that the war was not inconsistent with their loyalty to King George and the British Empire. To complicate matters, the majority of men in the Indian army, and the population of Egypt, were Muslim.

Britain's prime minister, H. H. Asquith, dismissively mocked the invasion in a letter: 'The Turks have been trying to throw a bridge across the Suez Canal and in that ingenious fashion to find a way into Egypt. The poor things and their would-be bridge were blown into smithereens, and they have retired to the desert'. By coincidence, on the other side of the Mediterranean, the British were about to reverse the roles and begin an offensive action against Turkey.

On 2 April in Cairo, not all Australians observed Good Friday as a Holy Day. Many were out to have a good time. One group, fed up with being fleeced, protested that they were being overcharged. A small punch-up quickly became a large fight, developing into what was described as a riot. A few houses went up in flames and three soldiers were killed. The next day Cairo was declared out of bounds to the Australians by the exasperated British authorities. However, historian John Laffin said that 'the Battle of the Wazzer' was not 'a first-class riot…[the men were] determined to exact some sort of revenge for certain injuries which they believed [they] had incurred in an infamous street… While they were ransacking a house, a story started that a Maori was stabbed there. This led to beds, mattresses and clothing being thrown into the street and bonfired. A number of mounted British Military Police arrived and used their revolvers but had the sense to withdraw...A Greek drinking shop was accidentally burned and the Egyptian fire brigade, which tried to put out the flaming bonfire, was roughly handled, but there was no serious trouble. Most of the Anzacs present were spectators...Burning the bedding of the brothels concerned was a public service...There has only once been a case of Diggers getting seriously out of hand and even that incident could have been prevented had the English staff officers understood something of the Digger temperament'.

A week after the Wasser riot, troops embarked for an unknown destination, rumoured to be on the other side of the Mediterranean. But everyone – even the Turks – knew the place was Gallipoli. The British invasion was referred to as 'the worst-kept secret in the war'. Even the price of wheat in Chicago dropped in anticipation of Russian ships sailing through 'the liberated Straits' with the Russian wheat crop from the Black Sea ports.

Originally the operation had been put under the aegis of what was designated the Constantinople Expeditionary Forces, so it was known that the purpose of the invasion was the capture of Constantinople, the enemy capital. In February and March, when the British navy tried to bombard the Gallipoli peninsula, the sailors had scrawled slogans such as 'Turkish Delight' or 'To Constantinople and the Harems' on the sides of the ships.

When the infantry and artillery departed from Mena, they began, as Major Arthur Olden later wrote in his book on the 10th Light Horse, *West Australian Cavalry in the War*, to 'move out on their great adventure, trained, equipped, eager and full of sympathy – some of it derisive – with the Light Horse at being left behind'. Horses, mules and donkeys were being brought in for officers, ambulance work and cartage, but the precipitous terrain behind the shore was unsuitable for mounted troops. They would be shipped over when the advance got closer to Constantinople. For the time being, the men of the Australian Light Horse brigades remained in Egypt with their horses, while the infantry troops of the Anzacs were to be the first troops to land at Gallipoli.

Frantic haste with the preparations for the Gallipoli invasion caused problem after problem. Even the maps and medical facilities were woefully inadequate. Lord Kitchener, the former high commissioner for Egypt who had become secretary of state for war, selected the chief-of-staff from his old Boer War days, 62-year-old Sir Ian Hamilton, as the commander-in-chief. Hamilton's record as a junior officer showed great courage and some tactical flair, but his success at that level was not replicated in the higher command. Beguiled by the clanship of British society and the sycophancy of the British officer class into succumbing to loyalty to his friends, he found it difficult to stand up to his seniors, especially those who had been his mentors in the past, such as Kitchener. When Kitchener told Hamilton who his chief-of-staff was to be, instead of rejecting the offer or demanding the right to chose his own man, he had little choice but to concur. This inability to assert his own will was to manifest itself over and over again during the Gallipoli campaign; Hamilton failed to impose his own rules on his generals.

B. H. Liddell Hart, in *The War in Outline*, criticised the lack of organisation and the inadequacy of the pre-campaign preparations:

> *At the War Office not a single preparatory step had been taken. [Hamilton] was hurried out to the Dardanelles at a day's notice. The information he had been sent comprised a pre-war handbook on the Turkish army, an old report on the forts, two tourist guide books on western Turkey and a map which proved inaccurate…On arrival in the Mediterranean, Hamilton found that his troops had been so chaotically distributed in their transports that they had to be sent to Alexandria for redistribution, thus entailing several weeks' further delay.*

As mines and patrols made close survey before the landings impossible, pre-invasion information about the territory and the strength of the Turkish resistance was inadequate. There were criticisms that the size of the Turkish forces had been underestimated. Aubrey Herbert, describing the troops and ships before the landing, wrote: 'The general impression amongst the intelligence is that we shall get a very bad knock...The intelligence and Hamilton don't seem to be in touch...It seems incredible that we are not better informed...'.

T. E. Lawrence headed the team collating the information for the maps and charts, and details of the topography for the invasion, and also acted as liaison officer between military intelligence and the Survey of Egypt, which produced and printed the maps. Their size was perfect – they could fold into an officer's map case – but their content was later greeted with criticism. The fact that some of the information about the geographical features of the area was inaccurate, inadequate – or both – cannot really be laid at Lawrence's door. Collation had been handicapped by old maps and lack of information. The only maps available were based on ones used in the Crimean War, 1853–56. Up-to-date knowledge gained from aerial reconnaissance reports of tents, trenches and gun batteries was woefully inadequate. However, after the first landing at Cape Helles, a set of Turkish maps was captured. It was reproduced in Cairo with anglicised names, and arrived in time for the landings at Suvla.

The first pre-landing casualty of the Gallipoli expedition was the poet Rupert Brooke. He was one of the earliest of more than one hundred thousand deaths occurring during the 'deliverance of Constantinople'. On 23 April, the eve of the departure for Gallipoli, he died of a septic infection from a mosquito bite on his lip. His coffin was taken to Skyros and carried to an olive grove by twelve Australian soldiers. The next day they sailed for Gallipoli. Had Brooke not died he would have been part of a branch of the Marine Light Infantry at Anzac Cove.

A 32-year-old idealist, with dazzling good looks, he was known as 'the handsomest young man in England', attracting attention wherever he went. A spell of fighting in Belgium had inspired him to write poems that conveyed the desperate sorrow of youth about to die. In his war sonnets he evoked a mystical idea of homeland, stressing what men were fighting for. His line, 'If I should die think only this of me', struck a cord of empathy with the brothers, sisters, mothers, fathers, wives and grandparents of the men who were at the Front.

Chapter Two

Arrival in Gallipoli

O n Friday 23 April, in Mudros Harbour, one of the mightiest seaborne invasions in history was about to commence. The first of 200 ships were off and moving forward to a tumult of excited and deafening cheers from the surrounding vessels, crammed with soldiers who would soon follow, including a French Division and the 29th British Division. Even the weather was auspicious. The wind, which had blown every cloud away, had now dropped, and the sky over this Greek island in the eastern Mediterranean was the brightest of blues. Ashore it seemed that all the spring flowers had burst into bloom at once.

This was the biggest offensive undertaken by Britain and France in the early stages of the war, and the Australians were to be the first troops going ashore. Their objective was historic: like the Crusaders before them, they were en route to capture Constantinople, the capital of Turkey and great city of the Islamic world. Their route was via Gallipoli, just 132 miles away. The peninsula of Gallipoli guards the three seas of antiquity: the Mediterranean, the Sea of Marmara and the Black Sea, the world's oldest maritime trade route and a magnet to merchants, pirates, conquerors and statesmen. Since ancient times, the dramatic headlands and rugged hills of Gallipoli have acted as a barrier between Europe and the Orient, between West and East, a gateway to Constantinople.

This new invasion was rightly considered by many strategists to be fraught with danger. Two years before World War I had even begun, the Italians had tried to storm Gallipoli but, like many before them, had been repulsed.

This time, nothing had been spared apart from the horses: men, seaplanes, battleships. At this stage, the majority of the animals landing with the troops were just beasts of burden; the cavalry would come later.

This was not just a simple advance into the heartland of Turkey, the centre of the Ottoman Empire, but a sophisticated diversionary tactic dreamt up by politicians and generals in London. Opening up a new front in the east would, they believed, shatter the stalemate in France. According to Churchill, then a 41-year-old aspiring politician, First Lord of the Admiralty and one of the main advocates of the operation, it would also attack Germany through the 'back door'. Another advantage was opening up the Black Sea to trade again. Russia could then ship out her wheat and be supplied with the munitions she so desperately needed.

The Russians, Greeks and Bulgarians also hoped to gain Constantinople, not only for its prized seaways, but because it had great religious significance and was the birthplace of Eastern Orthodoxy. Like Rome, Constantinople is built on seven hills. Only by occupying 'the city of the world's desire', taken by the Turks in 1453, could Russia be sure that her ships could safely sail from the Black Sea into the Aegean, the Mediterranean and beyond. Even the anti-Tsarist literary hero, Feodor Dostoevsky, wrote in 1876: 'It goes without staying that sooner or later Constantinople should be ours'.

No vessel can leave the Black Sea without first sailing through the Bosphorus, straddled by Constantinople. Having navigated the narrow channel, a ship next has to sail across the Sea of Marmara and finally through the thirteen-mile channel of the Dardanelles, which in earlier times was called the Hellespont. It had been sailed through by Jason and swum across by

Leander to visit his beloved Hero, deeds immortalised by many writers and poets.

Chanak and Troy lie on the Dardanelles' eastern Asiatic side and Gallipoli is on its western European bank. The nation holding either of these two banks – or both – controls all the shipping from southern Russia, Bulgaria and Rumania, including the rich basin of the Danube, the Crimean ports of Odessa and Sebastopol, and the mouths of four rivers: the Danube, the Dniester, the Dnieper, and the Don. As the icy expanses of the Baltic were not navigable in winter, these straits were essential for Russian trade.

For a century Britain had been Turkey's strong ally. The two countries had fought side by side in the Crimean War against Russia. This war had given the English language the word 'jingoism'. Crowds had gathered in Trafalgar Square in the early 1850s waving not the Union Jack but the Ottoman crescent and star flag singing:

> *We don't want to fight,*
> *But by jingo if we do,*
> *We've got the ships,*
> *We've got the men,*
> *We've got the money too.*
> *We've fought the bear before,*
> *And if we're Britons true,*
> *The Russians shall not have Constantinople!*

After the Crimean campaign, Britain maintained links with the Sultans in their palaces. When Russia attacked the Balkans via the Caucasus in 1877, Queen Victoria herself sent bandages to wounded Turkish soldiers. But in the same way that the decadent occupant of the throne of the House of Osman, Sultan Abdul Hamid II – Abdul 'the Damned' – had many wives and countless concubines in his harem, he also believed he could have more than one ally, even if one was in alliance with his old enemy, Russia. For thirty years this intriguer played off the European powers against each other. His successor indulged in similar games.

Many paradoxes resulted from Britain's closeness to Turkey. Firstly, she had trained the Turkish navy. Ever since 1911, seventy-two British naval advisers and staff under Rear-Admiral Arthur Limpus had been stationed in Constantinople, helping to modernise the Turkish navy. As a result, the British navy knew the seas they were about to invade very well indeed. Two years earlier, when the Italians had tried to take the Gallipoli peninsula, British officers had advised the Turks on how to defend it. However, as Edwardian attitudes still prevailed, it was considered ungentlemanly for Limpus to fight against the men he had taught to fight or the places he knew so well, so he never fought in the Gallipoli theatre.

Secondly, munitions manufacturer Vickers had been one of the suppliers of the Turkish arsenal, so a large number of the Turkish mines used in the Dardanelles to blow up British ships were made in the north of England. In 1915 British guns would also be among those used by the Turks against the British on the peninsula. Thirdly, two super-dreadnought battleships were nearing completion in the north of England. Ordered by Turkey in 1911, they were impounded by the British at the beginning of August 1914. These mighty vessels had been paid for by coins dropped into collection boxes in villages throughout Turkey. Britain's action outraged and embittered the nation.

The decks of the moving ships were overcrowded with raw Anzac troops who had never seen battle. The voices of over 10,000 patriots seemed to be raised as they sang 'Australia Will Be There', a song that became an emotive chant during the war:

> *On land or sea, wherever you be,*
> *Keep your eye on Germany!*
> *For England, Home and Beauty*
> *Have no cause to fear!*
> *Should auld acquaintance be forgot?*

No! No! No! No! No! Australia will be there!
Australia will be there!

When the singing faded, the bands kept playing and the troops kept cheering. Within a week, they thought, the Union Jack would be high above the domes and minarets of Constantinople. None of the men knew that the British, French and Russians had four weeks earlier concluded a secret agreement to hand over Constantinople and the nearby Turkish coasts to the Russians. This agreement, reached in London, completely reversed Britain's traditional policy of keeping Russia well out of Turkey. No longer was Britain preserving a barrier against Russian expansion. But it was war; and Russia was an ally, not an enemy. Nor did the Australian soldiers know that the Sultan had earlier proclaimed a *jihad*. Religion reared its head on both sides. As the ships neared their destination, men who had not attended a church service for years crowded onto the decks to sing the hymns in the 'Service Before Battle' and hear the chaplain pray for victory.

At midnight on 24/25 April, the ships were still moving. An hour or so passed. They halted. But had they landed on the correct beach? Did a current pull them too far up the coast? Had the landing cove been changed at the last minute? Had secrecy blocked information, so that officers were not sufficiently briefed about the right destination? Under a setting moon, they lowered themselves into the rowing boats, gripping the loose rope ladders that swayed with their weight. At about 3.30 am, steamboats started towing them the two-and-a-half miles to shore. Moving in darkness, they glided onto seashores of pebbles, about a mile north of Gaba Tepe, Ariburnu – the 'Cape of Bees', a name honouring the wild bumblebees which had made thousands of hives in holes eroded in the cliff-face. Soon, though, it would be known as Anzac Cove.

As dawn broke, the Australians were the first Allied troops to wade ashore on the beaches of the Gallipoli peninsula. Spasmodic shell and machine-gun fire whipped up the sand in front of the assault craft. The Turks were prepared to meet the invaders. Bullets hit the men, the water, and the shingle of the beach. Some men jumped out of the boats. But once they were in the water many were pulled down by the weight of their packs and drowned. Others in the boats and on the beach hardly dared raise their heads and look up. Some, defying bullets and shrapnel, ran across the pebbles, stumbling on fallen comrades. There was no cover. Men died trying to drag injured mates to a safer position. Some lay dead in the boats; others, unable to move, lay in agony on the beach. As the beach became piled with mutilated bodies, some of the injured were stacked onto linked barges. The sea around the cove was red with blood. Boats kept bringing more and more men. By 2 pm, 12,000 Anzacs were ashore – dead, injured and alive. Fighting went on ceaselessly, even in the dark, for forty-eight hours.

Leaving those who were incapacitated behind, the soldiers fixed bayonets and scrambled up the pathless cliffs, pulling at the dry crumbling earth. The inhospitable nature of the terrain challenged them. With their boots and clothes heavy with seawater, the men found much of the going very rough. Shinning up the deep sandstone chasms and gullies, they soon lost touch with each other, but managed to lever and pull themselves up by the tangle of low green scrub and a prickly holly-like bush with spiked leaves, which inflicted nasty scratches. As the soldiers clambered up, they came across patches of sweet-scented flowers, mostly yellow or mustard-coloured. The chain of communication collapsed. Neither messages from the officers on the beach, nor men and supplies, were getting through to the men surging forward over the hills. Disorganisation reigned. Each man high up in the scrub relied on personal endeavour. Communication between the command on the ships and beach headquarters was almost as ineffective.

While being peppered with bullets and shrapnel, some of the men managed to edge up to the uppermost ridge, where they caught glimpses of the Narrows, the mile-wide stretch of water immortalised by the English poet, Lord Byron, who had swum across it in 1810.

Next stop was to be Constantinople. But the Australian troops had to turn back or be killed, for close in the hinterland, riding at the head of his Division (around 12,000 men) towards them, was their nemesis, Mustafa Kemal.

The overall commander of the Turkish troops was Liman von Sanders, who would also often be in the fray, risking death and smelling the stench of the battles. Liman von Sanders was an unbending, resolute, stout, 64-year-old German general who brought monogrammed silk sheets on campaign and relished the 'von' with which the Kaiser had recently ennobled him. A year earlier he had been sent to Turkey to reorganise the Ottoman army. Apart from being fastidiously dressed and a cavalry officer, he had little in common with Kemal, then a 34-year-old with steely blue eyes, prominent cheekbones, an elegant nose and light brown hair, who more often than not was smoking a cigarette. The only son of a clerk at the Salonika Customs House, Kemal, like many well-educated Turks, was fluent in French, with polished manners and dignified deportment. Stubborn and thin-lipped, and adored by his soldiers, he was later to be referred to as 'the saviour of Gallipoli'. For seven and a half months he took the lead in the northern sector above Anzac Cove. Other Turkish and German officers also performed exceptionally at Gallipoli, but it was Kemal's name that was to stand out. Despite his abilities, Kemal was then only a divisional commander. There had been reluctance to send him to the front, as many Turks in authority regarded him as a somewhat dangerous person, a leader of the progressives. The Turkish minister of war, Enver Pasha, who in 1913 had staged a coup d'état that had given him, as war minister, effective power and control in Turkey, was always in two minds towards Kemal. Aware of Kemal's brilliance, he felt that one day Kemal might outshine him.

Although ambivalent about the West, Kemal had tried to adopt a few Western ways, even learning the waltz and taking ballroom dancing lessons. When he was a military attache in Bulgaria and in Constantinople, he had to shake off gossip about excesses of whisky drinking and women. But whatever his personal failings, once on the battlefield he inspired his troops. They would follow him to the ends of the Earth. Fellow officers, though, often found Kemal difficult, as he could not abide criticism.

Without Kemal's presence, the Australians might well have reached the far side of the hills and dominated the Narrows. Then, and only then, would they have cleared the channel of mines and conquered Constantinople. Kemal galloped here, there and everywhere building up a delaying force. Collecting the men from his two battalions wherever he found them, he pushed them into any gap. He kept thrusting them forward in a non-stop attack, wheeling field guns and howitzers into position. After a few hours, while his men – who, confusingly, also wore khaki uniforms – were briefly resting, Kemal sped ahead towards Chunuk Bair, where he saw another group retreating. For three hours they had been firing at the Australian soldiers landing on the beach, and they had not a bullet left.

The soldiers pointed at a line of Australians who were quickly advancing and were closer to Kemal than his own troops. Kemal gave the command to fix bayonets, lie down and keep the Australians at bay while a Turkish officer raced back to fetch the rest of the regiment, and more bullets and shells. Additional soldiers rushed into action with heavy guns, emptying them on the Anzacs as they tried to surge over the ridge, forcing them to scatter and take cover in the sparse scrub. Never did Kemal let up in his relentless defence. He sent two battalions forward to halt the invaders as they crawled and clawed up the steep slopes. Pushing forward the big howitzers to shell the beach, directing shrapnel and explosives on the incoming boats and men, Kemal stopped the Australian and New Zealand forces. As more Allied corpses piled up on the shingled beaches, he effectively froze the Australians and New Zealanders into an area close to the shore.

Half of the Australians and New Zealanders who landed during the first couple of days became casualties. A quarter of the Australians who perished there during the nine months of the campaign died in those ghastly first five days. In less than forty-eight hours, seven transports arrived at Alexandria, Egypt, carrying 3346 casualties. John Laffin, in *Damn the Dardanelles*, puts the figures for the three days 25–28 April as: killed – 2,500 men and 150 officers; wounded – 6,000 men and 250 officers. He does not, though, stipulate which army – the British as a whole, or the Anzacs in particular. The Turks, too, suffered terrible casualties.

The first objective of the Australians was to capture the third ridge of the Sari Bair range, a stepping stone towards the Narrows. 'The Narrows' became a place that haunted the Australians, always so physically close, yet unreachable. Kemal knew that whoever held those heights controlled the entire area – and ultimately the Dardanelles. In his diary, Kemal wrote that the decisive moment of the landing, the instant that he won the battle, was after he gave his famous order: 'I don't order you to attack, I order you to die. In the time it takes us to die, other troops and commanders can come and take our places'. As Islam is the only religion that has a specific doctrine of fighting for the faith, for martyrdom, many Turkish soldiers were quite willing to die. In confronting the Christian infidel, Kemal's soldiers were finding salvation, for the Koran says: 'The sword is the key to Heaven and Hell'. The Turks were a ferocious force in defending their homeland.

When ammunition ran out again, hand-to-hand fighting took its place. Finally the Anzacs were driven back to the coastal spurs and ridges. Confusion was rife. As both sides were camouflaged within the hills, it was difficult for gunners on ships to distinguish between their own men and the Turks. At such a distance, gunfire could not be sure of hitting foe rather than friend. So the huge guns at sea were not fully utilised. While the ships fulfilled their role by delivering every cartridge, ounce of food and supplies, and most of the water to the men, they were woefully inadequate at providing battle protection and support.

Men hit before landing could not be brought ashore, so remained in the boats as they plied back to the fleet bringing more and more troops. Not even the worst pessimist could have expected the flow of wounded that poured out from Gallipoli. Some boats – along with dirty, verminous transports, without doctors or stores – went from ship to ship, desperately searching for a place to offload the injured and dead. For example, Colonel Howse, ADMS 1st Australian Division, said that he was told by one non-commissioned officer (NCO) of one boat that he tried seven transports before getting the wounded taken on.

Many of the vessels moving the wounded were neither staffed nor equipped to take their pitiful cargoes. On the *Hindoo*, two medical officers with two surgical panniers cared for 800 casualties, many on the verge of death. Conditions on the SS *Lutzow* were worse. Here one lone veterinary surgeon was expected to care for 600 wounded during the four-day voyage to Egypt. One medical orderly on another vessel wrote that the boats were so jammed with bodies that as soon as a man died he was tossed as quickly as possible into the sea. Everywhere men suffered from the filth, the ineffective system of hygiene and lack of either water or someone to bring it to their parched mouths. On one ship there were between 400 and 500 wounded, with only one bedpan; wounds left untreated for seven days suppurated. This often caused deaths that would not normally have occurred with such injuries. Arrangements ashore were equally chaotic. On Gallipoli, the medical facilities were initially like those encountered by Florence Nightingale in the nearby Crimea sixty years earlier. Again the wounded were obliged to lie for days under shellfire, until transport could be found to take them. Only the numbers of the dead solved the problem of overcrowding.

In his diary, the official historian, C. E. W. Bean, wrote about the censorship that stopped the people in Australia knowing what was actually happening to their troops. 'People in Australia, when fifty casualties were published, seem by the latest reports to have been almost shocked. We know that by then the list was really 5,000 for this division alone...'

Appalled by hospital services that were strained and inadequate beyond belief, Mabel Brookes (later Dame) echoed the criticism that a great deal of the suffering was due to poor administration. Her husband, Norman, Australia's first international tennis star, who had won the Wimbledon championship in 1914, headed the Australian Red Cross in Cairo. Deeply moved by the uncomplaining heroism of the 17,000 wounded men who arrived in Egypt before the end of May, she recorded their pain in her memoirs, *Crowded Galleries*. Men lay in their drying and oozing blood, with no drugs to kill the pain, often without any blankets. Many were waiting for amputations. 'On 14 May, Luna Park [a temporary hospital in Heliopolis] with 1,750 patients had four medical officers, 15 sisters and 40 orderlies, mostly untrained. Kerosene tins were used for dressing trays and water was sterilised in dixies. Mudros took 6,000 cases irrespective of Cairo...the Red Cross in Egypt had not been sufficiently planned nor, indeed, had the whole medical service...'

Another hospital nearer Cairo, called the Atelier, took a thousand, while canvas was thrown over the tennis courts at the Ghezireh Sporting Club to take another 1250, and two Australian hospitals were improvised at Lemnos.

Apart from trying to keep the men alive, bedding, bedpans and other medical necessities had to be improvised and clothes had to be found for the men, most of whom had been separated from their kits.

Pinned down around Anzac Cove, the soldiers were unable to penetrate far inland. Their maximum achievement was about 1250 metres east of the beach. So dreadful were the casualties, so bleak the outlook, that the Anzac commander had sent a request to Hamilton on the *Queen Elizabeth*, on the first night, for permission to evacuate the men. Hamilton refused. They were to stay at their posts, 'dig in' and 'dig, dig, dig'.

The troops duly dug in. Instead of an advance to Constantinople, the troops were stuck in one place. This new front, which had been created to break the sour stalemate of trench warfare in France, turned into the same thing that had occurred in France – men deadlocked in trenches. Battle had deteriorated into the same trench-slogging match. Each man was in a trap, surrounded either by the sea or Turks. The sole way out was by boat. In his poignant memoirs Facey described the cat-and-mouse affair: 'We had to work hard digging new trenches...When daylight came the Turks would see that our line had moved closer. They would shell hell out of the trench for a day or two...'. With the combined strength of the British navy, army and new air force, combat developed into continual sniping, interrupted by short bursts of extreme and violent activity.

At Gallipoli, the army did not supply all the necessary ambulances for its wounded. The Red Cross supplied one, the poet John Masefield another. When war had broken out, he had volunteered as an orderly at a British Red Cross hospital in France. Horrified by the inadequacy of medical facilities, Masefield raised enough money in England to purchase a 32-horsepower twin-screw motorboat, two smaller launches and a barge. He drove the speedboat to Gallipoli himself, taking his small flotilla across the treacherous Bay of Biscay and around Gibraltar into the Mediterranean to reach his destination. Each night, under cover of darkness, the new ambulances sped across the sixty miles of sea to Gallipoli, to fetch British, French and Anzac wounded from the beaches.

Chapter Three

The Saddlebags and Horses are Left Behind

A ll attempts to progress beyond their slim beachhead and get over the hill to the Narrows on the other side, a hike of less than four miles, were in vain. Despite heavy losses and little hope of success, the Anzacs sustained a cheerful level of bravery, discipline and comradeship – 'mateship'. More men were landed; again their progress was halted and repulsed by Kemal. He was fast proving his skill as a military strategist.

With such heavy casualties, the British were revising their earlier poor assessment of the Turkish troops. Replacements were urgently needed, but there was opposition to the Light Horse brigades and New Zealand Mounted Rifles being sent for dismounted service. Having already vigorously opposed sending them to France, the commander in Egypt was reluctant to lose their vital role in protecting the Suez Canal. Destroying the hundred-mile long canal was a principal German objective, and ever since the Turkish attempt to close the Suez Canal in February, the British had feared further attacks. But when the idea of joining the other Australians in Gallipoli was placed before the men of the 10th Light Horse, they volunteered, 'to a man'.

Anxious to preserve their identity, the Light Horsemen parted sorrowfully from their animals, their bandoliers, their leggings and spurs. Usually there was a deep bond between each man and his horse. Many had travelled with their own cherished mounts from farms and stations in Australia, and affection and trust turned horses almost into extensions of their owners. To ensure that the horses were kept up to standard, 25 per cent of the men were to stay behind to groom and care for them.

On 16 May, 2,250 men and 106 officers from the 2nd Light Horse and the 10th Light Horse boarded a captured German steamer at Suez. The trip across the Mediterranean was far from pleasant. According to one man on board, the ship was 'in a terribly insanitary condition, having already made several hasty trips with very little opportunity of "cleaning up"'. On the eve of their arrival, the majority of men could not squeeze onto the deck for the usual prayers so they used these precious last minutes to sharpen their bayonets on revolving grindstones on the decks, to the singing of the hymn 'O God, Our Help in Ages Past'.

On 21 May, the Turks made a concerted effort to stop further Australians landing. But as more men were killed, more arrived. The men of the 10th Light Horse progressed towards the beach under light shrapnel in barges and pinnaces. For forty-eight hours they stayed in trenches near Plugge's Plateau. They then made their way to a place already christened Monash Gully, where their commander was Harry Chauvel, a small, wiry Queenslander who was to play a significant role in all the Light Horse regiments over the next four years. The grandson of a retired Indian army officer who had settled at Tabulam on the Clarence River, he had earlier proved himself in the Boer War. With the reserved manner of an English gentleman, Chauvel lacked the laconic laid-back bonhomie that endeared so many Australian officers to their soldiers. Henry Gullet, historian and author of the official Australian history of the campaign, said that although he became a great leader, 'he missed by his instinctive reserve the satisfaction of becoming a soldier's idol'.

As the 10th Light Horse arrived, thousands of sick and wounded were being evacuated. On 24 May, a brief armistice came into force, from 7.30 am to 4.30 am, so both the Turks and the Allies could retrieve corpses and rescue their wounded. Each side rushed to the bleak area of No Man's Land. Then slowly, and with sadness, they dragged and carried the limp, mutilated bodies to new burial grounds.

Five days later, at 3.20 am, the Turks rushed the trenches at Quinn's Post with bombs, accompanied by a rigorous battering by artillery fire in support. For three hours the men of the 10th held the Turks back, living up to their motto 'Percute et Percute Velociter' – 'Strike and Strike Swiftly' – even though their supplies of ammunition were low compared with those of the Turks. At last reinforcements arrived, at 7 am, but again there was not enough ammunition. Hour after hour the hail of shrapnel, machine-gun and rifle bullets and bombs rained down on the men.

In Gallipoli the weather was oppressively hot by the middle of July and the flies became unbearable. Diarrhoea – the 'Turkey Trot' – was increasing at an alarming rate, as were the numbers in the 'diarrhoea rest camp'. The Allies had few places in which to bury their dead, but in No-Man's Land, decomposing human bodies littered the parched land. These horrifying remains were close enough to see and, more gruesomely, close enough to smell; they were crawling with maggots, and blackening and swelling in the sun. The stench seared the nostrils. Most men had never seen anything to compare with the flies. Gigantic insects known as bluebottles flew from the rotting bodies, bringing with them dysentery, enteritis and all kinds of disease. As fly-proof latrines were not provided at Anzac Cove for the first three months, food could not avoid being contaminated, and no man could put any anything into his mouth free of flies.

At the beginning of August, when the 10th Light Horse was preparing to respond to further heavy shelling directed by the untiring Kemal, Major Olden, in his acclaimed history of the campaign, *Westralian Cavalry in the War*, wrote: 'All ranks 45 per cent physically below their normal standard'. In August, out of the 43,553 wounded and sick taken away from Gallipoli,

12,968 men were suffering from dysentery alone'. The Turks still seemed to possess a limitless amount of bombs, the heat continued to be overwhelming, the plague of flies even more so.

As he rode over to the ridges away from Anzac Cove above Suvla Bay, Kemal noted in his diary that 'for the first time in four months I was breathing air which was more or less pure and clear, because in the Ariburnu district and its neighbourhood, the air we breathed was polluted by the corruption of human corpses'. But soon the air around him above Suvla Bay was also putrid with the smell of the dead.

Suvla Bay, a shallow, open indentation in the thickest part of the peninsula, about two-and-a-half miles north of Anzac Cove, was the landing place for 30,000 men from the New Army and Territorial divisions on 6 August. The Turks were taken completely by surprise. If the British had moved quickly they would have pierced the Turks' front. But the commander, Sir Frederick Stopford, was caution personified. By the time he got his men moving, the Turks had blocked the gap and the opportunity was missed.

British theory was that the overall commander laid down the parameters, and the individual battles were controlled by lieutenant-generals (or the like). Even though Hamilton's instinct was to station himself at the bay at forward battle headquarters, his advisers insisted that it was better to stay back and keep in touch via the cable lines. So he left the running of this battle, which demanded great speed and initiative, to the ineptitude and dithering of Sir Frederick Stopford. If Hamilton had been there, he could have intervened to overrule Stopford and inject some urgency into the troops' moves. He failed to notice that Stopford's orders showed an ever-decreasing lack of urgency, and that the aims of his attack were continuously watered down. In contrast, Liman von Sanders had one local Turkish commander instantly dismissed when he became defeatist.

The British official historian, Brigadier-General Aspinal-Oglander, wrote that because of the delays and hesitation, 'the advantages gained by the surprise landing at Suvla had been thrown away. The IX Corps had trifled too long with time. The chance of gaining the high ground on very easy terms had disappeared. It was now to be a fight between forces of equal numbers, with the British troops...and the Turks in possession of every point of vantage...once surprise had gone there was little chance with anything approaching equal numbers of scoring a British success.' In just four days, out of the 50,000 British and Anzac troops engaged in the battles for Suvla Bay and Chunuk Bair, 2,000 were killed and 10,000 wounded. Over 22,000 sick and wounded were sent by ships to Egypt and Malta alone.

Impatience greeted this disastrous attempt to break out of Anzac Cove. It led a few weeks later, to the assault on the Nek, a ridge fifty yards wide with cliffs falling away on either side, where the opposing trenches of the Turkish and Australian troops were only twenty yards apart. The immediate instructions to the men of the 10th Light Horse were to cross the short space of No Man's Land and reach enemy trenches. The attack was to begin before dawn, in the half-light in which a man could barely see. Unfortunately, as Monash was to point out later, if the Australians could see to move, the opponent could see to shoot. The classic solution to this problem was for British artillery to smash the enemy's machine-guns and trenches before the men would charge. But this did not work. Guns from land and ship were too light, their fire too inaccurate. When the destroyer and the land guns opened fire in the direction of the Nek at 4 am, the shells missed the Turkish front line. In addition, for a reason never explained, the guns stopped seven minutes earlier than scheduled, at 4.23 am. It has been suggested that this may have been due to the Allied officers not managing something as basic as synchronising the time on their watches. Regardless of the cause of the lull, the Turkish troops took advantage of it and went forward to fortify their trenches.

The young soldiers waited to go 'over the top'. When the order was shouted, a line of 150 Australians charged across the ridge, but before they had covered ten yards Turkish gunfire mowed down the entire line. Most were killed. Minutes later the next line was ordered to follow. No reviewing officer could have faulted the way in which the men executed this command. But running and stumbling over the bodies of their fallen comrades, they too met the full blast of Turkish fire and were cut down. Next was the third line.

They too were mown down. Before launching the fourth line, the officer giving the orders, realising the futility of the task, asked for it to be cancelled. Under such a hail of well-aimed and well-distributed fire, men could not go forward even a few feet and live. The request was refused. The men were to go forward. They rose over the parapets, ready to assault. They too, like their comrades before them, were cut down.

By now the regimental colours of black, white and red were dark red with blood, as was the dry, parched earth. Orders were only then given to stop. The men were diverted to support troops at Monash Gully. Another scheme had miscarried. The bodies of the dead lay where they had fallen. The 10th Light Horse lost 136 men at the Nek, roughly half of their effective strength. Of these, eighty-four were killed or missing and fifty-two wounded. With 240 losses, the 8th Light Horse from Victoria lost two-thirds of their regiment. In all, 372 Australians were killed or wounded while the commanding Australian officer, Lieutenant-Colonel J. M. Anthill, stood by, refusing pleas to stop the men going over.

At nearby Quinn's Post, an entire line of fifty-four Queenslanders from the 2nd Light Horse Regiment, with the exception of one man, fell dead or wounded within a few paces of their trenches. Courage had been wasted. Commanders had not acted to minimise losses, nor had they met their objective. To make matters worse, in his despatch Hamilton failed to mention the 10th or the 2nd Light Horse, ignoring the fact that the attack had been disastrous for them. He briefly stated: 'The 8th Light Horse only accepted their repulse after losing three-fourths of the gallant band that sallied forth so bravely from Russell's Top'.

Olden later wrote sarcastically: '…never in the history of the Army has a more stunning effect been created in a unit with such suddenness than had that glorious debacle of August 7th among the wasted ranks of the 10th Regiment. Bitter as was the loss of their comrades…it was as nothing compared with the bitterness of the knowledge that their lives were offered up in vain'.

Hamilton continued to put a gloss on all that happened. He sent a report to London: 'As a result of the battles of August 1915, we had gained elbow-room and inflicted enormous losses on the enemy – how enormous we did not know at the time. But we had not succeeded in our main aim; to get command of the Narrows. The spirit of the Turks had, however, been broken, and they had been thrown entirely on the defensive'.

Robert Rhodes James, in *Gallipoli*, commented: 'Self-deception could hardly go further. Some of his staff officers now spoke openly at GHQ of engineering his removal. He had lost over 40,000 men in less than three weeks, and had gained little or nothing; ugly stories were circulating about the treatment of the wounded'.

Earlier in June, Aubrey Herbert had written, in a letter to his wife, that feelings against Hamilton were widespread, saying that 'Ian Hamilton has been here twice, I think for a quarter of an hour each time and has never been around the positions at all. GHQ are loathed'. Later, in another letter, Herbert added, 'Hamilton has the obstinacy of weak men. I have had one or two instances when I have seen how he and his staff believe what they want to believe in the face of all sense and evidence'. And on another occasion, he wrote: 'Rightly or wrongly, we thought that GHQ, living on its perfumed island, did not consider how great was the abomination of life upon the cramped and stinking battlefield that was our encampment, though this was not a charge that any man would have dreamed of bringing against Sir Ian Hamilton'.

Accused of leading 'from the rear' throughout the campaign, Hamilton based himself on board a cruising vessel or at headquarters on the *Aragon*. At that time, many British generals sat on padded office chairs more often than field stools. Often pictured in dress uniforms moving coloured pins on enormous ordnance surveys and charts, they relied on information about the Front from officers, who, keen on their own promotion, did not always give the true picture. According to A. J. P. Taylor: 'Few of the generals had heard a shot fired in anger; and they did not much increase their experience during the war – they remained far behind their armies at headquarters, drawing lines on maps, barking out orders over the telephone and surrounded by a sycophantic staff'.

Sir Ian Hamilton's biographer, John Lee, countered this by saying that 'throughout recorded history, front line soldiers have complained long and loud about staff officers. The criticism is often partial and inaccurate; all mistakes tend to be exaggerated, successes tend to be taken for granted. The idea that generals should command from the front lines is, of course, absurd in modern warfare. Ian Hamilton had a particularly difficult command and control problem, with his forces fighting in three separate localities and no room ashore for a general headquarters. When he settled for a base on Imbros Island, equidistant from Helles, Anzac and Suvla, his camp was run on Spartan lines to ensure that his immediate staff shared the discomfort of the troops'.

Troops huddled together, becoming enervated from privation and disease, from the everlasting racket of small arms and artillery fire, from the heavy labour of digging on top of the non-stop front line vigils, and the contaminated fly-ridden food. Weakened and overcrowded in their cramped up quarters around the shore, they were far below their normal capabilities.

The original £18 million borrowed from Britain to equip the first AIF had increased rapidly every week, and been followed by loan after loan for the troops at Gallipoli. Every bullet, every boot and every crumb of food put Australia further into debt. There was a feeling of quiet outrage among Australian politicians as the Bank of England refused to lend Australia more money to finance Australian troops fighting for Britain. According to Jack Lang, who later held the posts of both premier and treasurer of the New South Wales postwar parliament, when the amount had reached just on £50 million, the Bank of England declined further loans and the money had to be raised in Australia. The debt was increased further 'because of charges made by the British government for quartering the AIF in France, and on account of provisions supplied to the troops in France'. But such was the patriotism in Australia that not only were the loan monies raised, but the number of troops recruited increased.

Chapter Four

Departure from Gallipoli

M onash put some of the blame for the inefficiency at Gallipoli on the
hierarchical system in the British army. Like many Australian
soldiers, he could see the grave defects of 'jobs for the boys' and the jostling
for connection that riddled the British army, not to mention the social
snobbery and aspirations that went with the system. Written during a brief
leave in Lemnos, a critical letter home said:

> *In this island one can see the cult of inefficiency and muddle and
> red tape practised to a nicety. There are ever so many gentlemen
> earning their war medals on board luxurious transports, decked
> all over with...patches and arm-bands and lace, acting as deputy-
> acting-inspector-general-of-something-or-other.*

The *Aragon*, a magnificent South American liner anchored at Mudros harbour,
was, for a while, used as headquarters, and was said, jokingly, to be grounded
on empty wine and champagne bottles. In his next letter, Monash added:

...during the first forty-eight hours after the landing at Suvla, while there was an open road to the Dardanelles, and no opposition worth talking about, a whole army corps sat down on the beach, while its leaders were quarrelling about questions of seniority and precedence; and it was just this delay of forty-eight hours which enabled the Turks to bring up their last strategic reserve from Bulair and render futile the whole purpose of that landing, which was to protect the left flank of the Anzac advance. The failure to do this held up our further offensive. Cheerful, isn't it?

Monash' s remarks, in one of his many diary-letters, were pertinent:

Somebody in the House of Commons asked the other day, – 'Why are the Australian troops being sacrificed in such large numbers at the Dardanelles?' It's about time somebody began to ask questions, and it's about time too that somebody asked about the treatment of Australian soldiers in Tommy hospitals, for it's the absolute dizzy limit. Nothing could be better than our Australian or New Zealand or Canadian hospitals, but as to the British hospitals, here, well, the sooner they hang somebody for gross mismanagement the better.

The Australian public was not aware of the extent of the suffering, or the disaster that had taken place. Censors were told to suppress references to 'inadequate hospital treatment, camp troubles or criticism of the military planning'. The fact still remained that Australia had had no voice in any negotiations preceding the outbreak of war. When Britain had declared war on Germany, Australia, like the other dominions, had been automatically at war as well. During the Gallipoli campaign, senior Australian officers did not officially challenge orders from the British, nor did politicians in Australia make complaints about the hospital conditions. It has also been alleged that they did not prevent any military exploitation of their troops.

At Gallipoli, as in most battles, the majority of Australian soldiers were used as front-line soldiers; few were in supply and back-area duties. Ernest Scott, in the *Official History of Australia in the War 1914–19*, Vol. XI, said that 'The Australian casualties were higher in proportion to their numbers than those of any other portion of the British forces. This was probably due to the fact that the Australians were nearly all "front-line" troops, engaged throughout the war in heavy fighting'. Armies usually have a ratio of one-third front-line troops to two-thirds supply logistics and transport, etc. But as the Australian forces relied on Britain for these support troops, Australia had a larger percentage of men in the front lines.

There is a certain irony in the fact that no Australian had been part of the decision-making process to send Australian troops to Gallipoli, but it was an Australian journalist, Keith Murdoch (father of Rupert), who was a factor in the recall of Hamilton from Gallipoli. Despite his stammer and real shyness, Murdoch had become a respected journalist in Melbourne. When in Egypt, en route to London to take up a job with the Cable News service, he applied for permission to visit Anzac Cove for a few days.

While on the island of Imbros, the second British base for Gallipoli, Murdoch found that his feelings echoed those of Ellis Ashmead-Bartlett, one of the selected journalists permitted to accompany the troops to Gallipoli. Formerly with the *Daily Telegraph*, he had been appointed to cover operations for the whole of the London press, as well as for numerous other British, European and American newspapers. Previously he had said:

> *I thought there were limits to human stupidity but now I know there are none. The censorship has now passed beyond all reason. They won't let you give expression to the mildest opinions on any subjects…There are now at least four censors all of whom cut up your stuff…All hold different views and feel it is their duty to take out scraps. Thus only a few dry crumbs are left for the wretched public. The articles ressemble [sic] chicken out of which a thick nutritious broth has been extracted.*

Murdoch was struck not only by the squalor and flies, but also by the disparity between the truth and earlier news stories which hid the extent of the horrors. Seeing the suffering caused by the mismanagement of the campaign and knowing the ignorance about it in Whitehall, he smuggled out a letter from Ashmead-Bartlett to Prime Minister Asquith. But when Murdoch's ship docked at Marseilles, a British intelligence officer confiscated his papers. Undaunted, he continued to London, where he decided that writing a letter to the prime minister of Australia was not a violation of censorship. A copy was also sent to future prime minister, David Lloyd George, then minister for munitions, who was by now vehemently against the Gallipoli campaign.

The letter contained many flaws and errors. Its theme, though, that the Gallipoli expedition was heading for disaster under Hamilton's command, echoed the growing concern at what was going on in Gallipoli and coincided with a general feeling that the time had come to scrutinise those in high command. It also gave ammunition to the anti-Dardanelles faction. Lloyd George suggested that a copy be handed to the British prime minister. Asquith, who regarded Suvla Bay as a disgrace, in turn circulated it to British Cabinet ministers and the Imperial Defence Committee. He also wrote to Kitchener: 'I have read enough to satisfy me that the generals and staff engaged in the Suvla…ought to be court-martialled and dismissed from the Army'.

However, it must be remembered that Hamilton was not responsible for the decision to attack at Gallipoli, or for the shambles of the organisation; that was down to Kitchener. The lack of artillery ammunition was the responsibility of the British government, and the poor medical arrangements were due to the sheer volume of horrendous casualties. But Hamilton was responsible for not standing up to Kitchener and the British Cabinet, and for failing to impose his will on his battle commanders.

Not only was Hamilton sacked; he was given no further position of control during the war. Birdwood took temporary command of operations in mid-October, until the arrival of Sir Charles Monro, the new commander-in-chief. But the situation was still hopeless. The prediction in Murdoch's letter that not enough winter clothing and equipment would be supplied in time proved true. Men literally froze to death when the worst winter weather seen for decades in the area caused rough seas, making it difficult to land supplies and provisions. On reaching Gallipoli, Monro came to the conclusion that an early evacuation was eminently desirable.

Desperate to salvage the situation, Churchill continued to argue in favour of chemical warfare. At that stage, gas had only been used on the Western Front, not in the Middle East. According to Dr Yigal Sheffy, who has made a study of gas, Kitchener had earlier despatched a small amount of chlorine gas to Gallipoli to be used 'at the discretion of the local commander'. Hamilton, though, had kept the cylinders in store. After he had departed, a unit of chemical-warfare operators and 6,000 cylinders of chlorine gas (about 200 tons) arrived at Gallipoli. But they, too, remained sealed. The weather was against their use anyway. Apart from moral reasons that either Hamilton or Monro might have had for not using gas, gas is heavier than air and as the Turks held the higher positions, it would have floated back on the men who released it.

On 27 November it rained ceaselessly for twelve hours. Trenches turned into canals, dugouts became cisterns, and raging torrents ran through gullies. Men were knee-deep in water in the trenches. As work went on at night trying to drain them, the snows came, frost set in and the winds changed to northerlies. Flies disappeared completely with the drop in temperature, but the bullets increased in number. As the whiteness of the snow contrasted with the khaki uniforms, the soldiers were easier targets. Water was scarce, so the scant supplies of fuel were used to melt snow into drinking water. Not only were rough seas interrupting regular supplies arriving by boat, but at Suvla and Anzac the water mains had burst. One blizzard was so severe that over 200 men in open trenches at Suvla Plain died, frozen to death. Braziers made from old biscuit tins were not enough. The temperature remained below freezing for three days. Thirty-two-year-old 'Little Clem', Clement Attlee – the future Labour prime minister of Great Britain, and a captain with the 6th South Lancashire Regiment – wrote of how he had a foot inspection, making all men with sodden feet rub them with snow to increase circulation. He was already asserting authority. Criticising the hesitations in the chain of command at Gallipoli he said '...the right leaders were not chosen...hidebound generals were not the men to push through an adventure of this kind'.

In the first eight days of December alone, out of around 16,000 casualties, 12,000 were due to the weather. Once in hospital, hundreds of feet and entire limbs were amputated. A further blizzard lasted for three days. Without revealing the deaths and losses from exposure, an official report just stated 'Snow continues to fall, men taking it very well as first experience'.

The year 1915 was ruinous for the Allies. Germany, whose losses in France were less than half those of the total British and French casualties – over a one and a half million – was winning in France and had a firm grip on the Balkans and the Middle East. The British were reluctant to admit the ignominy of having to back out of Gallipoli. Kitchener finally made a visit in November and decided that withdrawal was the only sensible policy. But as Churchill, who opposed pulling out, said, 'Wars are not won by retreats'.

During eight months of fighting, over 43,000 Allied troops had been killed or had died of disease. Of the 410,000 British and 79,000 French soldiers who were landed, nearly every second man was a casualty. British casualties were 205,000 (115,000 killed, wounded or missing and 90,000 evacuated sick), including 28,000 Australians. The French had the worst ratio of casualties, with 47,000. The Turkish casualties were officially 251,000, but are often put as high as 350,000.

On 8 December 1915 Kitchener sent a signal to Gallipoli headquarters: 'Cabinet has decided to evacuate positions at Suvla and Anzac at once'. Later in that wintry month, the departure from the blood-soaked ridges and beaches was carried out without the loss of a single life. Each night thousands of men crept away under cover of darkness, until the whole 90,000, along with 200 guns and 5,000 horses, had departed. A skeleton army held the front line until the last possible moment. The British and French followed.

'Walk softly when you pass those graves so they won' t know we have gone,' murmured one Australian as he moved towards the waiting boats. Another whispered, 'I hope they won't hear us'. It is evident from going through letters from troopers written at this time that leaving behind around

10,000 Australian and New Zealanders in shallow graves meant that many a man hoped to get his 'own back' one day.

The Australians, according to C. E. W. Bean, were 'very sore at heart' when forsaking their dead, leaving them below rough sods of earth or scattered on the rugged Turkish headland. It had been impossible to retrieve all the dead. Some had been quickly tucked into the hillside where they fell; others just decomposed. Many corpses, though, had been tenderly buried beside little crosses made from wooden packing cases.

The mass exodus might not have been such a triumph if Mustafa Kemal had not headed off to Constantinople the day before the evacuation commenced. His departure had been hastened because of a falling out with Liman von Sanders. Andrew Mango, in his recent biography on Kemal, quotes him saying that he had realised that the Anzacs were…

> …about to withdraw, and so I had proposed an offensive. But they [the Germans] turned it down. This upset me. As I was also very tired, I came to Istanbul. If the enemy had withdrawn, as successfully as he has done now, while I was still there, I would have been even more upset. Lucky that I'm here.

Paradoxically, the two future world leaders who were at Gallipoli, Clem Attlee and Kemal, were never face to face. The last man but one to leave Gallipoli in December was Attlee. On 19 December, he led 205 men to the beach at 5.30 pm and embarked on HMS *Princess Irene*.

Gallipoli was not only the first battle in living memory that the Turks had won against a European power, it was also the first episode in Kemal's ascent – he had been crucial to the Turkish victory. Only seven years would pass before Kemal was to become president of Turkey. Attlee was to wait thirty years before he became Britain's second Labour prime minister.

Chapter Five

Three Conflicting Agreements

A dashing 28-year-old Turkish officer, Muhammad Sharif al-Faruqi of the 142nd Regiment, altered the direction of the war in the Middle East, which led to the first steps on the winding road to Damascus. Few deserters had ever had such influence on the course of war.

Officers were completely duped by him. At the beginning of the fourth month at Gallipoli, false information which he gave to Allied officers set the British on an unexpected route. Well educated, and from a prominent family in Mosul, the large city in northern Mesopotamia (now Iraq), this charmer with a wide smile and sincere expression managed to bring about a complete change in British policy towards the Arabs. Even though Arab nationalism was in its infancy, he painted a false picture of it, giving the impression that nationalism was the principal motivation of the majority of Arabs. The degree to which he managed to mislead the British can be seen in a letter dated 25 August, now in the Public Record Office in London, from

Hamilton to the war minister in London. David Fromkin, author of *A Peace to End all Peace*, goes as far as saying that: 'To the twentieth-century Middle East, he [al-Faruqi] left a legacy of misunderstanding that time has not yet entirely dissipated'.

Al-Faruqi exaggerated his standing in the Arab nationalist movement. His bogus statements became the springboard for Britain's involvement in the Revolt, and were just as far-reaching as the four conflicting agreements made by the British during the war: the Hussein–MacMahon correspondence in 1915, the Sykes–Picot Agreement in 1916, the Balfour Agreement in 1917 and the Declaration to Seven in 1918.

Not only was al-Faruqi's influence far-reaching, but its effect was felt quickly. On 20 August 1915, after the Suvla Bay landings at Gallipoli had petered out in sullen stagnation, al-Faruqi crossed No Man's Land. He ran quickly, waving a white flag on the pretext of leading a party rescuing dead soldiers for burial. After soldiers rushed towards him, he insisted that he should be treated as a deserter, not a prisoner-of-war. Without any of the reluctance typical in such situations, he agreed to immediate interrogation by English officers.

During his first grilling, al-Faruqi's revelations were manna from heaven. The year 1915 had been a time of almost unrivalled misfortune for the Allies – both on the Western Front and in the East – so British officers relished all the information al-Faruqi gave them. War Office documents show that in fluent French, he gave invaluable information, even details on the latest Turkish military moves. For instance, until he told them, the British had not known about the reorganisation of the Fourth Army in Syria, or of the establishment of new, but weak, divisions in northern Syria. He also provided facts on troop movements, reports of which had been imprecise and exaggerated until then.

But with the good came the bad. His brilliant intelligence on Turkish troop movements was countered by exaggerated reports about Arab nationalism. Having convinced the British of his credibility, al-Faruqi switched to fantasy. The information he gave did not include with any facts about either the mutual suspicion and feuds that often existed between tribes, or the fact that over the centuries the Arabs had seldom acted in unison.

The British had no trained professional interrogators; the bilingual officers, such as Aubrey Herbert, did their best. Lacking reliable means of substantiating al-Faruqi's claims, they accepted much of what he said. But it was also what the British wanted to hear, especially as it fitted in with their plan to free the Holy Cities, Mecca and Medina, allowing the 100 million Muslim subjects in the British Empire to continue making pilgrimages. Such a move would also greatly undermine the Sultan in Constantinople. As stated earlier, for three centuries the Sultans had kept constant control as Keepers of the Holy Places – along with holding the Prophet's mantle (cloak) – as possession of them was vital if they were to continue their dual role as rulers and religious leaders. Without Mecca and Medina, it would be difficult for the Sultans in Constantinople to maintain their position as the titular leaders of the Sunni Muslims.

The Sultan's standing relied on Sherif Hussein, the head of the Hashemite clan in the Hejaz sector of the Arabian Peninsula on the Red Sea, which contained Mecca and Medina. Large garrisons of troops were kept in the Hejaz by the Sultan to maintain order and ensure that Hussein remained subservient to Constantinople and did not transform his emirate into an autonomous or independent regional principality. Hussein was also kept subdued by the poverty of the region. The aridity of the dry, sandy country of the Hejaz made it dependent on imports, pilgrims and money – from wherever they could be found. The interest in the area shown by the British after the *jihad* was declared in November 1914 was more than welcome. Hussein immediately started negotiations that involved assurances of large sums of money and aid to help his country – and his family. Britain wanted Hussein to become independent of the Sultan but only control the Holy Cities and surrounding areas. However, Hussein wanted much more that. Because of this, negotiations for the British to aid a revolt to free the Holy Places were drawn out. By chance, as these negotiations were taking place, al-Faruqi in Gallipoli was giving information that would dramatically and decisively speed them up – and change their outcome.

During al-Faruqi's interrogation, he said that one of the first secret groups to be formed was Al Jamiyyah al Arabiyah al Fatat (the Young Arab Society, known as Al Fatat, not to be confused with the contemporary Al Fatah, or Fatah, of the Palestine Liberation Organisation). Another group was the al-'Ahd (the Covenant), a secret society of Arab officers with a special sign language, of which al-Faruqi was a member. He stressed that Arab intellectuals, many of them educated in Constantinople, were going further than urging the study of Arab history, literature and language; they were asking for the decentralisation of Ottoman administration and demanding a measure of automony within the existing framework. But after this, most of the information given by al-Faruqi was wishful thinking. As he told the story of the Arab underground movement, he painted a highly embellished picture of Arab nationalism. He said that complete Arab independence was the movement's one goal and that tens of thousands had gone underground to form a resistance. Groups engaged in subversive activities in Syria were stirring up mutinies and desertions in the Turkish army.

The British seemed to have forgotten the abject failure of the Turkish invasion of the Suez Canal, which had garnered no local Muslim support. Ten days after he had changed sides in Gallipoli, al-Faruqi sailed across the Mediterranean to Cairo, arriving on 1 September. He underwent further interrogations, including a grilling by the chief of the Arab Bureau, Gilbert Clayton, and by Lawrence. Much of what al-Faruqi said was similar to what had been related earlier by the leader of the al-'Ahd, Major Ali al-Misri, who was also now in Cairo. It also echoed certain aspirations related to the British by Sherif Hussein and members of al-Fatat.

But contrary to Hussein's wishes, the British planned only to help him gain control in the Hejaz. They had absolutely no plans to expand his borders or his control until al-Faruqi arrived in Cairo. They saw Hussein only as a self-interested tribal chief; he was certainly not a Garibaldi or a Bolivar.

At this time a blockade in the Red Sea against the Turks was isolating the area, but men and supplies were still arriving overland by single-track railway across the desert. A revolt in the Hejaz would isolate the Turkish forces in southern Arabia. So, at the beginning of September 1915, a polite and careful letter was sent from the British High Commissioner, Arthur MacMahon, in Cairo, to Hussein in Mecca.

Hussein, who could be obstinate, narrow-minded and suspicious, turned out to be more demanding than the diplomats had anticipated. While the British were then only considering a limited exercise, which would give the Sherif independence in the Hejaz, Hussein's burning ambition was to be king of a greater Arab nation with his sons, Ali, Abdullah, Feisal and Zeid as rulers of a confederation of Arab states.

The exaggerations put up by al-Faruqi were many. The late Professor Ellie Kedouri in *In the Anglo-Arab Labyrinth*, quotes him as saying '...we the Arab party are a power which cannot be disregarded. Ninety per cent of the [10,000] Arab officers in the Turkish army and a part of the Kurd officers are members of our society [the al-'Ahd.]' This has recently been proved to be inaccurate. Research by Tauber confirms that al-'Ahd at that time had only fifty members, of whom forty were officers – less than a meagre 1 per cent of the Arab officers in the Turkish army. Even though the number of dissatisfied Arab officers was probably larger than this figure indicates, the majority wanted reforms within the Ottoman Empire; they were not looking for independence. A small number were reluctant to join any groups because of fear of Turkish reprisals, while others were waiting to see which side would win the war. But whether disheartened, restless or ambivalent in their loyalties, there are few records of Arab officers deserting. Most who absconded from the Turkish army did so not for political reasons, but because of lack of food, maltreatment, or a longing to go home, away from the front line.

Secret information was gathered mainly by the men employed at the Arab Bureau in Cairo, including Lawrence, and directed by Clayton. No agents of any consequence were recruited during the Gallipoli campaign. Nor were they signed up later. Even the handful of Jewish agents in Palestine, despite their considerable heroism, did not supply significant information. Hidden eyes and ears were recruited, but the information given by them was second-hand, marginal, the result of casual encounters or accidental contacts. Good intelligence was hard to obtain due to fear of reprisal. Twenty-one Arabs were hanged in the city squares of Damascus and Beirut on the morning of 6 May 1915. Severe in dealing with any rebels, Djemal Pasha, the ruler in Damascus, had earned his title 'Djemal the Butcher' by sparing neither Muslim, Christian nor Jew from the scaffold. After rumblings of a revolt in June 1915, he had dispatched Arab officers to fronts in distant battlefields, such as Gallipoli or the Caucasus, or subjected them to beatings or torture.

Everything that Lawrence wrote and said was based on his assumption that the Arab uprising was a popular, established and widespread movement. Research has now shown that this was not the case. The question must be asked: why did British officials in Cairo, including Lawrence, rely on information from one deserter? They could have interviewed officers from a wider cross-section, such as the hundreds of Arab officers languishing in the prisoner-of-war camps, rather than al-Faruqi's handful of fellow Arab nationalists. Even after the war, Lawrence, who surely must have realised that al-Faruqi's statements were exaggerated, never qualified them or said that he had been misled.

Contrary to al-Faruqi's statements, membership of any of the established secret Arab organisations was small. Most importantly, the majority of Arab officers did not then care about Hussein's dynastic dreams. Despite the truth, Lawrence later told Liddlell Hart that he had been convinced by al-Faruqi's statements, adding that there could have been an Arab mutiny in 1915.

Lawrence's empathy with the Arabs worked very much in al-Faruqi's favour. His statements gave Lawrence something concrete; a basis on which he could fervently embrace Arab nationalism. It has often been suspected that the extent and importance of the Arab Revolt was exaggerated, but only since Professor Tauber's research (and he spent years studying the subject) has this suspicion been fully substantiated. Although many observers had noted it at the time, Tauber has showed that the majority of Arabian tribesmen only allowed themselves to be recruited in the Revolt when they were assured that there was gold to pay them. The common run of village and town Arabs remained loyal to the Ottoman state until it collapsed.

In Cairo, al-Faruqi warned the British that time was running out. Playing on unwarranted British fears that the Arabs would be given wholehearted backing by Britain's enemies, he stated that if the British did not give an answer promising the Arabs support within a few weeks, his society would be forced to accept the offers of the Germans. He painted a picture of a large section of Arabs fighting against other Arabs. It would be Constantinople and the Sultan versus the Sherif of the Hejaz, who would take Mecca and Medina. The two centres of the Islamic world would be at war. So much for the Sultan's *jihad*.

Clayton asked MacMahon to obtain instructions from London. An agreement was needed urgently. Kitchener sent authority to General Maxwell, 'empowering him in the name of the British government to deal with the Arabs and to try to ensure that their traditional loyalty to Britain would not be impaired'. Maxwell replied, reiterating that they believed there was 'a large and influential Arab party actually in the Turkish army'.

According to Professor Tauber, '...the arrival in Cairo of the deserter Muhammad Sharif al-Faruqi brought a complete turnabout in the British attitude towards Hussein and the Arab movement...Faruqi's crowning touch was his statement that the Turks and Germans would not dare to suppress the officers' movements and that they had even approached their leaders and agreed to grant all their demands...[when] they suppressed the Arab separatists the best they could...It is clear that Faruqi's statements to the British were permeated with inaccuracies, exaggerations, and lies'. With hindsight, it is difficult to understand how the men in Clayton's office did not see that al-Faruqi's statements were hollow and that Arab nationalism was in its infancy. Al-Faruqi, though, had given himself – and the movement – a new status. He stayed on in Cairo, where it was soon seen that he had a weakness for European mistresses. Throughout the remainder of the war he retained a paid position with British intelligence.

A comparison of MacMahon's first letter to Hussein (30 August) with his second (24 October) shows the extent of al-Faruqi's influence. The first letter to Hussein from MacMahon was full of ambiguities, with no commitment. The British had until then only wanted to stir up a limited Arab revolt, and contain it. Because of their emphasis on limitation, this early letter suggested that decisions about frontiers should be postponed until the end of the war. But Hussein, who saw through the charm and tricks of British diplomacy, said that he could not co-operate with the British on such vague terms. He wanted a full undertaking that all Arab lands under Ottoman control would be given self-rule.

Suddenly on 24 October, a letter written by MacMahon to Hussein met most of Hussein's demands. Known as 'the Hussein–MacMahon correspondence', these compromising letters were to be trawled out and discussed in parliaments and peace conferences for decades. The Arabs maintained that through MacMahon, the British High Commissioner in Egypt, virtually all the Arabic-speaking countries in the Middle East, with the exception of Lebanon, would be free to choose their own political future. Hussein, it is said, only rose against the Turks in June 1916 because he believed he had been given the word of the British government.

Persuading Hussein to revolt and cast off the Turkish yoke was a formidable task, as the Turkish garrison was ready to overwhelm any opposition by the Arabs. Bringing British ammunition and support troops by sea seemed to be the sole route. Royal Navy warships already patrolled the Red Sea to stop any enemy vessels entering the Suez Roads. Hussein not only lacked five components – arms, money, a strong army, capable leaders and imported foodstuffs – but his administrative abilities were far from impressive and his government, which was almost medieval with its layers of intrigue, showed little sign of social or economic progress. Nor did he have the power to stop marauding Bedouins robbing and exploiting pilgrims.

By the spring of 1916, messengers were continually plying between Hussein and Cairo. General Sir Reginald Wingate, who had earlier won fame in the Sudan, was given the title of General Officer Commanding Operations in the Hejaz – and the task of what was described as 'nourishing the revolt'. The British were becoming impatient.

Coinciding with the return of the Australians to Egypt from Gallipoli was the conclusion of the Sykes–Picot agreement between the French and the British. With optimism that they would eventually win the war, the British made plans for dividing up the Turkish provinces after they had been captured, even though, apart from Turkish losses to Russia around the Black Sea, there were no signs of Allied victory against the Turks. The respected member of parliament, Sir Mark Sykes, who negotiated on behalf of Britain appeared to disregard the earlier quid pro quo with the Arabs, which had been made only months before with the full knowledge of the British government. But at that time the agreements were not a source of conflict. Secrecy surrounding the Sykes–Picot agreement meant that Sherif Hussein did not realise that the land he considered pledged to the Arabs in the series of official letters was soon to be an issue. It was now in conflict with new zones of administration agreed to with the French. Attached to the Sykes–Picot agreement was a map with areas marked red for zones of British influence, blue for French influence. Palestine – the Holy Land, sacred to Muslim, Jew and Christian alike – was marked as a brown zone, with this explanation: 'Palestine, with the Holy Places, is separated from Turkish territory and subjected to special regime to be determined by agreement between Russia, France and Great Britain'.

France, as the traditional protector of all Catholics in the Levant, was the leading foreign power in Syria. In the past century France had established a network of schools and businesses both there and also around Jerusalem, while at the same time increasing her colonial ambitions in the Levant. However, France was not welcomed as a colonial power by the locals; they had heard of her subjection of the local population in Algeria.

There was irony in the fact that the British, 120 years after they had pushed Napoleon Bonaparte out of Egypt, were once again – although they and France were now allies – still holding the upper hand.

Chapter Six

Australian Troops and the English Officers

Oh the airman's game is a showman's game, for all of us watch him go,
With his roaring, soaring aeroplanes, and his bombs for the blokes below.
Over the railways and over the dumps, over the Hun and the Turk,
You'll hear him mutter 'What-ho she bumps!' when the Archies get to work.
But not of him is the song I sing, though he follows the eagle's flight,
And with shrapnel holes in his splintered wing comes home to his roost at night.
He may silver his wings on the shining stars; he may look from his clouds on high,
He may follow the flight of the wheeling kite in the blue Egyptian sky.
But he's only a hero built to plan, turned out by the Service Schools,
And I sing of the thankless, thankless man who hustles the Army Mules...
ARMY POEMS, A B PATERSON, *KIA-ORA-COO-EE*, APRIL 1918

The tattered remnants of the Light Horse brigades, reunited with their horses, resumed their role of mounted infantry and settled back into camp routine. Fresh remounts arrived, all saddles and harnesses were polished, and men exercised their horses by racing them around the sand dunes.

While in Europe the era of the horse in land warfare was gradually being superseded by machine-guns, tanks and other new technologies. In the Middle East, though, for the time being at least, the horse was still king of desert battles. For thousands of years, horses, mules, donkeys and camels had been the most common mode of transport in Arabia and the Holy Land. Apart from a few Rolls Royces and 'Tin Lizzie' Fords, anything on wheels was slow-moving on heavy sands and tended to get bogged down. Even the infantry soldiers resorted to putting removable wire soles (like snowshoes) on their boots. Trucks and motorcars, when driving over vast plains, mountains and sandy wastes, often ran out of fuel, broke axles and needed spare parts. Railways had been a godsend, but the tracks were few and far between.

The beginning of 1916 was a time of triumph for the Turks. As well as their victory at Gallipoli, they had defeated the British in Mesopotamia and the overthrow of Serbia had given them a direct supply of munitions from Germany. Using the troops released from Gallipoli, the Turks now planned a huge invasion of Egypt.

With renewed confidence from their success at Gallipoli, the Turks kept sending reinforcements south through Syria and Palestine to halt the British and Australian troops. Turkey wanted to ensure that she sustained her momentum in the Middle East by maintaining a multi-front war, with offensives in the Caucasus and in the Sinai.

An army of Turks, estimated at around a quarter of a million men, based in Southern Syria and Palestine, was moving towards Egypt. So started another segment in the long battle of the Australian Light Horse against the forces of the Ottoman Empire. For the time being, its action would be defensive, not offensive. Apart from the Australian Light Horse, there were twelve infantry divisions, two brigades of Indian infantry and some brigades of dismounted Yeomanry. Reinforcements were arriving regularly and some of the Australian regiments were over-strength. Any show of bad horsemanship resulted in a rider being transferred to other units – infantry, artillery or the new Camel Corps.

All effort was initially geared towards the protection of the Suez Canal. Although British control in Egypt still stopped just over the eastern border of the canal itself, in the Sinai Peninsula. Initially, despite agreements about the carve-up of Turkish territory, there were no immediate plans on the agenda for an all-out invasion to capture Syria or Palestine.

The repercussions from the British forces not pursuing the retreating Turkish forces after their invasion of the Suez Canal on 2 February were now being felt. Excuses given were that the troops had been untrained and unfit for such a mission, and that intelligence had not provided them with details of what reserves had been waiting in the desert. Wavell suggested that both troops and staff at that time had been 'new to the work and had not properly grasped the requirements for the conduct of desert warfare'. To ensure that critics would not have such grounds for complaint again, intense training began, always weighed down with haversacks, ammunition pouches, trenching spades, bayonets and rifles. Seldom, though, due to shortages of ammunition, was practice with real bullets.

Month after month, the men waited in camps in the Kantara vicinity while plans for an offensive were finalised. Restless and fed up, they spent their accumulated pay – and the rift between the Australians and the British officers widened. Australian wages, like the badge on the hat, showed a fresh attitude to military conventions. While the Australian rate for privates of 6 shillings a day was the highest in the world, that of the brigadier-generals, at £2 12s 6d a day, was below the rate paid to their British equivalents. The rural wage in Australia was only around 20 shillings a week and the average weekly Australian wage was £2 15s 7d, so the new Australian army rate of 6 shillings a day, of which 1 shilling was 'deferred' and the option of up to 4 shillings to wives or mothers, was particularly welcome to the rural poor. Australian lieutenants received £1 1s a day when overseas, and a captain £1 6s. The miserable rate of a shilling a day for British soldiers remained the same throughout the war – Australian privates were six times better off.

(Canadian privates received 4 shillings and 2 pence, and New Zealanders 5 shillings.)

When possible, men on leave visited the weekly race meetings at the Khedivial Sporting Club (Ghezira); the more ambitious took part in the races and placed and rode their horses in the stakes. Horses belonging to the 10th Light Horse that had come with their owners from Western Australia played a dashing role at the Saturday races outside Cairo. 'Babanooka', belonging to Colonel Todd, won four races in succession and became the best handicap horse in Egypt at the time. Other favourites from the 10th Light Horse were Lieutenant Norrish's 'Kojonup', Lieutenant MacDonald's 'Old Nick' and Major Olden's 'Yaboo' and 'Orchardor'.

Although they could attend the racetrack at Ghezira, the men in the ranks were banned from the tennis courts and wicker chairs on the lawns of the smarter clubs around the main clubhouse or the Turf Club. With their palm trees and aspidistras in pots, men in linen suits and women in crêpe-de-Chine dresses, thick damask tablecloths set with the heavy silver plate cutlery, these clubs were favourite attractions in Cairo. Many Australians thought they had the right to drink or eat in the same venues as officers. However, military administrators stopped all lower ranks entering them and the Long Bar at Shepheard's' Hotel, along with the dining room and the Hotel Continental. Shepheard's was the giddy centre of social life. Most other hotels were rented out as army office headquarters. However, some of the men who had been banned from the smart venues earlier could now enter, as they had risen in rank. The high death and casualty rate at Gallipoli had caused an acute shortage of officers, so troopers and lance corporals were among the new promotions.

Tales of indiscipline among the Australians in Egypt were countered by the Prince of Wales, the future Edward VIII, who himself was often impatient with ceremony, convention and 'Society'. While in Egypt in 1916 reporting on the defences of the Suez Canal, he called the AIF 'magnificent' and wrote that 'they have fought so d—d hard and are so keen, that it is hard to deal severely with them'. Stirred by their exuberance and cheerfulness, he burst out with, 'I'm not often given to these high-flown ideas, but really these Anzacs have impressed me so much!!'

A chain of discrimination from the British towards the Australians, then from the Australians towards the local population, was noticeable throughout the war. 'One lot of English would look down on other English, but all the English would look down on all the foreigners,' wrote James Aldridge in *Cairo*. 'All foreigners would look down on all Egyptians, and rich Egyptians looked down on middle-class Egyptians. And everybody of all races and classes looked down on the fellahin, who in fact dug and watered and nurtured the wealth the whole structure was built on.' Everyone seemed to be lording it over someone they thought inferior. The Australians scorned the Egyptians as 'wogs', while many English officers stood back with a certain disdain from the Australians with their aggressive familiarity. The Australians were often startled at the deference shown by the British tommy, who they saw as pale, puny and resigned to his inferior position. They could hardly believe that the tommy, self-contained and subservient, was willing to obey orders without question.

Many British officers treated the Australians with disdain, denigrating them as crude and ill-mannered. But these 'brash colonials' who sometimes called officers by their first names, were unimpressed by any superior airs. Their disregard for stiff military protocol was shown by their being slow to salute or use the word 'sir', an indifference to dress regulations, resentfulness when given unnecessary orders, carelessness about carrying passes and daring to answer back.

With their defiant egalitarianism, Australians saw the military master–servant relationship as oppressive.

Despite reforms, the British army generally remained a class-structured entity. Aristocratic traditions, wealth, social distinction and well-cut uniforms still counted. With few exceptions, status conferred by birth and schooling remained the prerequisite for choosing the upper ranks of the military.

In Europe the war was going badly for the Allies, including the Australian forces stationed there. At that stage, while the Light Horse regiments remained in Egypt, four infantry divisions of Australians faced the horrors of trench warfare in France. Out of the total of 222,000 Australians overseas, only 42,424 remained with the Egyptian Expeditionary Forces. They were part of the fourteen divisions placed under the command of Sir Archibald Murray, the new commander-in-chief, who had taken over from Sir John Maxwell. He was seen by many of the Australians as the personification of the pompous 'Colonel Blimp' type of British officer.

The Anzac Mounted Division was now no longer comprised exclusively of Australian and New Zealand riders, but also included Scottish and English cavalry. As well as the 1st, 2nd and 3rd Light Horse Brigades and the New Zealand Mounted Rifle Brigade, it included the Royal Horse Artillery Brigade of the Inverness, Ayrshire and Somerset Batteries. Chauvel was placed in command.

For a few months Egypt was relatively quiet, apart from the intermittent mine-laying raids on the canal by the Turks, which had started in 1915. Their priority was defending north-eastern Turkey against the Russians; their major assault on Egypt – using newly released troops from Gallipoli – was thought to have been delayed. But suddenly reconnaissance aircraft spotted 25,000 Turkish soldiers swarming towards Egypt under another German commander, Kress von Kressenstein. Wearily they trudged along the oldest road in the world – the vaguely marked highway connecting Africa with Asia that ran across the Sinai Desert to what was often referred to as 'that beastly place' Kantara, on the canal. Since pre-Biblical times, standing between the huge area inundated by the Nile and the fringe of the sand dunes, Kantara had been the entrance to the thousands of miles of desert. Invaders – Babylonians, Assyrians, Persians, Greeks, the Roman legions, the Crusaders and Napoleon's chasseurs – had marched through this area. None had been immune to the desert's fine powdery dust. It pervaded everything, causing colic and irritation.

As the Turkish troops moved nearer, more trenches were dug. Digging holes in the sand needed relentless energy. The shifting loose sand on the sides was inclined to fall inside again as quickly as it was dug. As one group dug, another stood by with timber hurdles, covered with coarse grass matting reinforced with wire struts, and rushed them into the hole. Wider trenches with a wall of sandbags on either side were more durable. Most trenches were seven feet deep but vigilance was needed to stop them filling with sand when violent sandstorms, known as Khamseens, whipped up the fine grains and pervaded everything. These hot, dry, easterly sandstorms blow from the Arabian desert and usually last about three days. After even a couple of days, a trench would be almost full and need digging out again.

East of Port Said, the northern end of the Suez Canal, a tract of desert known as the Plain of Tina, lies below sea level. While the men were at Gallipoli, this was flooded with water from the canal to form a barrier to the enemy. Beyond this, for over 100 miles, extending nearly to Rafa and Gaza, is a coastal strip of terrifying sand dunes with rampart-like edges. Some rise to almost 400 feet. So steep are they, and so soft is the sand, that men could feel that they were drowning if they attempted to descend too quickly. A continuous spray of fine sand particles blew off the edges of the dunes, so their shapes were constantly changing. Winds could alter the contours and profiles so much that a man could lose his way. Horses grew expert at coping with the almost perpendicular slopes, often sinking up to the hocks. But in drifts a horse would sink to the shoulder. At the foot of many of the dunes were the very welcome hods, usually indicated by a clump of date palms. Here, by digging or sinking wells men could, with luck, find brackish water.

The strong defensive line east of the canal protected it from Turkish artillery fire, but required too many men. So an advance to Katia, a town inland from Romani, twenty-five miles east of the canal, was planned. On 23 April – two days before the first anniversary of the Anzac landings at Gallipoli – the Turks again repulsed the British with the Australian horsemen in the lead. Katia, which had been taken briefly, was lost. The obstinate Anatolian peasant-turned-Turkish infantryman, 'Johnny Turk', 'Jacko' or 'Joe Burke', was quite a match for the Allied soldiers, and continually halted progress. Turkish soldiers have been noted for their bravery and even when outnumbered and outgunned, they do not give up easily.

Turks were not the only enemy facing this immense moving army. There were two other unseen foes: lack of water, and dust – worse now that the long and hot dry season was beginning. The unforgiving conditions of the advance were only too familiar to many of the horsemen, who had been hardened to life on a pitiless terrain with scorching heat and little water in the interior of Australia, yet trying to stretch the insufficient water supplies here was a problem from start to finish. Dried-out tracks or desert and stony ground were usually no obstacle to them. But now they often had to call a halt. The men marvelled at how the last foreign troops along the Sinai Peninsula, those led by Napoleon Bonaparte with 12,000 men, thousands of captured horses and his new Camel Corps in 1798, had managed to cope.

As well as hunger, thirst, heat and dust, both man and beast also suffered from the flies and other insects. Lice and fleas gave rise to almost non-stop itching and acute discomfort. Scratched sores went septic. Rubbing with methylated spirits helped the bites, and kerosene was a well-tried antidote to lice. Sand often jammed weapons, and after firing fifteen to twenty shots, rifles were sometimes too hot to hold. Often there was not enough water for men to wash either their own bodies or their clothes, and a strong stench of unwashed bodies had to be endured.

As the men rode on, from time to time the din of aeroplanes drowned the howl of the jackals. Added to the difficulties of getting water and forage to the animals was a new logistical problem: transporting cans of petrol. Aircraft had been used throughout the war, but this was the first time that such a large advance of horses had to be finely co-ordinated with aeroplanes. Progress during the campaign would have been slower and the Allied casualties heavier without air support. This was not just due to the hammering and strafing by the pilots. Their aerial surveillance and their air-post service, dropping notes to troops and taking messages from them to General Headquarters, were also invaluable. The superb co-ordination of the air and ground forces was seen when a group of airmen actually made an improvised landing beside a cavalry advance.

Fierce fighting between the Australians and the Turks ended in an Allied victory and Katia was retaken. Kress von Kressentstein decided to pause while reinforcing his position with yet more artillery, machine-guns and anti-aircraft units. During this three-month lull, the British strengthened their position, ready for an advance across the final leg of the Sinai Peninsula. The daunting job of laying railway lines across the Sinai, along with hundreds of miles of pipes, hundreds of water butts and storage tanks, was commenced. Three hundred miles of standard-gauge track alone involved 40,000 tons of steel, imported, like the other components from Britain, across the submarine-infested Mediterranean. Every week, these new arteries, bringing guns, water, food and men across the desert, grew in length by just over ten miles. Construction involved using forced labour gangs from the total of 120,000 Egyptian fellahin conscripted – mostly against their will – into the Labour Corps during the war. Howard Carter, who had been assigned to a department which mobilised labour battalions, was horrified at their sordid recruitment and said that they were often brutally and callously treated. Peasants and small landowners were also hit by the requisitioning of corn, fodder, camels and donkeys.

Meanwhile, rumours circulated among the Bedouin that camel trains laden with gold sovereigns – later referred to in *The Times* as 'Lawrence's secret Arabian "slush fund"' – were heading to the Hejaz. The Arab army would have been stillborn without British arms and gold, let alone the support of the British, Australian and Indian infantry forces. Without this, many of the Arab soldiers would have gone home.

Chapter Seven

The Arab Revolt – Lawrence Joins Feisal

—⟨⟩⟨⟩⟨⟩—

Six weeks after the first anniversary of the Anzac landing at Gallipoli, Sherif Hussein hoisted his flag. So began the Arab Revolt. By coincidence, on the very same day, 16 June 1916, Kitchener, one of the loudest advocates for the British to push the Arab Revolt, was drowned at sea. Britain's support for the Arabs would have pleased him. Owing to assistance from the Royal Navy, Mecca and Jeddah were taken almost at once. Three weeks later, a small Egyptian army unit, with six field and six machine-guns, was on its way. Next, a flight of aeroplanes was sent, together with a bunch of former Arab officers from the Ottoman army who had been released from prisoner-of-war camps solely so that they could defy the Sultan's *jihad* and fight against Turkey.

The degree to which the British drove the Revolt, and how exaggerated al-Faruqi's claims were, can be seen by the difficulties encountered in persuading Arab officers to leave the safety of the prison camps to fight for Hussein.

Many demanded six months' pay (in advance) to be paid into bank accounts. Others declined to go, knowing that there could be reprisals against their families. Eventually al-Faruqi was given the task of persuading officers in the prison camps to enlist. However, on arrival in Jeddah, the first group of Muslim officers flatly refused to take up arms against fellow Muslims. After about a week, most were sent back to Cairo. But with a little propaganda from the Arab Bureau filtering into the prison camps, though, recruitment became more successful. The numbers of Arab irregulars waxed and waned. Reasons for this depended on the amount of British gold to be distributed, the likelihood of success, and the proximity of a campaign to a tribe's territory. The military backbone – the Arab regular army – remained small. It comprised a camel battalion, an infantry battalion mounted on mules, an unmounted infantry brigade and about eight guns. Despite tradition, it did not have a large number of men mounted on horses.

In the early months Wingate became the central British character masterminding the Arab Revolt and sending the Arabs minted gold, weapons and munitions. 'Wingate had no illusions at all as to the military capacity of the Arabs,' his son wrote in *Wingate of the Sudan*. 'If they did anything – and he was never optimistic – it would only be because trained officers, a hard core of specialised troops, and a sufficiency of modern weapons were supplied to them. There was also the question of finance. It was idle to suppose that Arab tribes, utterly unused to modern war, would think of risking their lives unless heavily bribed…and finally there was the supply of food…'.

The pro-Arab British policy expanded quickly. In October, additional English officers, including Lawrence, arrived to continue nourishing the Arab revolt. Their job was to assist Hussein, keep the Arab Bureau in Cairo informed, urge the Arabs on to capture the Turkish stronghold at Medina, and disrupt and cut the Hejaz railway – the vital link between Syria and the Holy Cities. Supplies came on trains all the way from Turkey itself, but the track was not yet continuous through to Constantinople. Goods still had to be off-loaded in a few parts of the mountains, but the railway ran through most of the Taurus Mountains to Aleppo and down to Riyak, where the gauge changed, and goods were trans-shipped into other carriages to Damascus. In the next two years this railway line would become both a constant target and a military route.

Lawrence was immediately given scope to implement his highly original ideas on guerrilla warfare. Blowing up the track was a quick way of reducing military activity, as the arrival of supplies, owing to shortages of fuel and rolling stock, was already precarious.

Unlike a conventional war hero, Lawrence was of slight build, with bright blue eyes and a curiously nervous smile, his fair hair parted and brushed to the side and plastered with grease. His six years living in Arab countries meant that he not only spoke Arabic but also happily sat cross-legged in true Oriental fashion and climbed onto a camel as easily as onto a motorbike. Lawrence not only gained the confidence of the Arabs, who called him 'el Aurans', 'Laurens Bey' or the 'Emir Dynamite', but also became close to Prince Feisal. David Howarth, in *The Desert King*, summarised Lawrence's role in the Revolt, saying that: 'With Lawrence's genius and Britain's wealth, the revolt went from strength to strength. Yet it was always hollow; it was always an expression of Lawrence's will and of British power, and never of any permanent Arab aspiration'.

In contrast to Lawrence, Feisal, who often wore belts full of jewelled pistols and daggers, had been raised in almost suffocating luxury. But being the third of four sons of an Arab ruling family, when his father eventually died, it was likely that he would be pushed aside into obscurity. Only the Arab separatist movement gave him a chance of coming to the fore and seizing a kingdom and a throne. Well educated, he was fluent in both French and Turkish, and felt himself equipped to take on a king's role.

The Royal Navy again came to the aid of the Arabs in the spring of 1917, when Feisal's main force moved northwards up the Red Sea coast from Yenbo to Wejh, where it posed a serious threat to Turkish lines of communication. Soon afterwards, Allied intelligence learned that the Turks were planning an imminent withdrawal from Medina. While this would be a victory for Hussein, British headquarters in Cairo feared that the Turkish forces there would be transferred to Palestine, where they would help oppose the British advance. To prevent them leaving Medina, Lawrence developed a new strategy. He would allow the Hejaz railway to keep working, but only just. Guerrilla raids would inflict minor damage at remote points, halting railway traffic for a few days at a time. Withdrawal of Turkish troops from Medina would then be virtually impossible as large numbers of Turkish soldiers and repair workers would need to be deployed along the line to defend it and keep it running. From then onwards the Turkish force in Medina was impotent – they only survived because they scraped up sparse local produce.

During the winter of 1916–17, Lawrence and the Arabs slowly progressed in a northerly direction. They were troubled by both the weakening condition of the camels and snakes. The valley of the Sirhan appeared to crawl with puff adders, cobras and horned vipers. Even though they killed about twenty snakes each day, seven men were bitten and three died. In a month Lawrence began 1400 miles on camel, riding about fifty miles a day.

In July 1917, Lawrence's star rose after the brilliant taking of Aqaba, the last position on the Red Sea coast held by the Turks. Here, while starting to show an emotional, almost impassioned dedication to his work, he proved that the method most suited to the Arabs then was guerrilla warfare. A few weeks later, Feisal moved to Aqaba with his troops and Lawrence commenced co-ordinating movements with the British.

The British continued to send the Arabs massive quantities of guns, bullets, gold and camels, together with bilingual army advisers. As well as Lawrence, other British officers involved in the campaign included Hubert Young, Pierce Charles Joyce, Malcolm Peake and the future peers Lord (George) Lloyd and Lord Winterton. They played various roles, from helping with strategy to acting as interpreters and as liaison officers between the British and the Arabs.

In Palestine, as well as riding a camel, Lawrence travelled in an armoured Rolls Royce, which was thought of then as four-wheel drives today – a high-quality vehicle for getting through the heavy sands. He believed that 'a Rolls in the desert was above rubies' and 'cars are magnificent fighting machines…'. Fascinated by speed, aeroplanes and engines – anything with a motor, a key and a petrol tank – Lawrence later proved himself to be a skilled mechanic. Once he raced on his motorbike against an aeroplane on an open road. His rush of excitement came from speed, the thrill of velocity. He never drank alcohol and only smoked on Christmas Eve, but he seized every excuse to move as fast as he could.

Lawrence was ten when he pieced together the fact that his parents were not married, and that like his brothers Frank, Arnold, Bob and Will, he was illegitimate. His mother's real name was Sarah Junner. A self-educated woman from the working classes who had run off with her employer, Thomas Chapman, after four years in his household as nursery governess, she stayed with her lover for thirty-five years. Chapman's income had to stretch to keep up a grand Irish household with a butler, a cook, a wife and four daughters, plus an English household with a mistress, a cook and five boys. Lawrence's tall, bearded, quiet 'ever-loving father' was a member of the Anglo-Irish aristocracy, an Old Etonian whose real name was Thomas Robert Tighe Chapman, grandson of an Irish baronet, soon to inherit the title. Less than 300 miles from Oxford was his family mansion, South Hill, near Delvin, in County Westmeath, surrounded by woods, bogs and rolling acres. His wife Edith, maliciously referred to by locals as 'the vinegar queen', lived there with their daughters.

For Lawrence, embracing Arab ways was almost a way of defying his possessive mother. Always religious and thrifty, she had longed for him to work with the Christian Mission Societies (his brother became a missionary). Lawrence, like his elder brother, Bob, had in his youth become a Sunday school teacher at nearby St Aldate's in Oxford and later an officer in the Boys' Brigade. But in the Middle East, instead of converting people of other faiths, Lawrence's tolerance allowed him to live amicably with Muslims and aid their cause.

Chapter Eight

'Banjo' Paterson Looks After the Horses

While Lawrence was slowly progressing by camel in a northerly direction, thousands of horses were being groomed for desert warfare. In Europe, however, nearly half a million cavalrymen who had ridden into World War I in France, Germany, Austro-Hungary, Russia, Britain, Belgium and Serbia had been forced to discard their horses, finding that they were no match for machine-guns, barbed wire and trenches. German machine-guns had butchered and decimated the horses when they had been brought into the assault at the Somme in 1916, and a year later at Arras with Allenby. The death of a horse often meant the death of the man riding him. If a horse failed, the man in the saddle could fall to the ground and be trampled by other horses or dragged along, sometimes clinging onto the stirrups of another rider.

As a soldier on horseback has always been an easier target than a single infantry man on the ground, when firearms had become more deadly, mounted attacks became fewer. But even though horses were seldom used in combat – the horses at the Battle of Ypres formed the grand closing curtain for their use on the Western Front – most nations continued to maintain cavalry up to the bitter end. Keeping them on battlefields, even in the twentieth century, was a nightmare of logistics. Whole baggage trains were taken up with shifting fodder, and often prevented other supplies, such as ammunition and medical stores, from getting through. During the four and a quarter years of World War I, British horses in Europe alone ate their way through 5.9 million tons of fodder and feed, even though most men in cavalry units had been switched to infantry roles in trench warfare.

The Eastern Front was better for horses in a warfare role. In August 1914, the Russian army boasted thirty-six cavalry divisions, and over 4000 cavalry charges were mounted in that area, including the shattering of the Austro-Hungarian Seventh Army by Russian cavalry at Gorodenko in April 1915. Later on, the use of horses by the Cossacks and the Red cavalrymen when fighting against the White Russians in the Russian Civil War was spectacularly successful. Over the rest of the continent, though, horses were employed mainly for reconnaissance or in rough terrain and places too difficult for motorised vehicles. But neither the Western nor Eastern Fronts sustained active cavalry on the scale of the Palestine/Syria campaign. Here the Allies were fighting an enemy with a centuries-old tradition of desert warfare, and success depended on the quality, care and preparation of these animals. The majority of the horses and mules used over the three years of the Palestine/Syria campaign passed under the control of Australia's most popular poet, A B 'Banjo' Paterson, the author of both *Waltzing Matilda* and *The Man from Snowy River*. But few books, either on a military or literary level, acknowledge his role. Nor do they mention the extraordinary contribution of the Remount Service, which he ran so well.

Paterson's mastery in the training and care of horses enhanced the performance of the British in the Middle East, yet there is no reference to this important work in Volume VII of *The Official History of Australia*. Even Geoffrey Dutton's *Australian Literature*, which gives details of Paterson's six months as a war correspondent in South Africa in 1899, dismisses his part in the Great War in a line: 'Served in 1914–18 war as ambulance driver and in AIF'. No details are given of the nearly four years he spent in the Middle East, where he ceaselessly purchased, requisitioned and prepared suitable horses for the army. As in most books, the only detailed information given on his military career is about his nine weeks as an ambulance driver in France, taking the injured on stretchers to the railway station at Boulogne-sur-Mer.

When Paterson signed up at the outbreak of war in 1914, he showed an unusual eagerness to get to the front. He had sold his property on the Murrumbidgee River quickly, and then obtained a position as honorary vet (with a certificate of competency) to accompany some of the 7882 horses travelling with the first contingent of Australian troops.

In late January 1915, Paterson, having gone on to England and found no post in the British army, on hearing that in Australia a unit of men was being formed to purchase, train and care for the horses in the Middle East, had hurriedly sailed home to Sydney. Without delay he was accepted and commissioned as a lieutenant into the 2nd Remount Unit, jokingly called the Horsedung Hussars. Paterson lopped two years off his age, changing his birthday from 17 February 1864 to 1866. His withered arm was not seen as a handicap. He soon rose in rank to a dignified major, complete with a swooping white moustache. Paterson was told that his main role would be caring for the horses so the men 'could get away to the Front...'. His unit comprised twenty-one officers, three veterinary officers, one medical officer and 816 other ranks, which included blacksmiths, saddlers and wagon-drivers. He was reassigned to a camp at Maribyrnong in Victoria before embarking on the *Orsova*, landing at Suez on 8 December 1915. The moment he arrived at the British base at Maadi, he and his unit took care of the riderless horses of the absent Light Horse brigades. But as his arrival coincided with the evacuation of Gallipoli, he explained, '...as we got here the Light Horse men all came back...and took charge of their own horses so we were not much in demand...'.

With their original purpose superseded, Paterson's units were, for a short time, absorbed into the British Remount Service, but in March 1916 he was made chief officer of the newly combined Remount Unit at the horse depot in the huge British base at Moascar, outside Cairo. His squadron was made up of what he described as 'rough riders, jackaroos, horse-breakers, ex-jockeys and buck-jumping riders from country shows, who wore their socks pulled up outside their riding breeches'.

Paterson's staff chose, acquired and trained horses, inuring them to the traumas of battle by putting them through rigid toughening-up processes and teaching them to respond to specific commands and calls. His passion for horses was supported by sound knowledge, theoretical and practical. The hardest task for the animals was to stand still when gunshot was flying close to their eyes and head, amidst the noise of gunfire or the smells of cordite or blood. They had a high chance of being injured or killed, so the job was in many ways demoralising for a horse lover. Paterson's prose and poetry had helped to make horses part of Australia's literary tradition and had brought the ethos of the Australian bush to a wide and varied audience. Now Paterson found ways of raising the profile of the warhorses. Supervising this rigid training was a dramatic contrast to his former years. Then he had written about the beauty and poetry of 'the brumbies', the horses of the Australian bush, which were wild and free, or about reckless rides pursuing wild horses, 'a rush of horses through the trees' when the hoof-beats echoed through the mountains.

Many of these war horses had to be broken – a process that was so dangerous that the roughriders had to wear special gear. Elastic-sided boots had smooth tops so that the rider's foot did not catch in the stirrups; saddles had raised pommels and the hind bows had thick pads for the thigh and knee. Paterson said that the majority in his unit only joined the army so they could work with horses, adding that some 'did not even know a sergeant-major from any other major' – they were 'a motley crowd'. Others were too old for the front or were for some other reason unfit, but skilled in horsemanship. One man was a station owner and former member of Federal Parliament, another had worked in a circus, another had poor eyesight. Paterson described them as 'the best lot of men that were ever got together to deal with rough horses'.

It is extraordinary that Paterson's role was overlooked, as when his verses had been published in *The Man from Snowy River* in Australia, the book had broken all sales records. According to Penguin's *Literature of Australia*, 'The first edition sold out in a fortnight; ten thousand copies were sold in its first year...It was not only the most successful collection of bush ballads ever published; it was also, in terms of sales, one of the most successful books of any kind ever published in Australia'. A London edition was on the bookshelves in 1896, and a reviewer in England claimed that Paterson had a bigger audience than any living poet in the English language except Rudyard Kipling, another colonial, who had been born in Bombay. Theodore 'Teddy' Roosevelt, the former president of the United States, said that he enjoyed the 'speed and gusto' of Paterson's ballads.

One American war reporter visiting Egypt described Paterson's universal popularity. 'As soon as I landed I asked every Australian officer that I met where Major Paterson was, for locating an individual member of an expeditionary force, no matter how well known he may be, is not always easy. Everyone knew him. I remember well I enquired at the Australian headquarters in Cairo how the man I asked turned to a comrade and said, "Say, where's Banjo now? He's at Moascar, isn't he?" Whether they had ever met him personally or not, he was "Banjo" to one and all...At Moascar...I found him...'

Paterson's robust poems, which were particularly well suited for recitation, stressed the idyllic existence of living on the land; above all, they were about the droving and rounding up of cattle. The verses highlight the excitement, but seldom the pain and the hardship. Forgotten are the long, lonely days for station hands such as my father, who worked as a jackaroo before his enlistment. He loved the trees, the landscape, and the birds and animals, especially the flocks of cockatoos. But nothing was less romantic, he said, than droving, that is, taking cattle to the abattoirs or the boiling-down works. For him 'the bush' was a harsh struggle. The months of heat and drought often dragged on well after the creeks and water holes had dried up, and sheep and cattle perished. Coupled with this were often pitiful wages and periods of hunger, thirst and loneliness. But Paterson's poems, lyrical and romantic, became national symbols of the bush, idealising it for town dwellers.

The privileged son of a station owner, Paterson had worked with horses in his youth before moving to Sydney in the 1890s to become a man-about-town with a desk job, as a solicitor. Apart from rowing and playing tennis, his leisure time was still spent with horses. He became a competent and fearless polo-player and amateur rider, winning several races at Randwick racecourse.

Paterson produced many more stories and reports during his six months as a correspondent in the Boer War than he did in the Middle East. Between 1915 and 1919 he wrote little that became well known. A couple of anecdotal articles appeared in 1934 in *Happy Dispatches*, a collection of journalistic pieces from his days in both the Boer War and First World War, but his rousing war ballad, *The Army Mules*, which was originally published in the Australian soldier-produced newspaper in the Middle East, *Kia-Ora-Cooee*, although often recited by soldiers, was not published in Australia until 1992. The authors of the *Oxford Companion to Australian Literature*, who gave him the accolade of being 'the chief folk-poet of Australia', do not mention him in their lengthy section on Australian war literature in World War I. It seems that when faced with the gruesome reality of being with an advancing army, Paterson lacked the inspiration that had come from his beloved bush. War put him off, but his passion for horses continued, as can be seen in the following quotes from *Happy Dispatches*:

> ...we are supposed to take horses out of the Depots and ride them quiet and get them into condition ready to issue to troops. We have 200 roughriders and 600 other ranks and curiously enough our roughriders really can ride. The buck rider shows that used to travel about Australia all closed down when the war broke out and the riders all joined this unit and we got a fine lot of horsemen. We get some rough sorts of horses too, I think everybody that had an incorrigible brute in his possession must have sold it to the army. I usually only ride horses intended for Generals and thus I get the pick of the mounts.

The unit became especially prominent when Paterson gave roughriding displays in public:

> ...*instead of being a sort of Parish outfit we became justly celebrated. Egyptian notables, wandering English celebrities, and aristocratic females of various types all vied in trying to secure invitations to our display...All joking apart, the work is hard, monotonous, and dangerous, and the men deserve every credit. I don't think the world ever saw such a lot of horsemen get together as I have in my squadron – Queensland horse-breakers and buck-jumping-show riders from New South Wales. It is queer to note the difference in the various States – the other squadron are Victorian, Tasmanian, and South Australian farmers and they are quite a different type from my lot – far easier to handle; having had the real rough horses to deal with they cannot touch my men at horse work. We (my squadron) won five out of seven events open to all troops in Egypt at a show the other day. In the wrestling on horseback one of my Queenslanders, a big half-caste named Nev [not Ned] Kelly, pulled the English tommies off their horses like picking apples off a tree...I have never had to tell a man twice to get on a horse no matter how hostile the animal appeared; in fact they dearly like to do a bit of "grandstand" work even though they risk their necks by it.*

Sadly, official army files do not identify or commend any horse that took part in that campaign by name. Their sole identification was branding on the rump and a number engraved on the front left hoof. Scant records remain of the 136,000 horses shipped from Australia to Britain, Egypt, India and France between 1914 and 1918. Only one came back.

More dangerous than riding, though, was being airborne. Paterson felt a deep sympathy for the young, enthusiastic pilots. The saddest job for his wife, Alice, who was a nursing aide in a hospital at nearby Ismailia, was 'constantly making shrouds' for the men, often killed on their first solo flights in the fragile aircraft. Paterson wrote: 'The life of a pilot, computed in flying hours, is pitifully short; many of them are killed while learning'. To help these young men have a good time he 'let them have riding horses and we occasionally turn out quite a creditable hunt with the Saluki hounds after jackals'.

Following the progress of the young pilots closely, Paterson also wrote in *Happy Dispatches*: 'Everything is being hurried up. The big English flying school near our camp has been ordered to turn out as many pilots as quickly as possible...'. In each open cockpit was usually a pilot and an observer, wearing helmets and protective goggles. The observers, who were often trainee pilots, acted as spotters and assistants, dropping bombs out of cockpits, firing their Lewis machine-guns – or later releasing bombs from containers beneath the wings of larger aircraft, such as the Handley Page bomber.

He added: 'There is an average of eighteen planes in the air all day long, just above our heads. The din is indescribable, but the horses never look up, or otherwise take the slightest notice of the planes'.

Paterson was full of scorn for the puffed-up generals booked into the bedrooms of the grand hotels in Cairo, such as Shepheard's. He criticised the ninety or so 'busy about such jobs as reporting upon the waste of jam tins...others became town commandants, or examiners of an army diet. So many were they that there was little room for junior officers in the hotel and no room at all for non-coms or the rank and file. These latter riff-raff were forbidden to enter the hotel, even to buy a beer or to meet a friend, lest they should come between the wind and the nobility of the staff officers. This created a very unpleasant feeling and the troops rioted outside Shepheard's by way of voicing their protest'.

Paterson also told how two of the Australian officers played a practical joke on the English at Shepheard's one night after an order had been put out as 'O.C. of dress and deportment...that officers were on no account to wear socks that did not match the rest of their clothing'. The two men went to the hotel one night and 'made all present – generals included – hold up their feet to show their socks. They said that they were to see that the new order was being observed. Not a man dared keep his foot down, and the jokers got away with it'. No officer dared complain that he had been tricked.

Although Paterson was himself an esteemed officer, like many other Australians he had a defiant independence, especially when standing up to the demands of his seniors, explaining with sarcasm: 'No officer, not even a staff popinjay or a brigadier, should be allowed to select a horse for himself. We had to issue the horses. The best had to go to the fighting men; the next best to the staff; and the culls and rejects to the men on lines of communication, camp-commandants, doctors, water-supply officers, and such-like...'.

Paterson, like other soldiers, was very protective towards the horses. The attachment that each soldier had to his horse was enormous. His horse was not merely a part of war armoury, or transport. He was much more than an animated machine, much more than something to carry him into battle. He was a mate. Through suffering and deprivation, a bond developed between man and beast, a feeling of affection and trust, a real partnership. J M Brereton summarises that special relationship in *The Horse in War*:

> *On campaign, riding and tending the same horse for months on end, sleeping in the open only a few yards behind the picket lines at night, and suffering the same privations, the soldier came to regard his horse almost as an extension of his own being.*

As will be seen in the following chapters, this bond between horse and man developed over the campaign, only to end in tragedy – both for the horses and for the men who loved them.

Chapter Nine

The Two Battles of Gaza

On 18 July 1916, reconnaissance aircraft raced back with the news – over 8000 Turks were making their way towards the Australian Light Horse. A week later the Turks advanced to within about ten miles of Romani. In a surprise raid they struck the British Sinai railhead. After a ten-day lull, bitter fighting between the Australians and the Turks was renewed in the sand dunes. Romani was kept. On 8 August the *Sunday Observer* published a report by the English journalist W T Massey:

> *The brunt of the fighting was borne by the Anzac mounted troops. These magnificent horsemen had been anxious to follow their comrades to France, but they were retained in Egypt because they are ideal soldiery for work in front of our defences. And they acquitted themselves magnificently.*

Failures at Katia and Bir-el-Abd soon soured this brilliant victory. Undaunted, General Sir Archibald Murray withdrew his headquarters from

Ismailia to the Savoy Hotel in Cairo and put all troops east of Suez under the command of Major-General C M Dobell who, despite lack of experience, received promotion to Lieutenant-General; the very able Lieutenant-General Sir Philip Chetwode, an Old Etonian (who even in uniform smoked using an ivory cigarette holder), was made GOC of the Desert Column. He later became immensely popular with the men because he always went forward with them, but like many English officers, he took time to adjust to the casual ways of the Australians. He once complained in a letter to Chauvel that 'Not only do your men fail to salute me when I ride through your camps, but they laugh at my orderlies'.

El Arish, the largest enemy centre near the Egyptian border, was taken easily. A troop of mounted Light Horsemen rode twenty-five miles across the desert on a moonless night. Instead of putting up a fight, the Turks retreated to the town of Magdhaba, but it, too, was soon taken. Recognition of Chauvel, sometimes described as 'the finest cavalry general of the century', for keeping the advance across the Sinai moving came a few weeks later – a telegram arrived informing him of a knighthood for 'services and the gallantry of your Division at El Arish, Magdhaba and Rafa'.

But the lack of water continued to cause problems, and yet again the horses were near dead with thirst. As the wells were nearly empty, some mounted soldiers were forced to return to El Arish. On the long ride back, on their third night in the saddle, the men, guided by luminous prismatic compasses and the stars, slept, the reins thrown on the necks of the horses. Staggering into the camp, the horses showed off their excellent memory of places by taking their riders back to wells they already knew. There was merriment all around when the men found that the Christmas presents from Australia had arrived – cigarettes and chocolates stuffed into billies. But Harry Bostock of the 10th Light Horse related in his candid memoirs *The Great Ride* that a horse had already given himself a Christmas feast by eating all Harry's bread and biscuits the night before.

The deep affection given to the horses is illustrated by a drawing made of 'Galloping Jack' Royston's charger, sitting beside him, outside his tent, drinking out of his cup of tea. Although nearly sixty, Royston, a boisterous

South African who commanded the 2nd Light Horse, was said to have once ridden – and exhausted – fourteen horses in one day.

By early 1917, the Sinai Peninsula was cleared of all organised Turkish forces. At the Battle of Magruntein, British losses were 487, and 1600 prisoners were taken. For the first time since the defeats at Gallipoli, morale among the Light Horse was high. They had now pushed the Turks out of the Sinai Desert, and 120 miles of the railway and pipeline from Kantara was completed. The defensive action of the past twelve months had now achieved its aim and created a vast buffer zone east of the Suez Canal. Would any order come from London to extend the offensive and commence an invasion into Palestine? Syria? The majority of politicians were 'Westerners' – they believed that Allied forces should be concentrated in the main theatre of war, the Western Front; the 'Easterners', led by Lloyd George, argued that extra effort should be put into the war against Turkey. Among the reasons for stepping up the campaign was the fact that the Egyptian Expeditionary Force had done so well. Another was that Lloyd George considered Palestine a 'soft spot' – and a distraction from the slaughter in France and Belgium. Liberating a place of such religious significance would also offset the depressing bulletins from the continent, and the idea of the Holy City becoming part of a new British colony was challenging.

The re-conquest of Palestine – and by implication the re-establishment of Christendom in the Holy Land – had always been something dear to the heart of many of the British. Yet despite the enthusiasm for the Holy Land, instructions were only for a limited offensive; continuing into the heart of Palestine or Syria was not then mentioned. Orders were just to take the desert gateway of Palestine – the ancient Philistine city of Gaza – and a line running from the ridges of the coast to the town of Beersheba of the Seven Wells. The hill of Alimuntar, to the south-east of Gaza, where Samson had carried the gates of the city when the Philistines tried to shut him in, was now converted into a formidable fortress. Until a few months earlier, about 40,000 people had lived in the town. The Turks, fearing that the population would hinder the positions of their army, had forced most of the inhabitants to evacuate. They had even gone through the streets cracking whips to hasten them on their way.

Over fifteen months had passed since the Allies had been evacuated from Gallipoli and they were still on the Mediterranean coast, still fighting the same enemy. At least here, west of Gaza, at the edge of the desert, the men found luxuriant plantations of figs, almonds and lemons. The horses, which had not seen forage since crossing the canal, could, finally, be fed properly. Fields, especially in the Wadi Ghuzze area, were bright with spring flowers, and green with wheat and barley.

But the Australian Light Horse was restless and needed desperately to gain a sizeable victory over the Turks. Perhaps this would be achieved now they were about to turn their backs on the neverending sands of the Sinai? Further east the British had retaken Baghdad a few weeks earlier, so British prestige was growing in Arab eyes.

There was also dissension and opposition dividing the command in Damascus itself. As the Allies prepared for battle under new conditions, they did not realise that on 23 February, Mustafa Kemal, their old foe from Gallipoli, had reached Damascus and was plotting to contain the Arab Revolt that was spreading northwards. Kemal, wanting to reinforce troops along the Hejaz railway. He vehemently opposed the latest Turkish proposals on strategy. Indeed he was speechless when he read the report stressing that because of 'the strain of keeping relief trains and equipment on the Medina line weakening our main front, Sinai, we are not in a position to defend the Palestine front and keep Medina. In any case, if we lose Palestine, we lose Medina, for the British will control the railway. It is better to evacuate Medina now, and move the forces to Palestine where we might be able to defend the Sinai front more successfully'.

Kemal refused to take command of Medina for the evacuation. Back in Constantinople the very idea of abandoning this Holy City was also heartbreaking to the Sultan, who wept. Kemal, refusing to go south, stayed in the Damascus area until General von Falkenhayen arrived and took command. With him came more elaborate defence plans, all of which Kemal believed were unworkable (rightly, as it turned out). Furious and frustrated

Kemal resigned and went back to Constantinople, so he was not in the Gaza area to face the Australians. Confrontation would have to wait another eighteen months.

On 26 March, with the Australian Light Horse in the lead, the advance on Gaza began. The Turks were strongly entrenched in a position extending for about thirty miles inland, extending from Gaza and the coastal sector into a strong fortress surrounded by trenches and rolls of barbed wire. Due to erroneous intelligence, Murray believed that the Turks would not put up stiff resistance, and anticipated that they were likely to pull back to the Jaffa–Jerusalem line. He miscalculated badly. The British withdrew after the loss of nearly 4000 men. Gaza was a Turkish victory, but to save face, Murray sent London an optimistic and ambiguous account of the battle. His confidence misled the Cabinet into believing that success would be achieved by trying again. This time the instructions were even more ambitious: to advance past Gaza, and in the same swoop continue well into Palestine and capture Jerusalem.

Three weeks later, at dawn on 19 April, the second Battle of Gaza began. While the 7th regiment were moving to the right flank towards El Dammath, enemy planes dropped bombs on the Allied horses. Heavy shelling followed. Immediately British howitzers at the gates of the ancient city pelted the Turkish army trenches with a cloud of asphyxiating gas. They fired their entire load – 250 to 350 shells – in thirty minutes. When the British infantry advanced, they found, to their horror, that the Turks were still manning the positions that had been gassed. The gas had evaporated, or blown away. The German general, Kress von Kressenstein, then the commander of the Ottoman forces, later said that soldiers had had no idea that they were under a gas attack. Chemical warfare had failed dismally.

One squadron of Australians which started moving down the Gaza–Khalasa road so they could watch for movements from Beersheba – they were nearly overwhelmed. A huge cloud of dust moved towards them, at enormous speed. At around 2.25 pm it looked as if thousands of horses were galloping at breakneck speed from Beersheba towards the Australians. The hooves cut up the loose soil of the road and for a moment it looked as if the

Australians would be saved because the Turks could not see them. But in half an hour a huge body of enemy horses and men were still storming towards them. Would they come within range of the British machine-guns? The enemy horses slowed their pace, the dust dropped and the advance became cautious, slow. Suddenly the Australians realised that a living screen of men was enveloping them. A barrage of bullets filled the air. Scouts galloped furiously towards the ridges in the rear for protection. Then they relaxed a little. It was all show. The Turkish cavalry on their beautiful sure-footed Arab horses were followed by men, either dismounted or mounted, on camels and donkeys, some even on mares with foals at foot. But instead of a cavalry attack, shells from mountain guns were screaming over the heads of the Allies, bursting close to the horses at the rear. The position was now clearly untenable. There was not one inch of cover for man or horse on the flat-topped hill.

The Australians withdrew. The Turks, drawing their swords, galloped in pursuit, to be quickly repulsed and driven back by machine-guns and two armoured cars. But the enemy's guns responded and continued to shell heavily. Fighting continued in the dark. Next morning the men began digging trenches. Further north, in the town of Gaza itself, the Allied troops retreated. And thus ended the second Battle of Gaza. British losses were at least 6444 men against the Turkish losses of about 2,000 men. In theory this battle should have been a walkover for the British, yet once again the Turks had beaten one of the most technologically advanced armies in the world.

The period that followed the two Gaza defeats, April to November 1917, was one of comparatively little fighting. But the front still had to be held. To do this, frequent reconnaissance and demonstrations against the Turks were carried out in the vast No Man's Land between the British line and Palestine.

For the first few weeks the majority of troops were engaged in strenuous digging and wiring to make the line secure. Their spirits, which had been already lowered with the two defeats, became frayed as temperatures increased with the summer and the earth got drier and dustier. It was soon just a colourless brown area of powdery soil. The vitality of the men was reduced not only by terrible heat but also an almost continuous fog of light dust that penetrated and smothered everything, including the lips, lungs and lining of the noses of the men and horses.

Again there was the constant problem of temporary sanitary arrangements in desert conditions for tens of thousands of men and horses. There were no stones, no earth, just sand and more sand, and the tentacles of a straggly plant referred to as 'camel weed'. Each latrine, incinerator and grease-trap involved enormous amounts of digging. Things improved when a large earth incinerator was dug and five-seater latrines and pits were replaced with portable buckets with fly-proof automatic lids. Privacy was provided by galvanized iron and hessian sandbags.

Staying in the suffocating air with no change of scenery lowered morale even further. Breaks were rare and facilities for recreation few. The shortage of transport meant that leave out of the country could seldom be granted. So-called rest days were still spent watering and grooming the horses. But suddenly food rations, and conditions generally improved and rest camps were opened by the ambulance brigade on a Mediterranean beach at Tel el Marakeb, and on the cliffs just to the north of Khan Yunus. Even though everything was improvised for the men it was as welcome as the Ritz or the Savoy. Tents were lashed together, and matting huts made instant recreation rooms. A piano, books, cards and a variety of games arrived from the Red Cross. The surf was lacking but men could swim and wash themselves in the sea, there were no parades, and their only duty was to keep their beds tidy. Following the success of this camp, a larger rest camp was formed at Port Said for all troops of the Desert Mounted Corps. In just sixteen weeks, nearly 9000 men passed through these rest camps. On 20 June the duties of the ambulance brigade were shared with a completely new medical unit, the Australian Camel Field Ambulance.

The tragic and dreadful second battle of Gaza coincided with three events that were to directly and indirectly shape the Palestine and Syria campaign: the Russian Revolution, which took Russia out of the war and caused the contents of the Sykes–Picot agreement to be made public; the appointment of Allenby to the Middle East campaign; and the gathering of representatives from the British Empire at the Imperial War Conference, which held fourteen meetings between 20 March and 2 May. These meetings led to new thinking – that Palestine could be a crossroads of the British Empire.

The 300-year-old Romanov dynasty had ended when the Tsar abdicated a week after revolution broke out in Russia on 8 March 1917. The Bolsheviks, led by Lenin (whose brother had been executed by Tsar Nicolas's father), then overturned the moderate provisional government. In the Tsar's office, many secret papers were found. One bundle was already irrelevant – papers relating to Sazonov's 1915 agreement with the British over the distribution of Turkish territory to Russia. The other papers, however, the agreement made by Monsieur Georges Picot and Sir Mark Sykes, had a stinging relevance to the present. Realising that the Arabs had no inkling of the British promising their lands to the French – and knowing about the earlier correspondence between Hussein and McMahon – the Bolsheviks decided to leak the contents. This would affect not only Arab attitudes to the British but also Anglo–French dealings, as the French were unaware of agreements made with the Arabs by the British.

Morgan Price Phillips, the distinguished Russian correspondent for the *Manchester Guardian*, was allowed to borrow the documents until the next day. He worked through the night translating them and cabled the contents to Manchester. The editor, having managed to get these damning words past the censor, published them in full at the end of November 1917. But for some reason they had little impact at the time. *The Times* decided not to embarrass the government further by giving details of the papers' content, but they were also published in the Russian revolutionary paper, *Izvestia*.

The Turks, seeing the agreements as an example of Christian treachery, ensured that the Arabs were quickly made aware of them. As predicted, the faith of the Arabs in the British was destroyed and Lawrence had to explain to Feisal and the other Arabs why the British had double-crossed them. However, without British gold the Arabs would not be able to pay their troops, buy bullets or guns or have the support of aeroplanes, so they had little choice but to continue fighting with the British – and hope that circumstances and time would override the agreement. In addition, they would not have had any chance of victory standing alone, and stood a high risk of being defeated, captured or killed by the revengeful Turks.

Meanwhile, Leopold Amery, then a 44-year-old member of parliament and an assistant secretary to the War Cabinet, argued that although a million soldiers were from countries in the British Empire, these countries had no say in their management of their troops, or where they fought. As a result, the Imperial War Cabinet was convened at 10 Downing Street after Lloyd George decided that the dominions should get a voice: 'We feel that the time has come when the dominions ought to be more formally consulted…'.

Among the delegates was the South African representative, General Jan Smuts. Twenty years earlier, he had been one of Britain's enemies in the Boer War. A deeply cultured man, educated at the universities of Holland, Heidelberg and Cambridge, he was a Zionist of the calibre of Balfour or Robert Cecil, and his presence strengthened the pro-Zionist side in the War Cabinet. Smuts argued that Palestine should be a British colony. The Holy Land would create a 'land bridge' between India and Egypt, bringing together the empires of Africa and Asia. In the atlases of the world, it would result in a non-stop ribbon of British Empire 'pink' between the Atlantic and the Pacific oceans. Lloyd George, in his *War Memoirs*, wrote that Smuts had expressed 'decided views as to the strategical importance of Palestine in the British Empire…' This was similar to ideas expressed earlier by imperially minded Britons such as Lord Kitchener, who thought it was also a good northern barrier protecting the Suez Canal.

Plans for an even larger invasion into the Holy Land were soon under way. The war was still going badly for the Allies in France. Nobody knew for certain who would ultimately win. Mutinies were threatening the fighting spirit of the French army, and the German and Austrian forces were about to break through the Italian lines. The public still required a victory to offset the horrific news on the Western Front. What could be more uplifting than the capture of the Holy Land – and making it a British colony?

The de Bunsen committee put forward yet another reason for the Holy Land to be a British colony. It recommended that Palestine be held so it could be used as a land route for troop movements from the Mediterranean to the

Persian Gulf and India. In addition, creating a Jewish homeland there could counter any French establishment in Syria – a rational reason to block the French from taking too much territory in the Levant. Jews would also create a reliable and strong client population, and bring with them much outside investment. The fact that the British were planning virtually a Jewish state within a country which was more than 90 per cent Arab was not seen then as a problem.

As Leo Emery's edited diaries reveal, Smuts received a letter from Amery, saying that 'if we are going to do a big thing quickly in the Palestine direction [we need] a more dashing general'. An exasperated War Office sacked Murray. Smuts was offered the command but refused it, his excuse being that he believed he would not be given enough troops. But many thought he preferred his political role in London. Allenby, who was second choice, at first thought his recall from France was because of his poor performance at Arras, where he had sustained immense losses for trivial gains. Much to his surprise, when he reached London, instead of a reprimand he found he was to command the new thrust into the Holy Land. When he visited 10 Downing Street, Lloyd George made the much-quoted remark that the capture of Jerusalem was wanted 'as a Christmas present for the British nation'. He had less than six months to get through the Gaza/Beersheba gateway, up the coast and over the hilly country to the Holy City. Contrary to Smuts' fears, he was told he would be given whatever reinforcements he required. As will be seen, the numbers that Allenby thought necessary were highly inflated. Once more, inaccurate intelligence reports as to the strength of the opposing Turkish army would complicate the efforts of the British. The Middle East presented a melancholy and alarming challenge.

Chapter Ten

Allenby Instructed to 'Take Jerusalem Before Christmas'

Allenby took over command in Cairo at midnight on 28 June 1917. Immediately after his arrival, according to Paterson, no longer were 'troops rioting, officers disregarding orders…'. He described Allenby at fifty-seven as 'a sinewy well set-up man, at least six feet high, and broad and strong as a London policeman', adding that he was 'a great lonely figure of a man, riding silently in front of an obviously terrified staff'. Despite its persisting image of aristocratic amateurism, the British cavalry regiments in Britain were traditionally the most elite, and Allenby, like the majority of senior Allied officers in World War I was a cavalry officer. But unlike most, his reputation preceded him. Nobody dared contradict him. His explosive temperament had earned him the nickname of 'the Bull', and he was said to make even brigadiers shake. Inspections by Allenby were often dreaded for their thoroughness. Methodical, scholarly and rigid in his ways, he was from the school of polished brasses, spic and span uniforms and flawless webbing belts, and castigated anyone who split infinitives (even in telegrams) or looked untidy. A chinstrap not kept down, let alone a man on horseback wearing shorts, could send him into a rage. Whenever he was to make a personal inspection of his forces, a two-letter message – 'B.L.' - was passed out to all units – 'Bull Loose'. Henry Gullett, in the *Official History*, said Allenby 'went through the hot, dusty camps in his army like a strong, fresh, reviving wind. He would dash up in his car to a Light Horse regiment, shake hands with a few officers, inspect hurriedly, but with a sure eye to good and bad points, the horses or perhaps a single squadron, and be gone in a few minutes, leaving a great trail of dust behind him'.

Dignified, with a clipped moustache and immaculate uniform with gold braid and tabs, he had a formidable presence. But he was respected throughout the ranks. While men trusted and almost revered him as a military leader, he was also admired for his skill as an ornithologist, his ability to quote from the Greek classics in the original and his knowledge of the Bible, which he read without fail every day. In the Middle East, unhampered by other senior officials, he enjoyed being boss and flourished in a truly independent command. During his massive clean-up, Allenby moved 'the Shepheard's Hotel generals' with scant ceremony. Army headquarters were relocated from Cairo 150 miles nearer to the front. Making it clear that he was not an 'office chair general', he told Paterson: 'I'd like to get closer, where I can have a look at the enemy occasionally'. Allenby was usually accompanied by his military secretary, the grandson of Baron Meyer de Rothschild, Lieutenant-Colonel Lord Dalmeny (son of the Earl of Rosebery) and his chief-of-staff, Brigadier-General Archibald Wavell, the future Lord Wavell, who had been blinded in one eye in 1916.

'Allenby,' said Paterson, 'had been through the shambles of Mons where he had dismounted his cavalry and thrown them into the fighting line in a vain effort to stop the German rush. He had lost his son in the war; and being a full-fleshed man, the heat of Egypt tried him severely, and made him harder than ever. Where he had been granite before he was steel now'.

Allenby put the men through stiff training and issued unexpected new rules. Men found themselves on long marches while getting into the habit of working on a limited water ration. But an order was an order, a regulation was a regulation, and it had to be obeyed without question. The command from Allenby forbidding horses to be tied to trees had to be carried out even though the men did not like hobble-chaining their mounts.

The ruling that caused the most upset was the one prohibiting horsemen, even in the tropical heat, from riding in khaki shorts, which Allenby called 'cut-trousers'. Shorts, they grumbled, were the only suitable clothing in excessive heat. Allenby's argument was that cuts could turn septic in the heat and that bare legs when riding were often scratched. His argument was later proved invalid. Septic sores, or 'Barcoo' as the Australians called them, had been prevalent at Gallipoli, reappeared to some extent in 1916, and become common in the summer of 1917, but mostly on the hands, not on the legs. The condition rapidly disappeared at the end of 1917 once the troops moved into an area rich in oranges – the Jaffa–Ramleh region – giving the men an instant supply of vitamin C.

Allenby's emphasis on appearance, uniforms and correct behaviour was enough to make him clash with many Australians, who had little regard for these things. These men were fighting for their country, their lives – what did it matter what they were wearing? Yet they respected him, and in spite of the tension of the long rides and the long marches, the morale of the men rose. But if a third British attack against the Turkish fortified defence system of Gaza failed, the whole action stood in danger of fizzling out. Already extra troops had arrived from the Salonika Front and Aden.

Early in October, a series of telegrams from London instructed Allenby to quicken his pace. As the autumn leaves began to fall in Europe and the winter rains were about to turn the battlefields of candle-lit trenches into wildernesses of mud, the War Cabinet wanted to hasten a diversion. This was especially necessary because in France, Haig's Passchendaele battle had achieved little but had sustained appalling losses. However, enthusiasm in London lessened when the war cabinet received a reply from Allenby. To eliminate Turkey from the war during the coming winter, he would need thirteen more divisions – about a quarter of a million extra men. The demand, like so many similar requests from other generals during the war, was pushed aside.

During the highly structured preparations for the third battle of Gaza, it was instilled in everyone that the Holy City would fall within days, and that the occupation of the Jaffa–Jerusalem line was an immediate objective. During this time, Allenby met Lawrence in Cairo, where they co-ordinated plans for British and Arab advances across the River Jordan.

Lawrence had gone to Cairo for a brief rest. He had been in Arabia for four months without a break, and in the last month alone, he had clocked up 1400 miles on the back of a camel. Fed up with vermin, he 'wanted a bath, and something with ice in it to drink: to change these clothes, all sticking to my saddle sores in filthiness: to eat something more tractable than green date and camel sinew'. Lawrence's unemotional feelings about eating his own camels was revealed in the piece which he wrote in the *Army Quarterly* in 1920:

> *...and there was never a fear of starvation, for each of us was*
> *riding on two hundred pounds of potential meat, and when food*
> *lacked we would stop and eat the weakest of our camels.*
> *Exhausted camel is poor food, but cheaper killing than a fat one,*
> *and we had to remember that our future efficiency depended on*
> *the number of good camels at our disposal. They lived on grazing*
> *as we marched (we never gave them grain or fodder), and after*
> *their six weeks on the road they would be worn thin, and have to*
> *be sent to pasture for some months' rest, while we called out*
> *another tribe in replacement, or found fresh riding-beasts.*

Lawrence anticipated there would be shock at his own appearance, as is evident from his description of his first meeting with Allenby: 'He was hardly prepared for anything so odd as myself – a little bare-footed, silk-shirted man offering to hobble the enemy by his preaching if given stores and arms, and a fund of two hundred thousand sovereigns to convince and control his converts...Allenby could not make out how much was genuine performer and how much charlatan. The problem was working behind his eyes, and I left him unhelped to solve it'.

Allenby then started a weeding-out process, trying general after general, 'as a man would try hat after hat in a hat shop before he bought one', according to Paterson in *Happy Dispatches*. 'Each commander had just one chance. The most important command in the whole show was that of the mounted division. This division would be the spearhead of the attack...' Paterson added that now that the Desert Column was going to be enlarged into a corps, the prospect of the appointment going to his fellow Australian officer and old school friend, Chauvel, was discussed. 'Up and down, disputin' and contendin', as Paterson put it. In *Happy Dispatches* Paterson quoted one 'brass-bound brigadier' as saying, 'They'll never give it to Chauvel. Fancy giving the command of the biggest mounted force in the world's history to an Australian. Chauvel's sound, but he's such a sticky old frog'. Chauvel was given a try-out on 'a sideshow'. Omitting the name of the general who was also given a trial, Paterson continued, 'So definite was the idea of Chauvel's impending clash that one general – himself an Australian – went up with an orderly to the fight at Beersheba where Chauvel was in command. I happened to go up in the train with this general, who had married into the English aristocracy and thought himself next in order for the cavalry command'. According to Paterson, Chauvel's anonymous competitor said, 'This chap Chauvel, he's too damn slow. I've just come along to see how things turn out'. After many hurdles and tests, Allenby gave Chauvel the command of the largest body of mounted troops ever launched in an advance in the British army. He was to begin the longed-for breakthrough – and quickly.

The enemy line on the Gaza Front was formidable. The Turks had used the long months since their previous victory to extend their defensive line of strong earthworks as far inland as Beersheba. Jerusalem could not be taken until this line was broken. Allenby adopted the strategy that was drawn up just prior to his arrival by Chetwode and Brigadier-General Guy Dawnay. The main effort would be concentrated inland on the less fortified defences of Beersheba, still a scanty and poor Arab village. Despite its elaborate wells, which date back thousands of years to the time of the patriarch, Abraham, and the railhead and some modern buildings erected by German engineers, it was a backward, miserable place.

The unremitting shortage of water continued to dictate strategy, which would have been different if intelligence had been better. Due to the vast numbers of animals and men, and the lack of sufficient water, the wells would have to be captured before the Germans ruined them. These wells were the only local natural water supply, and the availability of water was essential for the second phase of the advance northwards.

Equally critical was information and intelligence about the size, strength and whereabouts of the Turkish battalions they were about to attack. One particular source of intelligence came to an end in September 1917 when a carrier pigeon used by the Jewish spy Sarah Aaronsohn fell into the hands of the Turks. Sarah was tortured with, according to Vladimir Jabotinsky, in *The Story of the Jewish Legion*, 'medieval brutality for two whole days in Zichron Jacob, by beating her with bamboo sticks, by placing hot boiled eggs under her armpits, and by the devil knows what else...'. She shot herself to spare her aged father additional beatings.

Earlier, she and her colleagues had provided the British with details of Turkish defences around Beersheba, data on the weather, on the location of water sources and malarial swamps, and on the condition of routes to Beersheba from the Negev. But Yigal Sheffy, who recently analysed the strategy in the campaign, says that the British plan was based on inaccurate information. They overestimated the numbers of Turkish soldiers and miscalculated their positions. After the Russian Revolution, Turkey, seeing the withdrawal of Russian troops as an opportunity to expand the territory near their homeland, had transferred thousands of troops north to the shores of the Caspian Sea.

There was a certain amount of irony in the fact that troops under Allenby should be organising a mounted charge. His previous cavalry sweep, near Monchy-le-Preux in France, had been a disaster. Line upon line of mounted men, equipped with lances and sabres, had charged into Germans, and were met with a barrage of bullets and death. It was sometimes said that he had shown that he was out of touch with what cavalry could do in a modern mechanised war. But defenders of the role of cavalry in Europe say that in the closing months of the battle which became known as First Ypres, they had acted as a fire brigade, moving up and down the line plugging gaps, using the same rifle as the infantry – the Short-Magazine Lee-Enfield (SMLE) – so helping prevent a German breakthrough.

But in Palestine there was no argument about the role of horses. They were the most effective transport over the deserts in warfare. Conditions for native horses in these Arab lands were often dreadful. Byron's great-granddaughter, Judith, Lady Wentworth, described the plight of the horses in Cairo. She ran Sheykh Obeyd, the stud set up at Heliopolis in 1882 by her mother, Byron's granddaughter Anne, and her father, the explorer/poet Wilfred Blunt. In *The Authentic Arabian Horse*, Lady Wentworth wrote of indifference to horses in Egypt:

> *The native habit of tethering horses and hobbling them in the full glare of a torrid sun (with a temperature of perhaps 120°F in the shade) destroys the strongest constitution and often kills them outright. The flaming rays beat upon their defenceless heads…Ceaseless buzzing flies swarm round the horses in myriads. Closely hobbled with tightly drawn ropes they can only move by laborious hopping with arched backs.Half-starved and half-blinded with glare and flies, the horses are in a sorry condition of thirst and misery. Yet no-one gives two thoughts to their condition. It is the custom of the country, and the owners would be astonished to be told they were cruel.*

The promise made in November 1917 by Britain's foreign secretary, Arthur James Balfour, in the Declaration that bears his name, stating that the government would 'view with favour the establishment in Palestine of a national home for the Jewish people…' is usually seen as the first public indication of the British government's backing for a Jewish homeland. But the Balfour Declaration could, at that stage, only be a mere paper promise, for the country they were inviting the Jews to inhabit was still in the hands of the Turks. Many battles would have to be fought against the Turks before Palestine could be linked to the British Empire. The terrible fact had to be acknowledged that the British were still west of Gaza, the desert gateway to Palestine. Eighteen months had passed since British forces had advanced from the Suez Canal across the sand dunes of the Sinai Peninsula. 'Wriggling across the desert like giant pythons', were the words used by military historian B H Liddell Hart to describe the sluggish pace of their advance.

Lloyd George had quickly found that British strategy coincided with Zionist needs, something pointed out to him by Dr Chaim Weizmann, head of the British Zionist Federation and a brilliant chemist. Lloyd George initially promoted the idea of colonising the Holy Land and turning it into a Jewish homeland. Instilled with religion during his fundamentalist Welsh Christian upbringing, he preferred the Old Testament to the New, and once remarked that he was more familiar with the names of the towns in the Holy Land than those on the Western Front. But there was nothing new in politicians being interested in restoring the Jews to the Holy Land. Lord Shaftesbury and the late Lord Derby had been among the nineteenth century Christians who believed in the 'restoration' of the Jewish people to Eretz to Israel as a fulfilment of prophecy.

Apart from tactical motives, there was a strong belief that the idea of a homeland would win over influential Jews in Germany, Russia and the United States to Britain's side. It was then commonly thought that Jews wielded enormous influence. This was summed up by Lord Robert Cecil, the Foreign Office under-secretary: 'I do not think it is easy to exaggerate the international power of the Jews'. At the time, arguments in favour of the Jewish homeland were plentiful. Restoring an ancient and persecuted people to their lost country was an inspiring vision to those who had been steeped in the Bible from childhood. For some Christians, expanding the Jewish population in Palestine would fulfil ancient prophecies such as Isaiah's prediction that the Gentiles would bring the Jewish people back to their land (Isaiah 49). The most famous of all the supporters was Arthur James Balfour, historically minded Scot whose mother had read to him from the Bible every day during his early childhood, and who had sung psalms about remembering Zion. Balfour, like Lloyd George, had seen the virtues of the Jewish Return before, through the persuasive arguments by the ever-popular Weizmann. But Balfour ran with the scheme only after sentiment in its favour was established by Lloyd George in the War Cabinet, and only after the concept had the support of the president of the United States of America.

The taking of Jerusalem would mean that the government in London could make a tangible move towards creating a Jewish Homeland. A Zionist Commission, comprising both Jews and non-Jewish English officials, would help the new military administration in Jerusalem. It was headed by Weizmann, who complete with top hat and morning jacket, assumed the air of an English gentleman; Major Ormsby-Gore was the official intermediary between the commission and general headquarters. Another effective member was Major James Rothschild, the multi-millionaire son of Baron Edmond, and one of the richest men in the world, who combined his job with the commission with his role as a senior officer.

The advance of the Australian Light Horse was fulfilling the heartfelt wish of millions of Jews in exile. A longing to return to Israel, the land of their ancestors, had persisted among the Jewish Diaspora for nearly 2000 years. For centuries every Jew in Europe had uttered the words 'Next year in Jerusalem!' in the annual ritual Yom Kippur greeting. Now it was about to become a reality. Not only did Allenby receive extra aeroplanes, battalions and battleships, but also 10,000 cans of asphyxiating gas.

Chapter Eleven

Beersheba!

A cts of deception were staged to mislead the Turks into believing that the main British attack – the big push towards Jerusalem – would take place elsewhere. Aiming to make it appear that Beersheba would still be the target, in order to lure the Turks into moving their main body of troops there, the controversial English intelligence officer, Richard Meinertzhagen, carried out a celebrated ruse. While out patrolling on his horse, risking capture, he dropped a haversack of bloodstained dummy documents in the path of Turkish scouts.

On 24 October 1917, the much-awaited thrust to Jerusalem began with the planned attack on Beersheba. Overhead aeroplane patrols kept the sky above the huge area free of German planes. Success would depend not only on keeping the enemy ignorant of the massive troop numbers in the area, but also on speed.

After Beersheba the riders would be in the saddle for days on end, perhaps weeks. The course was set – non-stop to the Holy City. They were to travel light so they could move rapidly, and they were to carry no luxuries such as tents. Even though the days were still hot, the night air was now chilly and would soon be bitterly cold; the riders were allowed no comforts except their greatcoats. All blankets and spares of any sort were sent to kit stores for safekeeping. Items such as ropes and cooking pots were to follow behind.

According to *The Australian Army Medical Services in the War 1914–18*, the three corps on the eve of the operation comprised 100,189 men:

Desert Mounted Corps	745 officers, 17,935 others
XX Corps	1435 officers, 44,171 others
XXI Corps	1154 officers, 34,759 others

In addition to well over 6000 horses, 30,000 camels and thousands of mules, there were then about 11,600 horses in the Desert Mounted Corps. This included the Anzac Mounted Division (5,000 cavalrymen) and the Australian Mounted Division (5,000 cavalrymen) and the 7th Mounted Brigade (1,000 cavalrymen). The Anzacs continued to act as the spearhead of the expeditionary force. Often they were thirty or forty miles ahead of the main infantry unit.

After riding for most of the night on 28th, at 2.30 am the men were given a break of just over two hours at a town called Khalasa. The horses were off-saddled, and after a rest, they were again mounted. The field ambulances, always behind them, swayed and bumped along. Breakfast was just a few scratched hard biscuits and tea – a common meal when on the move.

The cavalry were to encircle and occupy Beersheba, which was held by two Turkish infantry divisions, and then, while also encircling Gaza, start a push forward in a north-westerly direction. The challenge was taken on with a new light-hearted attitude, summarised by an Australian officer and later quoted by Paterson in *Happy Dispatches*: 'It is all or nothing with us. We have to smash right through the Turks and come out on the other side. I think Julius Caesar would have funked trying it. If we get held up we'll be out of provisions and horse-feed in a couple of days, and then you can write to me at Constantinople. [Townsend and the officers captured in Mesopotamia were already imprisoned there.] But don't worry; we'll get through all right.

We're more frightened of Allenby behind us than we are of the Turks in front. We'll go through Palestine looking over our shoulders, and the first thing you'll know we'll be in Damascus.' On 31 October, Chauvel ordered four infantry and two cavalry divisions to take Beersheba (as portrayed in Ian Jones's film *The Lighthorsemen* in 1987 – made nearly forty years after the film by Chauvel's nephew, *Forty Thousand Horsemen*). The Light Horse was to seize the wells at sunset. Instructions given were almost straight out of the *Cavalry Training Manual* of 1907: 'It must be accepted as a principle that the rifle, effective as it is, cannot replace the effect produced by the speed of the horse, the magnetism of the charge and the terror of cold steel'.

At most, the Turks expected a feint of one division and one mounted division against Beersheba. They knew an attack was coming but had not guessed its size or weight. As the bombardment at Gaza had been becoming more intense every day, the Turks had diverted their main body of troops there, especially after the arrival of three large warships – HMS *Grafton* and two destroyers, *Staunch* and *Comet*, along with the river gunboats *Ladybird* and *Amphis*. The result of this, as will be seen, is that the Beersheba garrison lost heart. They were completely overwhelmed and, according to Wavell, 'failed to make proper use of their strong position. Certainly the majority of the enemy infantry did not put up as stout a fight as usual. The 27th Division, which constituted the main part of the garrison, was an Arab formation, and Arab troops were never such doughty opponents as the Anatolian Turks. The Turkish artillery, however, shot well'.

Despite the disparity in numbers – only 4,000 Turkish soldiers and 28 field guns as against 58,500 allied men and 242 guns – the Turks were managing to keep the Allies at bay. The afternoon dragged on. If the Allies did not break through into Beersheba to the wells before nightfall, the horses would have a twelve-hour trek back to water at Khalasa and Asluj. Chauvel responded positively to Brigadier Grant's suggestion that his men forget caution and make a charge across the trenches to take the town.

Just before dusk, at 4.30 pm after an all-day battle, 800 men of the 4th and 5th regiments waited. Lacking either swords or lances, they had bayonets fixed to their rifles. The charge did not begin with a classic knee-to-knee line-up, as in traditional cavalry charges, nor with the order 'Draw swords – form line – gallop!' The horses started off at a brisk canter at first. With horses spread out about 1,200 yards across the gently sloping land, the whole spectacle had more of the appearance of a cross-country outing. But when they were about a mile and a half from the trenches, Grant gave the order to charge. There was a rush, a sound like thunder, as the men dug in their spurs and swept forward at fantastic speed. Horses galloped under shrapnel, over trenches and men.

The onslaught had a devastating effect on the Turks, who were standing and crouching almost awestruck, finding it difficult to aim their guns to match the speed of the charge. The ground shook with the thundering hoofs. Men were hidden from each other by dust and gun smoke. Dense clouds of dust raised by the leading squadrons formed a concealing screen and protected the riders from accurate fire. So intense was the speed, so dreadful the noise, that it blocked out the agonies of thirst for both man and horse.

While some men arched their backs as they pulled their horses up to jump over the wide trenches, others, using the heads of their horses as cover from flying projectiles, lay flat on the animals' necks. Some men, shot out of their saddles, crashed to the ground. The horses, their saddles empty, galloped on, seeking the security of the herd. When the Turks did manage to set their sights accurately, the middle of a horse's body usually received the first bullet. But, miraculously, relatively few horses were hit. The wounded animals, with blood pouring from their bellies, kept galloping, bursting their hearts to keep pace with their mates. Loyal to the last, they kept going until they dropped. A small number of men, who had horses shot from under them, came crashing to the ground, breaking legs, arms and backs. Some men pulled themselves out from under their fallen mounts and, seizing rifle and bayonet, continued the fight. As vulnerability during a charge is usually highest when it stops, when the combined action of man and horse loses its impetus, most injuries and deaths occurred on the ground at the end of the charge or when fighting around the trenches. In all, only seventy of the horses and thirty-one of the men were killed, with thirty-six men wounded.

When some of the men dismounted, a hand-to-hand contest started. Pushing their advantage, the horsemen threw themselves from their mounts and scythed their way through the disintegrating ranks of Turkish infantry. Again and again the bayonets of the Australian rifles thrust and stabbed as they cut the Turks down. Turkish resistance was finally broken, and the commander ordered a general withdrawal.

The rest of the riders galloped straight on into Beersheba. Taking 800 horses, the Australians felt they had paved the way for their comrades to win a similar victory at Gaza in a few days' time. Of the seven good wells in the town, the Turks had blown up five on the night of the 31st, and the remaining two had been prepared for demolition, but the men arrived just before the wicks had been fired. The whole place was full of hidden explosives – booby traps and trip-wires. Mines had been dug into the sand and even under doorsteps. Luckily, most of the wires had not been attached to their detonators, due to the absence of the German engineer who had laid them.

Exhausted, the Australians all had a feeling of achievement in having participated in the overthrow of the Turks, and the men were grateful to Grant and Chauvel. Paterson explained that Chauvel had belied 'his reputation of being a sticky old frog', adding that 'towards the end of the day I came upon his rival, still accompanied by an orderly, walking disconsolately through the empty streets of Beersheba'.

Summarising the attack, Paterson added: 'The New Zealanders whose horses had not had a drink for seventy-two hours, and the Australians who were in much the same fix, rode right over the Turkish trenches at full gallop – against the principles of war you understand – but it still came off. And that, after all, is the great test of any operation – does it come off?'

The men of the Light Horse, having hurled back the Turks, were in a euphoric mood. They believed that there had been no finer feat in the war in the Middle East and were buoyed up by optimism for a future in which their horses had a role. Although transport and water were difficult, the men managed to prepare a sort of victory feast and found fowls, goats, sheep, pigeons, and even a few oxen to throw into their pots.

Despite the capture of Beersheba and the wells there, the men could not rest, nor could the horses or men get enough to drink. The supply from the wells was unequal to the demand. Even with lorries supplementing the wells with 400-gallon tanks and ferrying water round the clock from the head of the pipeline, there was not enough for nearly 60,000 men and 100,000 horses. The Desert Mounted Corps was withdrawn into reserve and the Anzac Mounted Division was diverted to take their place. They went on to seize the trench systems nearby at Kauwukah and Rushdi. After a certain amount of opposition they occupied the line Bir el Marruneh-Towal abu Jerwal, capturing 179 prisoners and four machine-guns. The shortage of horsepower continued to be acute. To help out, a mobile camel force of Lewis gunners, machine-gunners and a few Sudanese Arab scouts augmented them, but they could not keep up with the horses.

With Beersheba captured, the second phase of the operation, the capture of Gaza itself, was begun. First the formidable trench system and barriers, and the huge strip of No Man's Land, which was over half a mile wide, had to be breached. Meinertzhagen used aeroplanes to drop messages concealed in thousands of small cigarette packets. Little did the Turks realise that the cigarettes that arrived before the final battle were laced with grains of opium. Meinertzhagen claimed that troops at both Gaza and Tel esh Sheria were 'drowsy and fuddled'. This state, though, is more likely to have been due to the 10,000 cans of poisonous gas used by Allenby, which unlike the first gas used in the second battle of Gaza, was dramatically effective.

Everything augured well for the Allies on the night of 1–2 November. Even the moon was small and low, giving ideal light for a night raid. At 11 pm, the third battle of Gaza began when the 156th Brigade assaulted and captured Umbrella Hill. Fighting continued all night. By 6.30 am, a long line of support trenches were in Allied hands. Gaza, at last, had fallen.

At first light the men found the fortress of Gaza abandoned. The eight months of holding out were over. The Turks were withdrawing north, scrambling over the coastal plain. Even though the water supply in the wells at Beersheba was inadequate – all shaving and washing were forbidden – the men pushed their thirsty horses on in pursuit of the retreating enemy. But they did not achieve their aim of rolling back the Turks as far as Jerusalem in one continuous advance. Fighting rearguard actions with machine-guns, the Turks hindered the progress of the Australians and the horses were constantly inhibited by the lack of water.

Victory, though, would have few results unless the enemy was pursued; otherwise it would re-establish another entrenched line. The Turks knew that they were more likely to defeat the Allies if they could keep men and horses away from water long enough. Constantly, they smashed up the winding devices on wells. The only way to draw water was to drop a canvas bucket suspended on a rope or a telephone wire down about 150 feet – and then only a small amount was retrieved. The tedious process of bailing had to be kept up until the horses had drunk sufficient and all the water bottles were filled.

But when it came to advancing on the enemy's exposed left flank around Sharia and Hareira, because the bulk of the horses were in the Beersheba area, the three infantry divisions did not have adequate cavalry support to exploit the breakthrough. On top of this, the Anzac Mounted Division met with more opposition than had been expected. Again there was not enough water. Grudgingly, because of the acute shortage, the Australian Mounted Division remained around Beersheba.

On the morning of 8 November, the pursuit continued with a vengeance. The Turks had got ahead in the night. It seemed that they were determined to keep the horses engaged so they could not drink. The Anzac Division was directed to Bureir, about twelve miles north-east of Gaza, with the Australian Mounted and 60th Divisions on the left. Taking advantage of a slight rise in the ground to the east of the enemy position, an order was given to charge. As the horses thundered over the rise, the Turks sprang to their guns and swung them round, firing point-blank into the charging horsemen. Men were shot out of their saddles. Riderless horses rolled bloodshot eyes, searching for help. Those shot fell on their haunches. Unable to move, they raised their heads with a last whinny. The rest of the horses thundered over the rise, racing down upon the flank of the enemy guns. A battery of field and mountain guns on a low hill between the two batteries, and three heavy

howitzers behind, emptied their contents. The infantry blazed away with
their rifles till they were cut down. There was no thought of surrender. Every
man stuck to his gun or rifle to the last.

Then, as the official British historian, Cyril Falls, wrote: 'Then matters
began to go really wrong. The cavalry became unduly dispersed and was
handicapped by the same adverse factor of insufficient water supply that
dogged the Egyptian Expeditionary Force from first to last.' Allenby could
not follow up the victory of Gaza to full advantage. Because the British forces
were scattered and the horses were in a sorry state, suffering from the effects
of dehydration, the Turkish armies in southern Palestine could not be
pursued quickly enough. Again and again the Turks were given space and
time in which to retire for another fight. So dreadful was the shortage of
water that a month after the fall of Gaza, the bulk of the British soldiers, both
mounted and infantry, were brought to a complete standstill. Without water
they could not move forward. Horses, efficient though they were, suffered
terrible deprivations.

Lack of water is worse for a horse than insufficient food. Some, as said
earlier, went seventy-two hours without a drink. But they kept on carrying
their heavy burden. After more than a couple of days with no liquid, the
tongues of horses were swollen and they struggled for breath. As well as colic
from dehydration, many had sore backs because they had remained saddled
for days. The injury rate was also high. In the temperate northern
hemisphere, regulations allowed the cavalry to carry a maximum of twenty-
two stone. Regardless of temperatures ranging from freezing to over 50ºC, in
the desert campaign, the maximum for horses was only two stone less.

The Australian attitude to horses was far removed from that of the
English. In England, finely bred horses were associated with recreation,
wealth, privilege, fox-hunting, the aristocracy and sport, whereas in Australia
horses were a means of existence. Horses had opened up the country.
Without them as transport, or to speed stockmen around huge properties
with few fences, there would have been no cattle and sheep stations in
Australia. Riding as an art had never been confined to just the rich in
Australia. But in Britain there had been huge improvements in horse

management in the decade before the war. The terrible loss of horses in the Boer War had shown how necessary it was, for instance, to avoid elementary faults such as tiring their horses unnecessarily. The Commission of Enquiry after that war reported that the problem lay in over-reliance on the riding school and not enough fieldwork – 'the German method' as it was known. Lord Baden-Powell, who had seen the problem for himself in South Africa and was afterwards appointed Inspector of Cavalry in Great Britain and Ireland, urged hunting as a school of practical horsemastership 'in economising the powers of the horse and judging when to nurse him and when to let him go'. By 1914 British cavalry on the march had led their horses almost as much as they rode them. By contrast, the French cavalry's horses were exhausted, many beyond recovery. By the end of September, some regiments were said actually to stink, so bad were their saddle sores.

On 9 November, water difficulties called a halt for twenty-four hours. Unless the rains came early, everyone knew that they would not make Jerusalem by Christmas. Although there were wells in most villages, they were often 200 feet deep, and the only methods of drawing water from them was very time-consuming. It could take a whole night to water a squadron.

The *Official History* published in Britain states that between 1917 and 1918, the horses 'revealed a power of resistance to the extremes of climate and an endurance in great marches without water that their most sanguine advocates could not have prophesied…Horses of all three mounted divisions went seventy-two hours without water and did continuous work during that period. The horses of the Lincolnshire Yeomanry hold the record of eighty-four hours for this feat of endurance. Those of the Dorsetshire Yeomanry covered sixty miles in fifty-four hours without water. Even when water was to be had, the majority of these horses were watered once daily only, and in many cases received very small quantities of food during the pursuit.'

The bulk of men and horses were kept near the coast so as to be backed up by the naval guns, and by supplies that came in surfboats rowed in off the ships by Pacific Islanders from Rarotonga in the Cook Islands.

But by the time the pursuit – and the invasion into the heart of the Holy Land – began again in earnest, the Turks, too, had had time to regain strength. Much advantage had been lost. But on the horsemen went, cantering, trotting and walking through clouds of dust over desert plains, areas of empty waste and past sunbeaten monuments. There was no time to examine the ruins of crumbling walls and arches. Riding steadily, they continued up the stern, barren hills and across the trackless rocky moorland of the mountain country, broken by terrifying, steep ravines and stony valleys.

On 15 November, a fast trot northwards brought the 10th Light Horse to the end of the Plain of Philistia, to Jaffa. The old port through which Herod had imported the cedars of Lebanon was now occupied by the weary troops. Unlike Beersheba with its empty deserted houses, Jaffa was a bustling metropolis. For the first time, the Desert Mounted Corps faced the task of organising a large and busy town captured from the Turks. Jaffa had good streets and a well-built Jewish and European quarter, plus an old section where some streets were not wide enough for two people to ride abreast. The modern part of the town was up to date, with large shops, a German bank, schools and town gardens with a bandstand. Most of the wealthy people – Germans and Turks – had cleared out, including Baron Ustinov (the grandfather of the actor Peter Ustinov), who owned the Park Hotel. He was now a pilot with the German air force. Gangs of sweepers were set to work by the British and soon six newly erected large rubbish incinerators were smoking away. The New Zealanders took over the sole civil hospital, which was efficiently run by the French, with two nurses.

To advance inland and go straight across the hills and mountains to Jerusalem was considered too bold. There were no good maps, no reliable intelligence. Everyone remembered the fate of the Crusaders. Caution was needed. Even the War Cabinet in London sent a telegram to Allenby, warning against committing his army too far for its strength and adding that troops, because of the worsening situation on the Western Front, might need to be withdrawn in the New Year. Determined, Allenby pushed on. Just as the historic advance over those treacherous rocky hills began on 18 November, the much-prayed for rain came. But it came in torrents. The greatcoats were not waterproof and the men were wet for days on end. How they longed for a tent or a blanket. At night, exhausted, wet and cold, they either found a hole or some sort of shelter somewhere, or spent a miserable night sitting up against a wall or each other, comforted, if they were lucky, with a hot cup of tea and a tin of bully beef and biscuits.

So heavy was the rain that it swept away bridges and culverts. Arabs who had lived in the area all their lives said they had never seen anything like it. Earth was turned into mud; the loamy soil became a slippery, slimy surface. Lurching with their heavy loads, horses, mules and camels squelched their way through mud, losing their footing. Often struggling horses slipped and went down on their knees, breaking their legs. Taking the animals at a slow trot did not stop them from skidding, falling and injuring their legs. Even without the bad weather, these hills were anything but cavalry country. In many places the horses had to be pulled and pushed up the slippery slopes. The camels were cruelly hampered by their delicate cushion-like feet, which tore and bled if they walked across any rough surface, especially stony ground.

Mud hindered not only the animals, but also the vehicles. There was only one proper road. It, too, turned into mud. Wheels frequently got stuck. Stones had to be put under them when they were bogged, then men and horses had to heave and jerk them forward. The narrow wheels of the ambulance carts were twisted and the axles were damaged.

There was no real front, and there were no pitched head-on battles, just constant attrition. This was guerrilla warfare country. Everywhere there were boulders, rocks and scrub, which gave excellent cover to the Turkish riflemen. With every step, a soldier could be sniped at by the hidden enemy. Never had fifty miles – the distance between Jaffa and Jerusalem – seemed so far.

It was desperately hard going in those hills. Struggling against the rough terrain was as tough as getting through the walls of bullets. At times it seemed they would never get to the Holy City. Both the human death toll and the suffering of the animals was beyond comprehension by modern standards. Over 18,000 Allied casualties occurred while turning the Turks out of the defensive positions on those perilous mountain roads. As the terrain and the

Although Australia had had no voice in the negotiations preceding World War I, far from objecting to being drafted into future battles without consultation, she was a keen participator. Patriotism and war fever gripped young and old alike. My father, like thousands of others, put his age up so he could go and fight.

Sentiment for the war was overwhelmingly pro-British, as was seen by the support offered, even by my grandmother, Cassie Robertson. She did her bit for the war by posing for an advertisement as an alluring Britannia in a flowing white Grecian robe. With long dark tresses almost covering a Union Jack shield and surrounded by uniformed cadets in khaki hats, she enticed loyal subjects to show allegiance to the gruff but likeable George V who had visited Australia twice in his youth.

British cavalry officers and all ranks from the Australian Light Horse were the first choice for pilots since 'good hands' were required to handle the primitive aircraft, as well as pluck and nerve. Ross Smith (pilot) and Lieutenant Mustard in their Bristol fighter, Palestine 1918. (AWM A658)

The prospects of success against the Turks in the Middle East were more realistic when General Sir Edmund Allenby arrived in Egypt in 1917 and took over from General Archibald Murray. Here he is seen inspecting a captured German Albatross aircraft (fuel tank missing from top wing). (AWM HO3817)

Prince Feisal, the son of Sherif Hussein who became Lawrence's friend and leader of the Arab Irregulars, played a prominent role in the Arab revolt 1916–18 and became King of Iraq in 1921. He is seen here in the summer of 1918 with his aide de camp at the 'Dead Sea Post'. (AWM B56)

By chance, for the first time since 1915, the very two men who had led troops against the Australians at Gallipoli, the German Otto Liman von Sanders and the Turk, Lieutenant Colonel Mustafa Kemal, were again commanding the Turkish troops. Here, just before his defeat, Liman von Sanders visits positions in Haifa. (AWM H13382 – donor German War Museum Bufa 11032)

The air was often heavy with the nauseating smell of unburied corpses of men and beasts. This photograph from my father's personal collection shows preparation of a mass grave for fallen Turkish soldiers. For Australia, World War I remains the most costly conflict ever in terms of deaths and casualties.

Colonel T E Lawrence, 'Lawrence of Arabia', usually overshadows the roles played by the Australian horsemen and rest of the 12,000 mounted troops in the battle-filled fortnight preceding the fall of Damascus. One reason for the Gallipoli invasion and the Syrian invasion not being seen as part of the overall campaign against the Turks is that the taking of Damascus was, and still is, strongly associated with Lawrence of Arabia and the Arabs. (AWM B2170)

If Mustafa Kemal (fourth from left), described as a throwback to the Tartars, the grey wolf of Turkish legend, had not seized the high ground at Gallipoli and held the heights above Anzac Cove, the Australians might well have succeeded and taken Gun Ridge. Then they would have reached over to the far side of the hills and dominated the Narrows. On the road to Damascus in 1918 the tables were finally turned.

The shortage of water meant there was little to spare for washing clothes or bodies – the troops bathed naked whenever they could. For weeks men were only given half a gallon of water a day for all purposes and the stench of unwashed men and clothes was constant.

The great courage of the horses enabled them to survive the most terrible deprivations, and their swiftness was such that the 1918 campaign has been called the 'quick win' of the World War I. The first three-day period from 19 to 21 September was especially notable for its speed and distance covered: sixty-five miles from Jaffa – home of the world's favourite orange – to the Sea of Galilee. At one stage the Desert Mounted Corps rode fifty-eight miles in thirty-four hours without unsaddling. (AWM B260)

Horses, under the careful guidance of their riders, grew expert at descending the almost perpendicular slopes of sand dunes. After Gallipoli, burning in the memories of many of the Light Horsemen, was the desire to conclude the job started there and to win through over the Turks. Many a soldier west of Suez had been waiting for the final offensive. In 1918 they had a capable leader and enough men to have a 'fair go'.

This photograph is from the archive of the official Australian war photographer, Frank Hurley (1885-1962), whose name became famous for defining the heroic nature of the conflict. *(Frank Hurley Collection, State Library of New South Wales)*

Australian soldiers were always distinguishable by their hat. As a substitute to the British cap that offered little shading, the Australians wore a brimmed hat. While British badges were steeped in history, the 'rising sun' badge on the hat came from a jam pot. *(Frank Hurley Collection, State Library of New South Wales)*

dreadful weather restricted the use of horses, infantry would dominate the taking of Jerusalem. But conditions were so bad that even with restricted participation, in the last two months of 1917, 10,000 horses, camels, mules and donkeys (11.5 per cent of the total) became casualties, half of which died.

Only one Light Horse Regiment – the 10th Light Horse – represented Australia in the final attack on Jerusalem. Mile after mile they went up the wet, slippery, steep old Roman road, through the pass with its gorges and bluffs on either side. Littered everywhere and pushed to the side were the naked corpses of soldiers, horses, mules and donkeys abandoned by the retreating Turks. The Bedouin and Turks had stripped them of anything useful, but sometimes the British and the Australians found the odd trophy, such as a couple of groundsheets or a knife. Other scavengers, the birds of prey – hooded crows, buzzards, wolves and jackals – soon gorged on the flesh of both beast and man.

Even when in patches the road flattened out, the men had to tramp through what seemed like deeper mud and slush. Bursting shells and gunfire echoed and re-echoed through the hills and valleys. Wavell, in *Allenby: A Study in Greatness*, described the weariness: 'By November 24 it was obvious that neither Bulfin's fiery determination nor Barrow's resolute skill could make any further headway; and Allenby ordered a halt till fresh troops could be brought up...The three divisions in the hills had been fighting and marching continuously for three weeks, in extremes of heat and cold, over dusty plains and in harsh, stony hills, often on short rations of food and of water.' By the first week in December, three divisions of the 20th Corps under Chetwode were well set up in the hills looking towards the mountain city of Jerusalem at 2800 feet. The date set for taking Jerusalem was 8 December.

Men shivered in the cold and wet after a night march. At first light, most of the troops were three or four miles further along the Jericho road to the east, and others six or eight miles to the north. But two men who had gone ahead to scavenge some eggs for breakfast saw an amazing sight – two men waving a torn white sheet. Jerusalem had fallen without a shot being fired. A flag of truce had been improvised by snatching a sheet off a bed in a hospital. Once defeat was inevitable, the Turkish governor, fearful of possible harm to the Holy Places, had hastily retreated with his staff north-east to Damascus.

Applauded as a 'Christmas present to the British nation', the taking of Jerusalem stirred the imagination of the Christian world and hit the front pages of most newspapers in Europe. The bells of Westminster Abbey rang for the first time in three years, followed by thousands of church bells in England and across Europe. But little did the millions of Europeans who rejoiced know of the full horror of the assault over the hills – or of the jealousy and rivalry associated with the entry. As with the capture of other significant cities during the war, clear orders about who should enter first had been issued. Allenby had wanted the surrender of the city to be done correctly. But the 'Operation Orders for the Final Attack on Jerusalem' issued on 6 December had been ignored. These clearly stated: 'Entering JERUSALEM. 1. During and after the forthcoming operations no officers or troops are to go beyond the outskirts of JERUSALEM into the town except in case of urgent tactical necessity...'. Therefore he was angry when an unauthorised officer with troops entered the city prematurely. Allenby also insisted that Jerusalem remained under martial law. Within hours, different factions were trying to usurp power. The French and Italians assumed that as they were the traditional protectors of the Christian holy places in Jerusalem and elsewhere, they would now be in control. Allenby would not let them have their way. Now that Muslim police were no longer guarding the Church of the Holy Sepulchre or other holy places, the Arabs were worried that there would be a problem with the Jews and the Wailing Wall, the remnant of the second Temple, which had become the site of the magnificent Dome of the Rock, and the al-Aqsa mosque. Jerusalem is only slightly less holy to Muslims than Mecca and Medina. In 638 AD, the original Muslim conqueror of Jerusalem, Caliph Omar, dressed in worn and torn robes, had ridden a white camel as he came to mark the place where Mohammed had ascended on a white horse to heaven.

On 11 December, five days after the surrender, when Allenby made his official entry into the Holy City , on instructions from the War Office in London, he dismounted his horse before arriving at the Jaffa Gate and humbly walked through on foot, proclaiming the re-establishment of Crusader rule in Jerusalem after an interval of 730 years. This was a snub to the Kaiser, who nineteen years before had entered the Holy City mounted on a white horse, through a triumphal arch.

Spirits rose with the capture of Jerusalem, but conditions for the troops and horses, both in the mountains and on the plains around the coast, remained terrible. Water continued to turn plains into seas of mud and water. In more than one instance, men and horses were pulled down into mud pools and drowned. A raging storm on Christmas Eve and Christmas Day 1917 washed away parts of the railway and hundreds of camels in the transport columns lay down in the water and died. Neither food for the troops nor forage for the animals could be brought up. Horses continually standing up to their hocks in mud also suffered from the biting winds. There was little shelter. Tired and thin, they looked like scarecrows. Four days after Christmas, the Turks made an abortive attempt to retake the city, but they, too, were hampered by the rain and mud. Blue skies returned early in January. The horses were slowly nursed back into condition. By February, the front had been consolidated, and the infantry and horses had recovered from the hard fighting and cruel weather. Allenby was now determined to extend his line to the mighty River Jordan, take Jericho and the eastern shores of the Dead Sea.

The advance to Jericho began on 19 February – again in non-stop rain. Day and night the infantry met strong opposition from the Turks. By dark the Allies had advanced nearly three miles and were about a mile west of Talaat el Dumm – the Hill of Blood – above the Good Samaritan Inn. From here the road descends steeply, in a series of terrifying hairpin bends, to the valley nearly 3000 feet below. Further along at Jebel Kuruntul, the traditional Mount of Temptation, the mountains drop into a cliff a thousand feet high. Meanwhile, the Australian horsemen moving through the Wilderness of Jeshimon had reached El Muntar, about seven miles from the Dead Sea. Next day, as the infantry stormed Talaat el Dumm, a squadron of the New Zealand Brigade reached the north-west corner of the Dead Sea, the base for a fleet of German motor boats which were being used to tow huge grain barges. After continued fighting, the soldiers withdrew to a position running north and south astride the Jericho road, at Talaat al Dumm, and the Anzac Mounted Division returned to Bethlehem, leaving one regiment to patrol the valley.

Not until the first half of March, after continued fighting, was the lower Jordan Valley cleared of the enemy and the British line secured north of the Wadi el Auja, from the River Jordan to the mountains.

Unlikely though it seemed at the time, Lawrence, the non-conformist British army officer in Arab dress, and Allenby, in his highly polished riding boots, the strict and traditional face of the army, were soon to be linked. This was due to Lowell Thomas, an American journalist, who was sent to Europe, on government instructions, to write propaganda news stories – articles with an emotional pull to make the Americans more enthusiastic about their participation in the war. In April 1917, after two and a half years of hesitation, the United States had joined the Allies, even going so far as to introduce conscription. But for countless Americans the war still felt far away, remote and impersonal. To make it seem more immediate, propaganda projects were planned, including commissioning journalists such as Thomas to write stories with popular appeal. Pacifists could be turned into war enthusiasts if they believed they were fighting for 'Justice and Right'. Interest in the four million soldiers who were being trained and equipped was increasing. In Germany and England, propaganda campaigns were being raised to new levels, but the Americans topped them, even recruiting singers, musicians and actors such as Charlie Chaplin and Irving Berlin.

When Thomas arrived in France he was faced with a problem. The grotesque horrors of trench warfare, with its warrens of soldiers and stiff bodies rolled in mud-caked blankets, came as a shock. Because of censorship, he had had no concept of the horrendous conditions in which the men spent their days. Knowing that these scenes would put Americans off the war he searched for alternative material.

John Buchan, the great adventure story writer, who later became the author of the bestseller *The Thirty-Nine Steps* and Governor-General of Canada, and who was then the Director of the newly formed Department of Information in London, came up with a substitute for Thomas. He arranged for him, together with the cameraman Henry Chase, to travel to the Holy Land, where he would find two very special news stories to thrill the American public. The first featured Allenby, who was obligingly capturing Jerusalem 'by Christmas'; the second was the story of Lawrence, the idealistic British officer who usually wore full Arab dress and was helping Prince Feisal fight for Arab freedom against Turkish oppressors. Such stories from the desert sands, with a background of date palms, minarets and camels, set in the sunshine of the Bible land, would have a romantic appeal – something that the mud of Flanders so obviously lacked. Desert 'battle scenes', a consistent source of 'good news' for the Allies, were a contrast with the main theatres of war, which were synonymous with despair. There was also a state of euphoria that at last Britain was in control of the city sacred to the three great religions.

Ronald Storrs, the new governor of Jersusalem, introduced Lawrence to Thomas as the 'Uncrowned King of Arabia'. As well as articles, an official newsreel, *Allenby's Entry Into Jerusalem*, was screened throughout America and also in Britain, Australia, India and English-speaking outposts such as Singapore. Propaganda such as this, catering to mass audiences, aimed to counter the anti-war lobby, but some of the photographs taken by the official Australian photographer, Frank Hurley, who had earlier been the official photographer on the Mawson and Shackleton expeditions to the South Pole, showed the harsh realism of the war – Hurley was a man who wanted to tell the unvarnished truth about the war.

Chapter Twelve

My Father Arrives in Palestine

The Australian government was desperate to make up the numbers to maintain their battalions abroad. Horrendous casualty figures in France meant that a minimum of 5,500 new recruits was needed each month to keep up numbers. But by 1918, four years into the war, recruitment in Australia had dropped dramatically. In July 1915 the monthly figure had reached its peak, at 36,575. In 1916 the month with the highest intake was January, with 22,101. During the following year the top month was March, with 4,989. When my father, Robbie, enlisted in April, numbers were down to just 2,781. As not enough men of the right age were coming forward, older boys like my father were accepted. For Robbie, enlisting held the promise of a new life. He had felt lucky to find work on a cattle station, tough though it was, where he could lift his riding to the high standard required by the 10th Light Horse. After three years on a remote property set up with the opening up of stock routes in the Kimberley Ranges, he came to Perth to enlist.

Ever since a priest had hurried across the yard at Trinity College, run by the Christian Brothers in Perth, saying, 'Your mother hasn't paid the school fees again!' Robbie's one dream had been to ride his horse with the 10th Light Horse. His mother had endured an uphill struggle since 1906, when her husband had died of typhoid in Kalgoorlie.

Cutting a proud figure on his stocky grey horse, Robbie thought of himself as a natural horseman. Inured to hardship before working on the isolated station, he quickly became adept at breaking in colts, some of which were brumbies, the feral descendants of domesticated stock. A rebellious streak in him found an echo in these spirited animals. Untamed, unhindered by fences, they became a pest to station owners, depleting precious water resources and luring away domestic horses to join the wild mob.

Horses and the bush were in my father's blood. His Irish-born great-grandfather, Thomas McManus, wrote 'horsebreaker' as his occupation on his marriage certificate in Wollongong in 1847. Thomas's son, Jim, a stockman, died of concussion from an accidental fall while galloping up the Queensland coast in 1877 towards the goldmining town of Charters Towers, where branches of the McManus and O'Hara families settled. Another uncle was a gunsmith; and a second cousin was Jack Moses, instigator of 'Bush Week', writer of bush verse and sketches, who was to capture the character of the bush in his poems, such as *Nine Miles from Gundagai*, about the dog sitting on the tucker box.

Robbie's life on the station was far from idyllic. His sister Dorothy, in an oral history interview in 1980, said: 'My mother had sent my brother up to the bush – to the north-west, on a big station where he was very badly treated, physically beaten and so on. He became a roughrider; then he joined the Light Horse Cavalry when he was 15 [actually 16] and went to the war. My mother should never have signed the papers to let him go at that age'. Three trips to the pearling port of Broome had been his only change of scenery. In three years he never received a single visit from his mother or sister. Nor did Robbie ever see a white woman, unless he went to the coast. Women, like water, were scarce out bush. The usual consolation of alcohol did not appeal to him. But cards did. And singing – on the verandah, around a campfire and when they were droving.

While the majority of Australians had a loyalty to King and Country and many saw enlisting as a duty, others saw it as a romantic adventure in the style of the *Boys' Own Annual*. Many boys added one, two or three years to their age; my father added one. Neither birth certificates nor the year of birth were required, simply the age in years and months written on dotted lines. Recruits had to be at least five foot six inches tall, have a minimum chest measurement of thirty-four inches and pass a stringent medical examination. My father's attestation form contained error after error. Although christened a Roman Catholic, because of the hatred of his old school, he had put it and all priests behind him, writing on the form: 'Religion: Church of England'.

Recruiting may have been affected by the first report from the Dardanelles Commission in March 1917. With the exception of the Mesopotamia expedition, the Gallipoli invasion was the only campaign in World War I to prompt a special investigation in London. During its two sessions, which began on 23 August 1916 and stretched over eight months, 170 witnesses were interviewed during sixty-eight meetings. Andrew Fisher, the former Australian prime minister, was Australia's representative. Asquith's handling of the invasion and Kitchener's hesitancy in sending reinforcements and the shambles of the organisation were condemned. Demands from France had been given priority. But would pouring in more men and equipment really have helped? Over half a million men had been sent. The formula of more troops and guns had failed in trench warfare on the Western Front, so why would it have succeeded at Gallipoli? The only hope the Allies had had there was surprise, and that had been blown.

The Dardanelles Report was greeted with howls of anger in Lord Northcliffe's newspapers. 'Impeach the Old Gang!' cried the *Evening News*, while the *Weekly Dispatch* thought the Old Bailey an appropriate destination for many who had been involved. Only a report was published, not the evidence. Due to the fifty-year ruling on certain state papers, all evidence taken was hidden from public access and not taken to the Public Record Office in London until the end of the 1960s.

Robbie's enthusiastic entry into the war contrasted with the millions of men conscripted into the British army and navy under the new Military Service Act, which came into force in January 1916. As the net widened, the anti-war lobby grew. Australia was still the only nation on either side of the conflict that did not conscript its soldiers. The acrimonious debate over conscription became fierce after the government in Canberra put it to a referendum, confident that sentiments towards Britain would produce an affirmative answer. Newspapers were usually pro-conscription, as they risked prosecution if they published any articles deterring men from enlisting. But the power of the press was not as great as expected. The result was 'No Conscription'. When a second referendum was held, the campaign became even more bitter. Trade unionists and socialists argued that no Australian should fight in a battle between the King and his cousin the Kaiser. They believed that lives were being squandered by pursuing vague objectives – a capitalist struggle not worth one drop of working-class blood. Again the 'No Conscription' vote won.

The Protestant churches tended to back conscription, while the Roman Catholic Church, though divided, was opposed to it. As some of the most vocal among the Catholics were of Irish descent – over a quarter of the Australian population was then of Irish descent (including my father) – repercussions of the severe way in which the British authorities had dealt with the Easter rebellion in 1916 in Ireland reverberated throughout Australia. In Dublin fifteen Irish rebel leaders had been shot by firing squads following the failure of that famous rebellion in Easter 1916.

Disillusioned though Robbie became later on, when he walked up the gangplank of the *Wiltshire* on 10 June 1918, with bands playing and his rifle slung over his shoulder, he was exhilarated.

This hired British steamship had been converted to a troop carrier nearly four years earlier, and had by now become rather shabby. On board were twenty officers, two nursing sisters, two nurses and 643 men listed as 'General Service Reinforcements' for Egypt.

He found his hammock in a long, badly ventilated cabin below the waterline. As the ship throbbed, quivered and creaked its way across the

Indian Ocean, the suffocating heat below decks was worse at night. At dusk, to ensure that there was no possibility of the ship being seen, especially by aircraft, hinged iron covers were screwed down on all portholes so that no light was visible. Nor could any air get in. Even before the Equator, the troop quarters were being compared to ovens. After their coaling stop in Colombo, each day seemed more stifling than the last. Shovelling coal into the ship's boiler was the worst job. A shortage of sailors to man the bunkers caused the soldiers to be rostered so that each did a stint.

Every Sunday the ship's captain held a Divine Service. Whether rough or smooth conditions prevailed, morning parades took place on deck at 6.30 am. Mutton for tea and a concert on Wednesday nights broke the boredom of the repetitive stews served in the galley, washed down with mugs of tea. And there was always the singing and a pack of cards.

Conditions for both animals and soldiers aboard the ships were dreadful. But for some reason there were no horses in the hold of this ship. Usually hundreds of these poor creatures were housed on five decks, three below the waterline, two above. On the bottom deck, known as 'Little Hell', each horse was secured with ropes to counter the heavy roll of the sea. Stalls were spread with coconut matting. Despite special baskets for manure and a timetable for emptying them, the stench was horrific. Cleaning out the stalls, heaving the manure through a chute in the bulwark and exercising horses was more than testing for those caring for the animals.

The distress of dim light, intolerable heat and the oppressive lack of ventilation seemed worse when crossing the Equator. Men often suffered with their horses, especially during rough weather and when the vessel rolled and pitched. Dozens of horses were lost on voyages through sickness and accidents. Embarkation and disembarkation were particularly dangerous times, especially when vessels were unable to moor alongside a quay, and horses had to be swung on or off board with cumbersome pulleys, tackle and slings.

Robbie set foot at Suez on 17 July 1918. He considered himself to be, like other 'diggers', part of a unique unit from a faraway place with the special quality of 'Australianness'. Survival in the bush had brought out his 'making the best of it' skills, such as resourcefulness, independence and 'mateship' – sticking with your mates through thick and thin. It also gave them fieldcraft: a good eye, together with the ability to judge distance, time and space, and knowledge such as the fact that banks of a stream are soundest in a neighbourhood of trees, an appreciation of how the land as a whole lies – what is 'dead' ground, which are the covered approaches, etc.

Coping with a hostile environment had also given men a practical bent. If water was short, instead of washing knives, forks, spoons, plates and saucepans in soap and water, they cleaned them with sand or dirt. They could quickly tie corks to hats with string to keep the flies off the face while being indifferent to snakes, adders, great stinging spiders, six-inch centipedes and scorpions. Hastily putting together enough sticks for a fire to boil a 'billy' anywhere was never a challenge and most could cook a stolen sheep without being noticed. They would skin and prepare a sheep and cut it into quarters, then dig a hole about knee deep. A fire would be made in this. Once it burned down to hot ashes the mutton, wrapped in wet sacking, would be placed in the hole and covered up. Henry Bostock in his memoirs *The Great Ride* said they usually placed a saddle over the top 'just in case the Military Police paid us a visit'.

In Europe, as in the Middle East, the stalemate seemed everlasting. In Britain, industry and civilians were suffering from lack of supplies through the German 'sink at sight' U-boat campaign. In Germany food supplies had not recovered from the bad harvest and harsh weather of their 'Turnip Winter', now made worse by the British naval blockade. Rumours were increasing about powdered straw and sawdust in the gritty grey bread; coal was being swallowed up in war industries, leaving meagre amounts for civilians.

But in other ways Germany was doing well. In particular, Germany no longer had an Eastern Front to face, as the Bolsheviks in Russia had signed an armistice before Christmas; Rumania, which had earlier switched alliances and joined the Allies in August 1916, had collapsed. Germany was sure she could now smash the impasse in France – if she could get her men into action before ships brought the Americans across the Atlantic. The Germans were moving a million men and 3000 artillery pieces with great rapidity from the Eastern Front to the Western Front.

In despair, the Allies waited for 'the tanks and the Americans'. On 21 March 1918, the long-expected German offensive to take Paris opened. The results for France and Britain were disastrous, and led to a split in the coalition government. The director of military operations at the War Office accused Lloyd George of misleading the country by falsifying the numbers of British troops in France. Evidence pointed to the director being correct.

Desperately short of manpower, the British needed hardened, experienced troops. What better than those in the Middle East? Sixty thousand suntanned men, including six of the regiments of the Yeomanry Mounted Division, exchanged a mobile life in the desert for a harrowing existence in the trenches in France. Sassoon described their departure: '…these men who ask only to go home to their farms, towns, parks, manors, flats, mansions, cottages, granges, etc., are doomed to suffer far worse things than any they've yet known. Fortunately the fact that the Western Front is over two thousand miles nearer Leicester Square seems to console them…the whole landscape of the near future bristling with unimaginable perils and horrors, and overshadowed by the gloom of death'.

The prospects, however, continued to appear almost hopeless. To restore shaken morale, Haig gave out what became known as the 'Backs to the Wall' message. Again the British considered alternative places to force a decision. The Supreme War Council met at Versailles in February and passed a plan of campaign for the early part of 1918 – to stand on the defensive in the West and to deal Turkey a knockout blow in Palestine. But for two years British troops had slowly advanced around the eastern Mediterranean coast towards Damascus and were still far from driving Turkey out of the war. With extra troops and resources, could Damascus and Aleppo be taken? Soon a new energy was directed towards Syria – and a final showdown with the Turks. If all went well, Turkey would soon be out of the war. If all went badly…it hardly bore thinking about.

The Turks were proving a stubborn enemy. The line in Palestine, held by an estimated 40,000 Turkish soldiers, stretched inland from the

Mediterranean. Tens of thousands of other troops were holding other strategic places.

After Jerusalem, Allenby failed to maintain either the momentum or the advance. It is generally said that in March and April 1918, a few raids that failed took place and the troops prepared for the big offensive. This is nonsense. In March, Allenby had sent troops beyond the River Jordan, but they were pushed back. In April a second advance also failed miserably. Cyril Falls says that Allenby was not 'altogether candid in describing these operations as "raids", because he had meant to retain most of the ground won, including Amman on the Hedjaz [sic] Railway and Es Salt'. In both of these operations Allenby was let down by Lawrence and the Arabs. Rex Hall, who later became ADC to Chauvel, in his memoirs *The Desert Hath Pearls* wrote:

> *On Sunday, 24 March, we left the Jordan Valley on the most arduous task for both men and animals the Brigade was to carry out — the First Raid on Amman...we had been told by higher command that in our attack on the enemy's southern sectors we could expect T E Lawrence and his Arabs to come up from the south, and so to prevent reinforcements by road or rail from that direction. During the Wednesday, we looked in vain through our binoculars. Instead of the Arabs coming, the resourceful German engineers had overnight shaped wooden pieces into the gaps which had been blown by our engineers in each rail, thereby allowing trains with reinforcements to come into Amman. Three more days passed and still no Arabs. A week later, GHQ informed us that Lawrence had apologised and that he would be sure to co-operate, if Allenby gave him another chance. Consequently the raid on Es Salt was made a month later, but again no Arabs.*

On 1 April the air forces of the British navy and army became an independent body, the Royal Air Force. German air superiority, which had kept the British back for nearly two years in the Middle East, was now a thing of the past. The Palestine Brigade consisted of two wings – seven squadrons – of which one was Australian. The most effective and constant pilots were those in the Australian Flying Corps, which had eighteen Bristol fighters and one giant Handley Page, piloted by Captain Ross Smith from Adelaide. Carrying sixteen 112 lb bombs and a huge petrol tank, it outflew and outgunned all the other planes and could remain in the air for eight hours. Cyril Falls wrote in *Armageddon: 1918* that one of the functions of the Australian pilots was their 'brilliant and unceasing support of Lawrence's Arabs, who would have been well-nigh helpless without it for the bolder enterprises in which they were to engage…the Germans now found themselves outfought in the air'.

The Australians protected the extreme far right of Allenby's army when they joined Chaytor's Force, under the command of the quiet New Zealander, Major General G E Chaytor. Already there were two battalions of West Indians, a Scottish field artillery battery, an Indian mountain battery and the Anzac Mounted Division. Never was a day or night silent. The Turks on the other side of the valley, according to intelligence, had seventy cannon, including one terrifying piece of German machinery nicknamed 'Jericho Jane'. Chaytor's Force also had the ignominy of being fired on by British cannon, which had been taken from the British in March during an attack on the Turks north of the Dead Sea.

Soon the Australians were given a most unpleasant and dangerous assignment – the occupation of the Jordan Valley. Locals said no Europeans could exist there during the summer months – not just because of the immense heat but also because of the prevalence of malaria. Occupying this valley, one of the hottest places on earth, was a necessary preliminary to taking Amman (the Roman Philadelphia with its amphitheatre). Stationing the army there also cut off a Turkish line of retreat, as well as depriving them of supplies arriving by boat across the Dead Sea from the grain-bearing districts near Kerak. The Turks held the northern part of the wadi, as well as its right and left flanks.

Taking the road through the valleys leading to Jericho, the Australians made their way towards the deepest gash in the face of the earth. Here the

River Jordan flows down until it disappears into the Dead Sea, 1,290 feet below sea level. In summer, temperatures soared to between 43 and 52°C, leaving many men sometimes on the verge of unconsciousness because of dehydration. In addition to this, the fine dust caused coughing. Thirst took over from hunger – few men ate all their rations. Added to the excruciatingly dry heat and lack of shade was the searing wind of sandstorms. Brief and occasional though they were, they could peel skin off a man's face and arms. Enemy shelling was severe and constant, and added to this was the mental and physical strain, reducing the condition and vitality of the men to their lowest ebb since the Gallipoli days. The extreme desolation of nature appalled even the toughest man, and the Turks, who still held both sides of the Jordan, never stopped reminding the Australians of their superior position.

The rumour that no European man had ever spent a summer there persisted. There was no shade apart from the shadow of the sand dunes, the odd cluster of date palms and battered tents. The slightest breath of wind raised a cloud of dust.

The Jordan Valley tested the men's endurance and willpower, especially as there were not enough mosquito nets to go around and not enough crude oil to pour on stagnant pools of water to destroy the mosquitoes. Raids, rifle fire and enemy shelling broke the daily routine of digging, wiring and standing to arms before dawn. Day after day they patrolled, toiled and sweltered in the deathly valley, until malaria, disease, poisonous bites, bullets or bombs claimed them.

Soon the men were moved to near the ancient reservoirs of Solomon's Pools, built by King Solomon close to the limestone road leading to Beersheba. As well as their normal duties, the men were now given a new role – to destroy mosquitoes by ridding the area of stagnant pools and streams of water and pouring kerosene into drainage holes. The nearby town of Bethlehem was close enough for men to make visits to the Church of Nativity to see where Jesus Christ was born; it was a stark contrast to their harrowing life in the desert.

Everything, including the food, was full of grit, sand, insects and more insects: lice, fleas, loathsome sand flies and scorpions, not to mention spiders and snakes. Apart from these adversaries, there was still another irritation to contend with – the stiff attitude of the British officers which contrasted with the easy-going ways of the Australians. The difference between the British cavalry regiments, many of which still sported a pack of hounds, and the Australians, was particularly marked. In *The History of the British Cavalry*, the Marquess of Anglesey praises the closeness of Australian officers and soldiers in the Middle East. 'So long as they gave themselves no airs and were truly efficient, a close personal association with their men developed…The material differences between officers and men in camp and field were not very great…They had a little more space in their tents than the other ranks had in their "bivvies" and they could buy spirits, which the men were not allowed to do.'

Once again the horses were easier targets than men. On 7 May, shortly after dawn, six German aeroplanes flew low. This dropping bombs continued sporadically over the next few weeks. On 2 June, towards dusk, ten planes appeared and aimed about fifty bombs at the horses and the bivouac lines. Six horses were killed outright, and eighty were wounded, sixteen so badly that they had to be shot.

On 10 July the 10th Light Horse were moved from Solomon's Pools to Talaat el Dumm, opposite Jebel Kuruntal. On either side of the narrow valley are whitish-grey hills, which hide the strange, twisted, mutilated rocks, in parts rising into cliff-like hills. A Greek monastery was wedged into the side, near the top. This is the wilderness in which Jesus Christ was supposed to have spent his 'forty days and forty nights' struggling with the Devil.

Dust filled both the air and their noses. Malaria was rampant, as were the sandflies. Swimming in the Dead Sea was the best local diversion, even though the men found that although they could not sink in the salt-laden water, it would be easy to drown because feet rose right up. Courting the danger in the water, men played cautious pranks.

Meanwhile, Lawrence and the Arabs were continuing their grim camel rides through the sun-scorched lands. Lawrence's task was now much more than just cutting the Turkish steel rail track and fighting – it would be political and would spur the decision makers in London.

Chapter Thirteen

Lawrence and the
Australian Flying Corps

A mong the outstanding young pioneers in the sky was 26-year-old Captain Ross Smith, one of the many light horsemen-turned-pilots. This new 'cavalry in the sky' showed that a good air force could help not only destroy but also demoralise an enemy. As an observer and pilot with No 1 Squadron of the Australian Flying Corps, he flew Bristol fighters, but occasionally the much larger Handley Page 0/400 bomber. He was one of a group of Australians sent to aid Lawrence. By early 1918, Lawrence had so enriched the Arabs with British money and equipment that Feisal was not the only Arab who had great faith in him. Lawrence, who had again visited Allenby, had promised to co-ordinate the efforts of the Arab irregulars in the advances to Amman and to Damascus. Keeping in contact, though, was a problem. Military wirelesses lacked sufficient range, and aeroplanes could not be spared to run a daily letter service. Although wirelesses had been invented in 1895, they were still heavy and awkward to use. The lightweight two-way radio was a thing of the future.

One of Smith's first jobs was to fly Lawrence to a meeting with Allenby at a secret rendezvous in the desert. It was decided at this meeting that action would be taken to improve communications. The movements of the Arabs could be erratic, and often the Bedouin had to cover an area so wide that at times the columns were hundreds of miles apart. The telephone, being fixed, clumsy and time-consuming to set up, was unsuitable for mobile warfare. So communication between the British army and the Arab irregulars came to rely on messengers or carrier pigeons. Pigeons earned records for valour, speed and resourcefulness. At a time of great technological advances, countless men owed their lives to the tenacity of these little birds. They stayed in the air despite open wounds; often arriving with a note tied to a leg covered in blood, or with a leg or an eye missing. Experiments soon proved that the actual homes of pigeons were more important to them than the locations. 'Homing Pigeons' could find their homes, even when they had been relocated up to around fifty miles distant. So moveable horse-drawn and motor-drawn homes were introduced.

L. W. Sutherland, a former pilot, wrote about Lawrence and the pigeons in *Aces and Kings*. 'And what of the Arabs? Adroit thieves and keen marksmen who are inordinately fond of game of any description. How would the pigeons fare at their hands?' A few ended up on the table, but the pigeon postal service worked efficiently. Sutherland continued:

> *Well, one morning a crate of pigeons arrived at the squadron...*
> *Single birds were to be taken out in the machines and released from*
> *varying distances and at different heights...One of them we called*
> *'Jenny'. She became the pet of the squadron and was most carefully*
> *guarded in training. She had a sort of net for carriage in the*
> *machines. When the time came for the bird to be dispatched, the*
> *net would be lifted and the bird thrown up and back, down the*
> *slipstream...But once out Jenny would stick to the machine until*
> *she had sorted herself out, and then how she would streak for home!*

> *It was simple to deliver the birds to Lawrence at Azrak, but*
> *what of it when he moved? We got this necessary mobility by*
> *building small cane cages, with a kind of cell or compartment for*
> *each bird, and a parachute for the cages. So when the birds were*
> *to be delivered from aloft to the ground, we simply tossed the cages*
> *overboard, and the parachute did the rest.*

Jenny and her friends took messages to Lawrence over inhospitable country for distances of up to 300 miles. But when plans for the offensive were intensifying, the aeroplanes and the pigeon service ceased. The pilots had more urgent and pressing tasks – keeping the Germans out of the airspace above the Jordan Valley so that they would not get close enough to see that 15,000 of the horses were nothing but wood and wire.

The decline of troop numbers in Palestine caused by demands from the Western Front was remedied by boatloads of Indian units, both cavalry and infantry. India might have supplied more men to the Allied forces than Canada, Australia, New Zealand or South Africa, but apart from two divisions that went to France early on, Indians did not play a large role in France. Instead, they shone in Palestine and Mesopotamia, where they formed the bulk of the Egyptian Expeditionary Force (EEF). Despite their lack of success in France, their wide experience there meant that the troops that were sent from there contrasted dramatically with the majority of their compatriots who, it was joked, had never seen a rifle.

Instructing and integrating them was not easy. Few understood English, French or Arabic. A tremendous strain was put on a handful of officers who had served in India and could speak Hindustani or Urdu. An officer in signals was given a curt reply when he remarked that it took two years to turn an Indian into a signaller. Training was to take no more than two months. The job of turning the raw Indians into polished soldiers was given to Lieutenant-General Sir George Barrow, a former Indian cavalry officer. Much to everyone's surprise, in August 1918, after a raid was carried out to 'blood' and test four battalions, they were passed all set to fight.

On 21 August, the 10th received an order to move yet again, to Ludd, and a few days later they were resting at Talaat al Dumm in the relative coolness of night. They were soon passing under the walls of Jerusalem, built by Suleiman the Magnificent out of huge, ochre-coloured squared stones, some of which had once formed the outer wall of Herod's Temple. Once they set up camp at Ludd, almost daily reinforcements of men and horses from Moascar arrived. Among them was my father, Robbie. He arrived at dawn to see the Palestinian hills in all their beauty and glory – a relief after the sixteen-hour train journey, during which passengers had been covered with sand and soot from the engine. Facey in *A Fortunate Life* said that the only lavatories on the trains were primitive to say the least: 'Empty open trucks with about one foot of dry sand in the bottom were put in between the carriages...The sides of these sand trucks were only eighteen inches high'.

The anti-venereal crusade, initiated soon after the first Australians had arrived in Egypt, continued the next day with a lecture to all ranks on parade. Over two hundred miles from Cairo and living in an all-male camp, such dangers seemed remote. The entry in the regimental diary of 12 September '120 men sent to Surafend in the afternoon for disinfection' does not specify whether they were fumigated against lice or venereal disease. A delousing parade consisted of diving naked into a large canvas container full of water and chemicals; not unlike sheep dipping. Clothes were placed in a steamer and would emerge free of lice. If a delouser was not available, some men would put their shirts on inside out. This, according to Henry Bostock's memoirs, was called 'giving them a route march...it would take our passengers some time to change over'.

Despite the maintenance of routine, the men knew that battles were looming. On Sunday 15th, the last break before D Day, fourteen bags of sweet potatoes and 1,420 eggs were purchased to augment the tedious rations.

The extra weight of the swords was a problem. It was finally decided that the amount of ammunition carried would be reduced to ninety rounds with a second bandolier around the neck of each horse. At least the sword had no additional weight of ammunition, no need of resupply. Instructions were given that dismounted action would be resorted to only when mounted assault was impossible. To raise the morale of the men, the officers were told: 'The sight of a determined mounted advance and the fear of cold steel have a far greater and more lasting effect on the enemy than many bullets. The terror inspired by a cavalry charge extends far and wide, and is not confined to the troops immediately attacked'.

Swords were not the only anachronism in a war in which machine-guns and science were speeding up combat. The humble shovel and pickaxe were still used in trench digging. However, scientists were playing as important a role as soldiers. While at the beginning of the war forests had been felled to furnish the vital ingredient from timber for explosives – acetone – it had not been long before a chemist made it synthetically from maize. Nitrate imported from Chile, another crucial component, was diverted from being used as fertiliser until a chemist worked out how to make it synthetically too.

In most of Syria it rains only in winter, that is, between November and March, when the west wind blows in from the Mediterranean. For nearly eight months everything is dry, parched even, and in September/October, the tail end of the dry season, in many places there is not a single blade of grass. The heaviest rain is near the coast, where it falls in torrents; it decreases as the winds lessen, further east. After a distance of about 120 miles from the sea, so little rain falls that agriculture is virtually impossible, unless, as is the case in Damascus, the land is irrigated by rivers.

Allenby's plan depended on a rapid breakthrough on the north before the rains. He would conceal his intentions by acting out a charade of deception. This time he would surprise the Turks by smashing their lines in the west and hitting them from behind, while making it appear that the main attack was from the east. The operation had to be carried out before the rainy season began around the beginning of November, when water turned the dust into slippery mud, as had happened in the assault on Jerusalem the previous December.

Lawrence was on Allenby's right flank, just 100 miles from his base, so there was much planning between the two of them. The Arab irregulars were to protect this flank all the way into Syria. Messages were sent instructing them, as the third column, to prevent the escape of Turkish rolling stock by cutting the railway lines from Jenin and Haifa to Afuleh. The terrain of Syria, a land of high mountain ranges and narrow valleys running parallel to the coast, is so hazardous that it had protected the country from invasion for centuries. Lawrence and Allenby chose Deraa as the target for the Arab irregulars prior to taking Damascus. Blowing up the junction of the Jerusalem–Haifa–Damascus–Medina railways at Deraa would disrupt the Turkish logistical system and distract the attention of thousands of Turkish soldiers from Allenby's troops, who would still be moving in from the coast.

While the Australians in Palestine were preparing for the advance to Damascus, the majority of the Australian troops were in France, where they were getting quite a reputation; not only as good soldiers, but also for their personality and individuality. When Queensland-born Major-General Thomas Glasgow was ordered to make an assault at dusk he replied, 'If it was God Almighty who gave the order, we couldn't do it in daylight'. He got his way. The attack was under cover of the night.

The Australian Army Corps were leading some key Allied victories in France that began the German slide towards defeat. Not Haig in his polished riding boots, but a Jew from Melbourne was adding engineering precision to the art of modern warfare. Blending his skills as an engineer and a musician, Monash combined infantry, artillery, tanks and aircraft into 'the perfection of teamwork'. Although small in scale, his was certainly was a new kind of 'Allied victory'; as much won by the British tanks, artillery and aircraft as by the superb Australian/American infantry. By the excellence of its planning and combination of all arms into one efficient weapons system, it became a model that would be followed at Amiens on 8 August. It was this that began the German slide towards defeat, rather than the actual Battle of Hamel in France on 4 July 1918 itself. Six weeks after the Battle of Hamel, with the Australian Imperial Force as the spearhead of the British army, Monash was among the generals sustaining new victories. When knighted by King George V on the field on 15 August, he was the first general to be so honoured by a British monarch for over two centuries.

Chapter Fourteen

Preparations for
the Great Ride

S ome of the ruses used to mislead and deceive the Turks in order to make the vacated base look active verged on schoolboy practical jokes. Chaytor was given the job of making it appear that the big push would be coming eastwards from the Jordan Valley. Every man had to give the appearance of being one of a large number so that the Jordan Valley troop would still seem to be the bulk of the British army in the Middle East. Elaborate charades were staged. The Turks had no idea that there was any change to the vast numbers of the British forces in the Valley. Most of the men and horses had been moved already for a surprise attack from the west. At night they had slipped along the mountains and roads to flat areas near the coast, where they were hidden in groves of citrus and olive trees north of Jaffa and around Ludd.

Ingenious methods were dreamt up. Huge clouds of dust would make it appear that there were ten men where there was actually only one. Clouds of dust were sent into the air by bushes dragged behind mule-drawn sleighs between horse lines and water places. This helped create the illusion of massive troop movements. Patrols, often unnecessary, were constant. Other clever stunts included the erection of dummy tents; makeshift bridges flung across the river; extravagant amounts of forage ordered locally for horses even though most had been moved; a horse race was planned; unnecessary smoky fires were lit daily. Further false impressions were given with fictitious wireless messages from the old Desert Mounted Corps headquarters near Jericho. The most extreme of all the make-believe ploys were the staged marches. The recently arrived West Indian and Jewish battalions marched down the valley in the scorching sunlight one way, only to be moved back secretly at night in camouflaged lorries with muffled engines, ready to repeat the same ruse the next day. High security meant that the soldiers were not told that these activities were just to bluff the enemy, but most, of course, guessed. Pilots flew over each ploy to ensure that it would deceive any German planes that managed to get through on reconnaissance flights.

Other false leads were given with further wireless traffic. Fictitious messages were sent from the old Desert Mounted Corps headquarters near Jericho; a wireless receiving station had been set up earlier on the Great Pyramid itself to intercept enemy messages. The officers and the majority of the troops were now in the flat areas around Jaffa. All the rooms in the grand Hotel Fast beside the Jaffa Gate in Jerusalem were booked and after they were vacated of guests, had printed notices pinned to the bedroom doors with the letters 'GHQ' on them. False rumours were spread in the bazaars that the hotel would be Allenby's advance headquarters for the coming offensive. As early as May, the manager, Caesar, the famous head waiter from the Continental Hotel, Cairo, had received confidential instructions that all his accommodation would soon be urgently required. After two sentry boxes were placed at the entrance more whispers went through the bazaars to Turkish–German intelligence.

The cavalry divisions could not give vent to their high spirits, which resulted from being transferred away from the suffocating Jordan Valley. Hidden in groves of orange, lemon, almond and olives trees north of Jaffa on a five-mile front, they had to conceal all signs of their presence. Each man had to be still during daylight. Horses were kept hobbled as they drank from the irrigation channels. As fires were forbidden day and night, all cooking was done with smoke-free cubes. No order, no command was committed to paper. Sightseeing was forbidden. As camels tend to pierce the air with raucous calls and rumblings, none were present. Nor were there any mules. No new tents were put up. The long days were spent playing cards and looking into the horizon through binoculars – some could see the city and old citadel of Jaffa far in the distance. Trying to find relief from the oppressive heat and the boredom of waiting was testing. The inactivity of these men from the Desert Mounted Corps in hiding on the coast was in contrast to the non-stop activity of their colleagues in the Anzac Division, left in the still sweltering Jordan Valley.

After the Desert Mounted Corps horses had left the Jordan Valley, where they had spent the summer, they were replaced with 15,000 dummies ingeniously made from wooden frames, stakes and sticks – complete with real horse-rugs and nosebags. Australian pilots kept up a constant presence in the air, as the hoax would be visible from any low-flying aircraft. Only from a certain height did the shadows of the wooden 'horses' give the appearance of real animals. In the two months before the main offensive, the Australian planes shot down fifteen enemy planes and forced twenty-seven to the ground. In one hectic dogfight alone, two pairs of Australian pilots, including Ross Smith, took on seven enemy planes, shooting down four of them.

Both sides were well supplied with ammunition but were low on water and food. During preparations, Allenby had asked his senior administrative officer to report on the supply situation. On hearing an abrupt 'Extremely rocky, sir', he just grunted 'Well, you must do your best!' and gave instructions to push the troops forward on the shortest rations.

To add to the problems, the harvests had been poor. The fear of famine was widespread, and most men who usually worked the land had been conscripted into the Turkish army. While the Turks and their conscripted Arab soldiers survived on sparse supplies of dried legumes and mealy flour,

Lawrence's Arabs, also used to subsisting, often managed on a meagre fare of dates, camel milk, water, and, if they were lucky, a scrap of tough meat. As if by magic, the silent, stern German officers pulled unexpected supplies of tinned sausage, wine and crystallised fruits out of the sky, but only for their own consumption. Although he loathed the rations of Queensland bully beef and biscuits 'hard as wood', Robbie could not bring himself to swallow camel milk. A pennyworth of gritty, sticky dates was hidden in his left trouser pocket, to be savoured to the full – he could suck them for hours when thirsty.

The destination of Damascus was never spelt out. Secrecy was paramount. Bluff and deception were maintained, and Allenby continued to hoodwink the enemy. He kept the bulk of troops together on the eastern flank for one terrifying main thrust. Even on the eve of the offensive the Turks did not know of the British positions and were still preparing for an assault up the Jordan Valley. How could Mustafa Kemal have been hoodwinked in this way? The Sultan had reappointed him as head of the 7th Army, yet it had been late August before he had reached the Syrian Front. His confidence, and the fact that he was the sole Turkish commander who had never been beaten during World War I, were about to tempt fate.

After a brief stay at the grand and imposing Baron's Hotel in Aleppo, Kemal had travelled south to his new base at Nablus. His men were in a deplorable condition; Syria was in a pitiable state. The only way to beat Allenby would be to amalgamate the three weak armies, but Kemal lacked the authority from Constantinople to do this. Liman von Sanders, who had now clocked up over five years as head of the German military mission in Turkey, blocked his schemes. Antagonism between the German and the Turkish commanders was running high. Kemal had not wanted to serve under, near or with Liman von Sanders, who had succeeded von Falkenhayn in command of the Turkish armies in Palestine and Syria on 1 March. Tension was not confined to high command. Villagers and tribesmen were rebelling, and morale in the Turkish army was low. Feisal's army was said to be swelling daily with deserters – just how many will never be known. Deserters in the ranks were so numerous that orders were given to machine-gunners on lorries to shoot soldiers seen fleeing. Most deserters went home, but in the six weeks before the final push, 350 gave themselves up to the British (making a total of 800 during the war). Unlike going home, this offered safety from arrest.

Using Arab agents and political infiltrators who worked behind enemy lines, the British secret service was spreading both misinformation and discontent through communities in an attempt to disrupt Turkish rule. Liman von Sanders, in his candid war memoirs *Five Years in Turkey*, quotes Kemal's letter of 11 September, in which he wrote:

> *There is a lot of British propaganda. The British secret service is*
> *active everywhere. The population hates us... The British now*
> *think that they will defeat us by their propaganda, rather than by*
> *fighting. Every day from their aircraft they throw more leaflets*
> *than bombs, always referring to 'Enver and his gang'...*

The front-line Turkish troops were supported by 12,000 men on the left flank, with another 5,000 in reserve, and 10,000 men on the right flank. Kemal set to work hurriedly, ignoring the pain from his recurring kidney problem, directing troops from his bed. He wrote: 'Our army is very weak. Most of our formations are now reduced to one-fifth of their prescribed strength'. Recent research has revealed that morale and the ability to fight among the Turks were severally curtailed by disease among the troops, especially pellagra. Like scurvy, this is a disease caused by malnutrition, but manifests itself with severe dermatitis, diarrhoea and dementia.

On 17 September, an Indian sergeant, a deserter from General Barrow's battalion, warned some of the Turkish officers that the big attack would commence near the coast. He gave the time and place, and the fine points of the deception. A trusted officer, who had been fighting the English for three years and knew their ways, was convinced that the Indian was telling the truth. Kemal dragged himself from his sickbed. A warning was rushed to Nazareth to Liman von Sanders. Nonsense, he replied. This man was yet another ruse of the English.

The 10th Light Horse rode through the cactus-hedged roads and camped not far from the railway station at Ludd. All through Palestine and Syria, the formidable cactus hedges, about six feet tall, were still tangled with barbed wire put there earlier by the Germans. Clumps of almond trees in full leaf, and grey olive trees, heavy with ripening fruit, brightened the town. No entries in the Regimental Diary reveal that they were getting close to D-Day. The official 10th Light Horse War Diary records: '6/8/18: One of our planes bombed Baghalat. One man was wounded at trenches. Enemy shelled our position during the night but did no damage. Usual parties on defence works. 7/8/18: Intermittent shelling all day. Usual working parties at night. 2000 eggs, 900 lbs potatoes, 80 lbs tomatoes, 1074 lbs onion purchased from Regt. Funds were issued as comforts and made a welcome addition to the usual rations. 8/8/18: Our batteries heavily shelled roads and tracks behind the enemy line causing a considerable decrease in enemy movement. 10 men were evacuated to field ambulance. Mail arrived. Working parties improved the trenches and fences at night. Work now nearing completion. 9/8/18: An average day. Usual working parties at night. 12 men evacuated to field ambulance'.

Disregarding the excitement of the long-awaited advance, the regimental diary reads:

> No training parades...Move orders were received...Conference of all officers at BHQ [Battalion Headquarters] at 1500. 15 men were evacuated sick to Field Ambulance. Regiment moved out at 1800 and arrived at bivouac area...Lines down and bivouacked for night...To be ready to move at half hours notice...

Paterson's description of droving a contingent of his horses north to the Front gives a feeling of the tension:

> We are very near the climax now. I am taking a hundred horses up by road as there is not room for them on the trains; and ahead of me and behind me there are similar consignments of horses all

headed for the Front. I pass a flying depot where the boys are
leaving at daylight, each with his load of bombs to smash up the
Turks. Eight of them start off, but one boy's machine fails to make
altitude and he comes back for adjustments. As he lands, he rushes
over to us and says: 'Come on, let us have a drink...' [I] arrive at
the Front with my horses just in time to hand them over and see
the start of the expedition after all Allenby's months of preparation.

Announcing the advance, Allenby greeted the officers with the words: 'I came here, gentlemen, to wish you good luck, and to tell you that I consider you are on the eve of a great victory. Practically everything depends on the secrecy, rapidity and accuracy of the cavalry movement'.

Jerusalem and Ludd were still the limits at which British troops could be supplied from the bases in Egypt. The broad-gauge military railway line brought wagons crammed with food and ammunition to Ludd, while the new pipeline conveyed water from Kantara in Egypt. Urgent though the need was to extend this, work could not proceed until enough stockpiles – depots of bullets, shells and food – were built up. So the camels continued to be carriers, as they had been for thousands of years in the Holy Land, as did the plodding little pack donkeys that survived on a sparser diet than ponies and horses. The donkeys, laden with thousands of tons in preparation for the advance, plied backwards and forwards ceaselessly, often at night, to disguise activity. Unlike most other animals, they managed to keep their balance anywhere, even on slippery ground.

The Australian Light Horse, organised into the Desert Mounted Corps, prepared for the fight ahead. Men were 'conditioned' to the thirst they would experience en route. Habitual thirst, the officers mistakenly believed, hardened men; in reality, it made bodies excessively dehydrated and led to kidney stones and other problems. For weeks men were given only half a gallon of water a day for all purposes – and were reminded that each gallon weighs ten pounds.

Supplies for each man consisted of two days' rations, one emergency quota and two days' rations per horse. They had to travel light. Bad weather and freezing conditions in the mountains were predicted. Some memoirs say that each man had in his kit a greatcoat and a waterproof sheet; others that these, together with blankets, tents and horse rugs, were left behind. Surplus kit was dumped at divisional headquarters. Everything was done to spare the horses any extra weight, as the task of getting forage and water to such numbers of animals and men in an advance was a logistical nightmare. Ten thousand horses alone needed at least 55 tons of oats, around 50 tons of hay, 80 tons of straw and about 300 tons of fresh fodder per day – and there were many more than 10,000 mouths. However, Allenby's total army, which comprised 69,000 men, 540 guns, 62,000 horses, 44,000 mules, 36,000 camels, 12,000 donkeys and thousands of Egyptian labourers, was not yet fully mobilised for the final advance against the Turks in Palestine and Syria. The total moving forward on 19th April was 12,000 sabres, 57,000 rifles and 540 guns, in:

> The 4th and 5th Cavalry Divisions: partly composed of the
> Indian Cavalry regiments.
> The Australian Mounted Division: the Imperial Camel Corps
> brigade of Australian and New Zealand Companies, including the
> Scottish Horse as a machine-gun squadron.
> The Anzac (Australia and New Zealand Army Corps) Mounted
> Division.
> The 10th, 53rd, 54th, 60th, 75th, Lahore and Meerut Divisions.
> An Indian infantry brigade
> 6000 French troops
> Among the mounted units were the Dorset Yeomanry, the Jodhpur
> and Mysore Lancers, the French in their Régiment Mixte and
> Algerian units, two Jewish battalions, skilled Armenian and a
> smaller number of coloured troops from the British West Indies
> and South Africa.

Speed was imperative. Damascus had to be reached before the rains started, causing men and horses to lose their footing, and before malignant malaria took its deadly toll. Fourteen days was the incubation period for this dreaded disease. Precautions such as issuing men with mosquito nets and citronella oil and not leaving standing water around helped. Prevention was impossible. Malaria had already hit the Turkish forces, and their weakly nourished bodies offered scant resistance. Disease-carrying flies and mosquitoes were also the bane of the horses. The law prohibiting the docking of tails would not be implemented in Britain until thirty years later, and some unfortunate beasts were left with only a stump, unable to swish away troublesome insects.

On the eve of the advance, Barrow addressed the men with a 'you-can-do-it-chaps' speech, which in essence said that the British troops were better than the Turks. 'We have established a great moral superiority over the Turk…He has suffered severe defeat, and has been constantly forced to retire'. Then, with a touch of overconfidence, he added that the Turks had lost in every recent mounted advance. 'He dislikes our cold steel, and the sight of it makes his fire erratic. He cannot stop us from reaching him, and when once we reach him his fate is sealed.'

Only instructions for the following week were given. The main force was to be 12,000 horses. Barrow's 4th Cavalry would take Nablus and Kemal's base and then press on to Haifa. The capture of Nazareth and Liman von Sanders' headquarters would follow. Then by pushing east to Deraa Junction, they would meet up with the Arab irregulars, who by then would have further crippled communication by wrecking the Pilgrims' railway. The Australian Mounted Division, after passing west of Lake Tiberias (the Sea of Galilee), would cross the Jordan. Even at this stage the word 'Damascus' was still not mentioned.

The plan was for bombs, artillery and infantry to crash an almighty hole in the twenty-five mile long Turkish line, which was held by 7000 troops. Once the hole was wide enough, two mounted divisions would push north on the approach routes east of the Jordan; the other two mounted divisions were to break through the defensive line near the coastal plain. Speed would be a matter of life and death, but the terrain meant that progress in all but a few places would be slow. The Turkish positions in the Judaean Mountains for ten miles east and west north of the Jerusalem–Nablus road were in places of great natural strength, providing many hiding places. While the horses were rushing north, the Infantry Divisions were to break the centre of the line north of Jaffa. Then, when they had broken through, the 5th Light Horse Brigade was to make a beeline for Tul Keram, a rail junction.

On the night of April 18th, the 10th Light Horse, chosen as the vanguard of the advance into Syria, was ready to take up its position at the head of the Australian Mounted Division. They were told to get as much rest as possible and to be ready at 6.30 am. Reveille for the Light Horse would be at five.

Three main theatres of war – France, Palestine and Bulgaria – dominated the Allies' plans in September 1918. The Australian forces were involved in the first two. In London, in anticipation of victory, the foreign secretary, Arthur Balfour, asked the Foreign Office for a memorandum on the recent British pledges on the Arab lands. He hoped that the conflicting undertakings could somehow be reconciled without souring Britain's relationships. These undertakings now only included the MacMahon letters and other pledges to the Arabs, the Sykes–Picot agreement with the French and his own declaration to the Jews, known as the Balfour Declaration. The Russian Revolution had made the earlier Constantinople Agreement of March–April 1915, between Britain, Russia and France, null and void. The British tried to think of ways in which they could juggle all their promises. How could Britain keep her word to France and her pledges to the Arabs, let alone the Jews? Would one way out be to let it appear that the Arabs conquered Damascus?

Chapter Fifteen

The Great Ride Commences

T he order was shouted: 'Saddle up, everywhere!' 'Turn out! Saddle up everywhere!' Each man pulled on his boots and leggings. The darkness was broken by a glimmer of light from an officer's torch as he peered down at a folded map. Within two minutes each man had his belongings strapped to his saddle, which he carried to the horse-lines. Men fumbled, locating their horses in the dark. Then each saddle was strapped on – with a canvas water bucket and nosebag.

The campaign had begun at 1.15 am. Three Australian pilots smashed the enemy's central telephone exchange with sixteen bombs. At 4.30 am, a deafening roar of guns followed. The bombardment, the great offensive, had begun. Bursting shells and Turkish SOS signals lit up the sky. After a barrage from 400 guns, the infantry followed, sweeping the Turks out of their trenches, rolling them back northward and eastward. As the escaping Turks scrambled through narrow defiles, planes flew low, emptying their machine-guns into the retreating enemy columns and dropping bombs.

Despite the tremendous noise, the horses, except for the odd neighing, were silent, unlike the camels, which were braying loudly. Occasionally shuffling could be heard, sometimes a little soft whistling, the snorting of the horses, the creak of the saddles, or the clanging of the new scabbards. An hour passed. Then another. Some men were longing for a cigarette, but when the enemy was in the vicinity smoking was forbidden until full daylight. The men waited for the whistle.

Siegfried Sassoon had summed up the feelings soldiers experience before battle when he was in Palestine at the beginning of the year:

> ...the stabbing moments of realisation before battle...the ugly anticipations of wounds and failure, then the excitement and devil-may-care ardours before going into action, the mental gesturing and limelight postures of 'facing death'...then the disillusion and nerve-shattered exhaustion – broken in mind and body – the shock of seeing one's comrades killed and maimed. And, worst of all, the futile longing for home and comfort, the rat-in-a-trap feeling that escape will never come.

When the whistle finally came, the men and horses (three divisions of cavalry – the Australians and the 4th and 5th cavalry divisions) rode steadily for mile after mile, and finally plunged through a gap in the enemy's wire near Tabsor. The infantry and engineers who were clearing out the debris of the morning's battle greeted the men. Major Olden wrote that on reaching the wire of the Turkish defences, there were cheers and cries of 'Good luck!', which were heartily responded to by 'Same to you! We'll meet in Damascus!' Jokes were also made about the fleeing German officers, who might leave in their wake some superior food or wine.

The scene of the morning's great battle was now jumbled earth, broken equipment, corpses and a few parties of prisoners. The horses jumped over the now abandoned trenches and the tangles of barbed wire imported from German factories. Men and horses headed north into what has often been described as rather desolate-looking country. The slightest breath of wind raised a cloud of dust. Nor was there any shade from the relentless sun. Few trees were left standing. After the supplies of locomotive coal were cut off, the desperate Turks had chopped down anything that would burn as fuel for their steam trains, even ancient olive trees. Trains even ran on dried camel dung; for over a thousand years the Arabs had used animal dung as fuel, depriving the soil of its usual nutriments.

For wheeled traffic, the soft terrain was covered by wire netting, or the wire was placed on matting. The wheeled transport behind the horses included ambulances, ammunition wagons and water carts, supply vehicles and baggage. Speed, surprise and manoeuvrability were the key words in this advance. The 100,000 special shells containing chemicals for howitzers and heavy artillery were left behind in the ammunition stores.

The logistical system would be stretched as the men galloped ahead. Lagging miles behind, four abreast, were 2,200 camels with their load of 44,000 gallons of water. Slow as they were, these 'ships of the desert' were still the best water-carriers.

The men swept northwards over the sand hills to cut off the enemy's supplies and line of retreat. Maintaining the right distance from the man and horse in front was not always easy, but it was necessary. Horses dislike anything too close behind them and can demonstrate their displeasure with a kick or two.

Noise from rifle shots joined the sound of the hoof beats as the men rode north, quickening their pace. After thirty miles of cantering up the coastal corridor, men and horses swung inland to cut off the enemy's rear. Meanwhile, on the other side of Palestine, the Anzac mounted division under Chaytor remained in the Jordan Valley, holding down the right flank. The plan of the battle was likened to the infantry opening a door on its hinges and holding it open so the cavalry could ride through, across the mighty River Jordan and into Syria.

The constant fear was that wells or waterholes might have been poisoned, tainted with camel's urine, or simply be brackish and unpalatable. The cisterns in the villages, insufficient for the thousands of horses, were usually a disappointment. Some oases, too, were a source of frustration, while many waterholes were choked by waterweed or fouled by worms if frogs were not present to eat them. So each man shared his pitiful water ration from his canvas water bottle with his drooping horse. Normally horses drink a bucket of water three times a day – more in hot weather or with heavy work. As well as the discomfort of the actual thirst, the dehydration causes indigestion, loss of condition and intestinal fermentation.

The Australians were expert at living off the land, at making do, but at that time of the year little was left but withered grass and the odd clump of wild sorrel or leeks. Often in summer it is only the dew falling at night that preserves the miserable vegetation. Nor was there time to forage. Grapes and figs could be purchased from time to time at odd settlements; also a little tibben – chopped barley straw of scant nutritional value, but better than the wasted, thin grass which the horses ate so quickly that they swallowed stones caught in the base of the blades and roots.

The 10th Light Horse rode on. Stopping was dangerous. The route led through Khurbet es Zerkie and el Mughair to the small river of Nahr Iskanderun, which was crossed at 7.30 pm. The horses were watered from canvas buckets from the river. Near Sheikh Mohammed, both men and horses rested briefly. Some of the horses in the other groups were desperate for water, and at about 7 pm, the well-drawers started the lengthy process of watering the horses. Sleep was out of the question for man or horse. To save the backs of the horses, the girths were loosened. The 10th Light Horse remounted at 1 am to keep up the relentless pursuit. In front of them was a terrifying route over gigantic mountains.

Once on the rugged heights, the men started the difficult trek through the fourteen-mile long Musmus Pass. This famous thoroughfare, a shallow stony waste similar to an elevated ridge, rises from 300 feet above sea level to 1200 feet, with hills ascending abruptly from the track. Even though it had widened a little in the 3,377 years since the Pharaoh Thothmes III took his foot soldiers through, it was still a dangerous and tight place. Often men had to walk in single file. The slightest stumble could plunge man and beast headlong into an abyss, so the horses were cautiously led. Going over sheer, rocky mountains at night was perilous. Men kept losing sight of those in front. Now and then they had to take the loads from the horses to squeeze them through the track when it narrowed.

At 3 am, near the crest of the pass, about a hundred Turkish soldiers were sighted sitting around a fire, warming themselves in the chilly night air. They looked with astonishment at the turbaned Indian lancers. Almost instantly they laid down their arms. There was no resistance. The weary men and horses continued on and on, the men trying to ignore the pain of their saddle-sore buttocks and thighs.

The Musmus Pass opens onto the Plains of Esdraelon. This, in part, was one of the granaries of Palestine for hundreds of years, but in later times it had become a grazing ground for nomadic Bedouins. As the Light Horse emerged from the Pass, the men could see the hills of Nazareth in the distance, where they hoped to capture their old enemy from Gallipoli, Liman von Sanders. A thick, early morning mist made it difficult to view their immediate destination, the town of El Afuleh, but after taking another compass bearing, the men rode on along a dirt track.

As all communications had been bombed or cut the day before, and as the advance had been so rapid, it is said that the Germans had no idea that the advance had started until the arrival of the 18th Bengal Lancers on the outskirts of Nazareth, with the Royal Gloucester Hussars following close behind. Liman von Sanders only just avoided being captured and made a prisoner-of-war in his pyjamas. On hearing an alarm, he jumped out from between his silk sheets. Clad only in his night attire and armed with a torch, he ran from his headquarters, shouting for the driver of his car. Rushing back to dress, he grabbed some of his papers and then climbed back into the car, which was driven at high speed by his terrified chauffeur towards Tiberias. They got away, but most of von Sanders' staff were rounded up. Also seized, much to the delight of the Australians and English, were wooden cases of French champagne and dozens of bottles of sweet wine.

At 5.30 am, the leading riders of the 10th Light Horse came under fire – a large body of Turkish and German infantry, preparing to leave, had been sighted in an olive grove. This group left behind a number of Turkish troops who were instructed by the Germans to hold their position at all costs. The

Australians, backed up by a machine-gun squadron that opened fire, drew swords and charged. The Turks quickly surrendered and over 8000 prisoners were taken.

Liman von Sanders had managed an escape, but his fellow commander from Gallipoli was not faring as well. Machine-gun bullets from the planes were aimed at Kemal's 7th army, with its straggling column of horses, wagons, guns and infantry. As they withdrew helter-skelter along the precipitous road on the Wadi Fara, troops fled into the hills, but there was no cover to be found. Their formation disintegrated as strafing by the Australian planes intensified. The gorge was choked with burning lorries and guns. Later, British mopping-up troops found 87 wrecked guns, 55 disabled lorries, 4 staff cars, 75 carts, 637 four-wheeled wagons and scores of water carts and field kitchens.

The wheeled transport following the horses arrived at Jenin on 21 September with a full load of supplies, having travelled sixty-two miles.

Chetwode, after urging his infantry troops on to Nablus, gave the welcome order from his armoured car for his infantry troops to rest. But Allenby, who arrived in another armoured car from the opposite direction, asked why the men were lying on the roadside. Chetwode explained that they were utterly exhausted but pleased with themselves for having arrived ahead of schedule. Allenby, who relentlessly drove both men and horses to the utmost limits of their stamina, persuaded Chetwode to make the men, despite being dead beat and thirsty, go yet further – another ten miles.

The official diary of the 10th Light Horse Diary recorded that: 'The moon was now up and huge bodies of enemy were observed moving north along the Nablus road. This was blocked from movement from the south at a pass about three-quarters of a mile south of the town...they were immediately engaged and rapidly captured...small parties of our officers and men had now returned from their first escort duties and were sent down to the pass on the Nablus road where they in turn captured more large bodies of enemy troops. This movement was carried on throughout the night, all ranks working with courage and untiring energy, with the result that by daylight, nearly 7500 prisoners had been captured and sent to a compound.

All the roads and tracks leading out of the town were picquetted by detachments from the various squadrons and any of the available personnel...'.

Even during a brief halt, the Australians dismounted, and if there was time, loosened the girths around the horses. Each hour, if possible, the command was given: 'Dismount – spell for ten minutes!' One trooper noted that these rest breaks were as welcome to the men as the horses. At each halt the men tried to spend nine minutes fifty-five seconds on the ground asleep, with the right arm looped through the reins and the hand in a pocket, so the rein would jerk if the horse tried to wander off. Of all the tens of thousands of horses used by the Allies, the ones ridden by Australians had the lowest rate of sore backs. In contrast to the British, who usually rode at a trot through the desert sands, the Australians preferred a fast walk. This is not a natural step; it has to be patiently taught and requires sensitive hands.

By 25 April, six days on, the men and horses of the 10th Light Horse were feeling the strain and longing for a short bivouac. Yet again they rode through the night – another night foray – this time towards the town of Tiberias. Again there was much shouting in the dark to locate each other. As the sky lightened, they were happy to discover that their comrades, the 8th Light Horse Squadron, had already captured the town. The drowsy horses then proceeded to Lake Tiberias, well known to many of the men from the New Testament. All through the campaign, the Australians were constantly on the lookout for a beach or a lake. The troops took the opportunity of bathing in Lake Tiberias during this respite, freshening up ready for the horrors of the crossing of the River Jordan. The horses too had a swim. Some horses were anxious about going into the water, but soon revelled in it. As Edwin Gerard ('Trooper Gerardy') wrote in his *Riding Song*:

> *Horsemen took their mounts a-swimming,*
> *And the cup of joy was brimming*
> *Twenty miles from Tel-el-Farah, by the sea.*

Something that made the men feel at home but, paradoxically, increased their homesickness, was the pungent scent of the Australian eucalyptus trees. Feeling nostalgic, the men gathered around these trees and groomed their horses, smoked, chatted, ate their frugal rations, threw dice, played cards and found sticks to make a cooking fire. A fire always meant 'boiling the billy', brewing Australian tea in the time-honoured manner with a eucalyptus twig across the tin with some stones set beneath it.

The pace quickened for the Australian Mounted Division. Refreshed, they started again, ready for the final haul. Orders were given for the capture of Damascus, using the Tiberias–Damascus Road, which included part of the oldest road in the world – the caravan road to Mesopotamia that crossed the River Jordan. The way ahead was open until they reached Jisr Benat Yakuk, north of the Sea of Galilee – the Bridge of Jacob's Daughters in the Bible. This was where Napoleon's troops were halted in 1799, two days short of the fabled city. His vision of France ruling Syria was never fulfilled. The French blue, white and red tricolour may not have then flown over Damascus, but now, the French carried a flag with them, ready to hoist. The British, though, had secret and conflicting plans.

Meanwhile, Mustafa Kemal managed to widen the space between his men and the Australians. After personally supervising a withdrawal over the mighty Jordan, he stayed behind until his main body of men were across the river. Only then did he follow, shouting and yelling out orders to smash up the ancient bridge as he did so. The 11th English Cavalry Brigade sped along so quickly that they managed to cut off his rearguard, narrowly missing Kemal himself. Rapidly – almost at lightning speed – Kemal covered the stony ground to Damascus. Twice his rearguard troops were caught in defiles and slaughtered. Above him the Bristol fighters piloted by the Australians swept up and down, raking his columns with machine-gun fire and dropping bombs. The dominance that Kemal had achieved over the Australians at Gallipoli, three years ago, was completely reversed. He was losing – and had a good chance of being killed.

Still fighting the Turks, on foot, in the saddle, but also in the skies, were thousands of men who had fought in Gallipoli. Among light horsemen-turned-pilots who had fought on the ground at Gallipoli, were P J ('Ginty') McGinness and Wilmot Hudson Fysh. The following year, with the ground engineer, Arthur Baird, they were to start the Queensland and Northern Territory Aerial Services (QANTAS).

As the 10th Light Horse arrived at the Bridge of Jacob's Daughters, they came face to face with skilled German rearguard machine-gunners and engineers demolishing the 14th century three-arched grey stone bridge. The horsemen broke into a canter, then a gallop, then a race, in a frantic effort to save the viaduct. Bullets cut down men and horses. Men fought, slashing left and right with their sabres. The sickly smell of horse sweat mixed with fresh blood rose in the stifling heat. The thunder of the horses' hooves almost drowned the screech of artillery shells and the yells of stricken men. The Australians sent out two flanking brigades while the French colonial Spahis skirmished over the steep banks, where horses came crashing to the ground, breaking the legs, arms and backs of their riders.

Unable to either save or take the bridge, scouts were sent to find a place to ford the river. They could not locate an area shallow enough to cross and were about to stop when a local Arab told them of a place where the river would only come up to the bellies of the horses. The dangerously fast-moving currents were testing. Trying to get over to the east bank they again came under heavy fire. As it grew dark men plunged in and swam, leading their horses by the reins. A few drowned, but most of the men and horses got through the freezing water to the other side of the river.

Shivering and panting, they scrambled with their horses up the steep riverbanks, strewn with rocks and pebbly stones. An eerie gloom descended. The men rubbed down their horses, knowing that they themselves would have to stay in their wet clothes all through the now freezing night. The crossing, the terrain and the combat had unnerved the horses and they were difficult to calm. Even though they had been in the river, many had been too nervous or excited to drink. Next morning a mounted attack with swords was ruled out, as the horses were ill prepared for combat; a bayonet charge was ordered instead. The Turks were, as usual, no match in body-to-body fighting with cold steel. At last the Light Horse saw the rear of the German and

Turkish forces depart in lorries, followed by the small number of German machine-gunners who had been left behind to give them cover. The inhabitants of this area, the Circassians, were allies of the Turks, but they put up no resistance.

The country flattened out. Small stones got into the horses's shoes, causing suffering and pain. The farrier's equipment, including the horseshoeing forges, had not been able to keep up with the troops, let alone ford the river. Men had worked overtime with their hoof-picks, levering out small stones from the sore feet of their horse's hooves, but the shoes desperately needed repairing. Sore feet and the terrain on the road to Damascus slowed the horses down, giving the Turks an advantage. Then the dreaded malaria hit, earlier than expected. Some men, delirious with fever, started falling from their saddles, casualties not of war but sickness. A dose of quinine – which was readily available to the troops – was the only known medical treatment for malaria.

Meanwhile, Lawrence, with an increasing force of Arab irregulars, rode on towards Deraa. Describing the relief of reaching the pinnacle of his endeavours, he later wrote to his friend Hogarth: 'For a year and a half I had been in motion, riding a thousand miles a month upon camels: with added nervous hours in crazy aeroplanes, or rushing across country in powerful cars. In my last five actions I had been hit, and my body so dreaded further pain that now I had to force myself under fire. Generally I had been hungry; lately always cold; and frost and dirt had poisoned my hurts into a festering mass of sores'.

The British planes did not have a monopoly of the skies. German aircraft, too, were dropping large numbers of bombs on the Arab irregulars. Sometimes they flew only seventy or a hundred feet above the ground. As columns of dust and smoke burst out among the camels, the Arabs became so unsettled and terrified that Lawrence anticipated mass desertions. Quickly Ross Smith and some fellow Australians piloted Bristol fighters and a Handley Page over Lawrence's route. Smith was able to force a German aircraft to the ground; then, while the pilot and observer watched, he set it on fire with a Verey pistol.

Lawrence wrote in *Revolt in the Desert*:

> *Our Australians scrambled wildly to the yet-hot machines and*
> *started them in a moment. Ross Smith with his observer leaped*
> *into one and climbed like a cat up the sky... There were one*
> *enemy two-seater and two scouts. Ross Smith fastened on the big*
> *one and after five minutes of sharp machine-gun rattles, the*
> *German dived suddenly towards the railway line. As it flashed*
> *behind the low ridge, there broke out a pennon of smoke and from*
> *its falling place a soft dark cloud. An 'Ah' came from the Arabs*
> *about us. Five minutes later Ross Smith was back and jumped*
> *gaily out of his machine swearing that the Arab Front was the*
> *place. Our sausages were still hot; we ate them and drank*
> *tea... Ross Smith wished he might stay for ever on this Arab Front*
> *with an enemy every half hour... however he must go back for the*
> *Handley-Page with petrol, food and spares.*

The relentless bombing by the Australian-piloted planes allowed the Arab irregulars to keep on the track to Deraa. Once they arrived there, the Arabs started an orgy of killing unarmed and wounded Turks. Driven on by hatred and lust for revenge, they killed without pity any Turk – the armed, the stragglers, the wounded. Bitter hand-to-hand fighting was still taking place when General Barrow, commanding the 4th Cavalry Division, arrived on 28 September. He was horrified. In three days about 5,000 Turks had been killed. Although an experienced soldier, he had never seen anything to match the vicious cruelty. But he knew nothing of the massacres that the Turks had committed with Arab villagers as their defenceless victims. So he censored Lawrence for condoning them; according to many, unjustly. But it can also be argued that as Lawrence was regarded so highly, he could have influenced the Arabs to stop the slaughter. The Arab irregulars, though, were not part of the British army, so the *Manual of Military Law* did not apply to them. Also, they were not under Lawrence's direct command, but under the brilliant chief-of-staff, Nuri Bey, who went on to become prime minister of Iraq.

In the intervening time, Kemal had reached Damascus with a reduced personal escort, leaving his troops to follow. Held together only by his willpower and brutality, the tattered remnants of his army were hysterical with fear as overhead planes dropped more bombs, decimating his transport and artillery. Most of the men in the Turkish 7th and 8th armies had either been killed or been taken prisoners of war. Major-General Salt, who had previously witnessed the impact of Kemal in Gallipoli, commented that few escapees were not made prisoner, '…but, even if there had been only one, I am certain that one would have been Mustafa Kemal Pasha himself!!' How angry Kemal must have been at Liman von Sanders for not heeding his advice to accept the word of the Indian defector. A Turkish intelligence service map found by the British proved that Allenby's deception had worked. The day before the advance, the cavalry had been marked on the map in the Jordan Valley and only two infantry divisions were indicated in the coastal area.

During the last days of Turkish rule in Damascus, all pretence was dropped. The town knew that each hour was bringing closer the rolling boom of the cannon, and the sound and dust of the horsemen. The Turks blamed the Germans; the Germans blamed the Turks. The local population boycotted both Germans and Turks and stopped selling them goods. Liman von Sanders, realising that they could not hold the city, appointed an Arab administration. Djemal Pasha, the Turk who then ruled Damascus, had already fled. Kemal went to establish a new line at Riyak, but before he could do so, the news arrived that the British were in Beirut. The Turks were outflanked there already. Kemal saw that total annihilation was inevitable unless there was quick action. He planned to retreat the 200-odd miles to Aleppo, form a new line in the north, protect the roads into Turkey and give up Syria. He discussed the plans with von Sanders, who said he had no authority in such matters. There was no-one to make a decision. The Sultan and Enver were far, far away. Kemal assumed authority.

Prince Feisal's flags, which had been smuggled in earlier, along with propaganda messages, were hung over balconies. The Arab dislike of both the Germans and the Turks was no longer concealed. Morale among the Turks, Germans and Arabs dropped. Services in places such as hospitals collapsed, and flies, stench and misery increased. The dead were lying around on floors beside the living.

Hatred between the Germans and the Turks turned into a race for survival. The top priority for each official was to find getaway vehicles. In the scramble for transport, the Germans commandeered most. The local population, as Liman von Sanders later explained, gave vent to their anger against both the Germans and the Turks:

> *The attitude of the people of Damascus at that time had become threatening. Armed bands of Arabs arrived there daily which, though they did nothing but arrange fantasias and fire into the air, formed an ominous element in the city. The population was flooded with British leaflets, which described the bad situation in Bulgaria, and contained exaggerated news of the general German situation...*

Disturbances inside the city were increasing. Feisal's agents continued to provoke the excited population. Arab recruits in the Turkish army deserted their ranks in greater numbers than before and disappeared into the crowds of the city. Djemal Pasha's cruel sovereignty was at an end. As no Arab had ruled Syria for 2000 years, the idea of an Arab ruler instead of a Turk enlivened talk in the bazaars.

Damascus meant more than just triumph at the end of the long desert campaign. The very word 'Damascus' then symbolised the Orient. Nourished by two rivers, this city was seen as a place of rest and refreshment after a long weary haul, quite literally an oasis in the middle of the desert. In contrast to the bleak areas surrounding it, Damascus was well watered. The luxuriance of its green gardens, its olive groves and orchards was renowned. Lying on a plateau between desert and mountain, it is on the prehistoric trade route between Syria and Mesopotamia. Despite countless invasions over 4000 years, and battles that had often surged round her, the city had never been destroyed. For Muslims, Damascus was the starting point of the annual Syrian pilgrim caravan to Mecca; for Christians the city was synonymous with Saint Paul, who had his miraculous conversion on 'the road to Damascus'.

Outside the city, Feisal, who was making his way to Deraa with Lawrence, was plotting the hoped-for finalé of the Arab Revolt. Would Feisal enter Damascus as an Arab liberating Arabs – and be proclaimed king?

Chapter Sixteen

Damascus!

The Arabs knew that hastening to Damascus was important. In Chapter 101 of *Seven Pillars*, Lawrence explained exactly why. 'They promised to the Arabs, or rather to an unauthorised committee of seven Gothamites in Cairo, that the Arabs should keep, for their own, the territory they conquered from Turkey in the war. The glad news circulated over Syria.' He was referring to the seldom-mentioned Declaration of Seven made by the British in Cairo a few months earlier.

But on the evening of 30 September, the Arabs were days behind the Desert Mounted Corps. The Australians were, at last, within sight of Damascus. Shots started ringing through the air as soon as the Allied troops were drawn up at the top of the long ridge of the Barada Gorge. At first the Turks managed to repulse the Australians. Fighting grew in intensity as the narrow gorge below filled with fleeing Turks, and a few Germans. Whether on horse and on foot, in motorcars, cabs or carts, they surged forward with the force of a tidal wave. So that the road would be impassable, the Australians fired on the vehicles and carts in front. The result was a shambles.

When the refugees turned back to the city, they were caught by groups of local Arabs who were rebelling against centuries of oppressive rule.

Brigadier-General George Macarthur-Onslow described one scene: 'There was a train on the line, packed with Germans, but it was completely blocked by the mass of people who struggled and fought along the railway, and the engine driver had long since been submerged in the tide of frenzied Turks. Even the river was full of men and horses'.

At 10 pm the Australians were told to bivouac for the night. 'All ranks were greatly elated at the prospect of being the first troops to enter DAMASCUS...' were the words hastily scribbled in the regimental diary. 'The huge dumps of oil and ammunition [in the valley of Damascus below] which had been fired by the enemy burnt furiously, while every few minutes a big gun would be used against us.' Also in the rough camp was an unlikely guest – Lawrence, sleeping restlessly near his armoured Rolls Royce. But Lawrence and the Australians did not depart for Damascus together. The men of the 10th Light Horse Regiment were mounted before daybreak and were away well before him.

To prevent the enemy troops still in the city escaping, the Australians had been ordered to blockade all the exit points of the city but refrain from entering it. At 4 am they were saddled up and pushing on towards Damascus. Their strategy was to encircle the city in a clockwise direction to prevent any Turks retreating.

Crossing the river by a rickety wooden bridge, they sped on towards the outskirts of the city to block the Homs Road to Aleppo to the north-east, which appeared to be the only way by which the trapped Turks could still escape. The dramatic effect and noise created by a moving mass of horsemen were daunting. So thick were the dusty clouds stirred up by the horses' hooves that visibility was often difficult. Around Jerusalem the rains had come early that year, but not here. The whitish-grey dust was still thick. Continuing across the extremely exposed plain, the men reached the edge of the city.

Major Olden, who was at the head of the regiment, galloped forward. Realising that encircling the city was impossible, he took the risky decision to order the men of the 10th Light Horse to keep going into the city itself, ignorant of what sort of barrage or onslaught might break out. His initiative was another example of the spirit and dash that had become characteristic of Australians during the war.

Hearts hammering and mouths dry, the sound of the harness jangling, the men waited for the order to charge. Each man held his reins loosely. Then the command rang out. With drawn swords, the men dug in their spurs and the horses, manes flowing, rushed forward towards Damascus. (The spirit of this charge was later captured in the painting which is on the cover of this book.) More terrifying than the speed was the noise. The thrust of the horses had a devastating effect. So loud was the deafening rumble of the hoof beats, so thunderous, that it filled the sky, the space, the plain – everything. It rolled ahead in relentless waves. The city's 250,000 inhabitants heard the echo of the horses getting louder and louder as the men got closer to the city. Only hours had passed since the noise of explosions had filled the air – the Germans ensured that their ammunition would not fall into Allied hands by setting fire to it before their hurried retreat.

Remembering the old training advice that 'the moral effect on the enemy bears a distinct ratio to the pace at which the attack advances', the riders went like the wind. The official historian Henry Gullett observed that although the Australians had been ordered not to arrive in Damascus before 2 October, 'they travelled so fast...that they arrived by the 1st...'. Not only their speed but the sight of the great Australian horses coming at a gallop, the flashing swords, and the ring of shoes upon the metal, was impressive and helped subject the populace.

At the stately stone Hejaz railway station a train waited, apparently about to leave. Its occupants did not seem to know that the railway tracks had been cut just hours earlier. The pace of the Australian horsemen was momentarily checked by a burst of rifle fire from the garrison, and then by another from Turks protected by a stone wall to the right.

The quicker the men rode, the thicker the dust. Their newly issued double-edged swords at the ready, as they rounded a bend in the road, they confronted about 800 Turkish infantry. To the right a further mass of disheartened and demoralised Turkish troops – an estimated 12,000 – stood in the open parade ground of the barracks. Shortage of equipment meant that many of the Turkish soldiers, instead of wearing boots, just had sandals with rags wrapped around their feet. The Australians did not have the advantage of knowing that the Turkish commander, Mustafa Kemal, had already abandoned his men and fled north on the Homs Road. If Kemal had not seized the high ground at Gallipoli and held the heights above Anzac Cove, the Australians might well have succeeded and taken Gun Ridge. Now he was fleeing from them. For the Australians, it was the chance to conclude the job started at Gallipoli three and a half years earlier.

Some of the Turks, screaming 'Allah!', obviously still had some fight left in them, but most were so dispirited and worn out that their aim was not accurate.

Meanwhile, Lawrence, who was miles behind the Australians, was putting the finishing touches to his appearance, arranging his flowing robes, ready to make the grandest of entrances. In the habit of shaving using a canvas basin and a mirror hung on a pole, he had halted briefly to wash at a wayside brook and then proceeded towards Damascus. But his magnificent car was stopped. A non-commissioned Indian officer, mistaking Lawrence and his party for Turks, refused to let them pass and tried to make them prisoners. When set free, Lawrence's Rolls Royce could not catch up with the 10th Light Horse.

Rushing forward on horseback, the 10th Light Horsemen seemed engulfed by the dust and the terrible noise. They charged on. But as they advanced, the possibility increased that they would soon, within less than half an hour, be the first European force to take Damascus for over 1,000 years. Yet, rather than a unified exhilaration of anticipated victory, the various units of the Allies were competing to be the first inside the city.

While the French, the British, the Arabs and the Jews were united under the banner of the Egyptian Expeditionary Force, each country, each faction, even some of the officers, had strong leanings or secret agendas about what would happen to the land they were liberating. Allenby himself was fearful of French ambition towards Syria and, like so many British officers, had a predilection towards supporting the Arab army.

Paradoxically, 120 years earlier, in many of the same places, including Jaffa and Acre, Napoleon and the French had confronted the Turks and the English. Although the French and the British were now allies, the competition and jealousy between them had not diminished. Now not just Syria itself would be affected by the answer of who was first to Damascus, but the national and political prestige of Britain and France was also at stake.

Indeed, rivalry among the French, British and Arabs was matched by competition among officers. Jean Pichon, who was with the French Regiment Mixte de Marche de Cavalerie, attached to the Australian Light Horse, was perplexed. He likened the situation to a comedy, asking: 'Que se passe-t'-il?' Which country, which person, was going to have the credit? Was it to be the main British army, the scholar–hero Lawrence with his Arab irregulars, the French, the Indians, or the Australians?

The secret political agenda of the campaign was beginning to manifest itself. The orders from General Headquarters were clear: Feisal's Arab irregulars, accompanied by Lawrence, were to be first into the city. The Arabs, though, were still on their way from Deraa and Lawrence had not been sighted since the night before.

Orders were received by British and Australian troops that 'no troops were to enter DAMASCUS unless absolutely forced to do so'. The instructions to the Australian Mounted Division stated: 'While operating against the enemy about DAMASCUS, care will be taken to avoid entering the town if possible. Unless forced to do so for tactical reasons, no troops are to enter DAMASCUS. Brigadiers will arrange picquet [sic] all roads in their areas into the town to ensure this order being carried out'.

Because an order not to enter the city was similar in wording to that issued before the capture of Jerusalem, it would not have appeared strange. But neither the officers nor the men knew that the reasons behind the restrictive orders were different. The first were personal, the second political. Allenby had wanted no-one to accept the surrender of the Holy City before him. In contrast, the future of a whole country could depend on who entered Damascus first. Because of the Declaration to the Seven, there was more chance of installing a Hashemite regime in Damascus if it looked as if the

Arabs had entered first. And they were a means of the British exerting control over the area – and keeping the French out.

Barrow's instructions were more specific. Feisal and Lawrence's Arabs were 'to be allowed to enter DAMASCUS'. The war diary of the 29th Lancers in the 4th division for 1 October shows that similar instructions were duplicated: 'No troops were however allowed in the town during the day'. Did Allenby himself issue this order for a staged Arab entry to make it appear that the Arabs had caused the fall of Damascus? Or did it originate in the War Office in London?

With their plumed slouched hats and rattling swords, the Australians made an impressive entrance. Arriving at one of the main streets with houses on either side, the men turned their horses and reined in from their headlong gallop. Unshaven, with eyes bloodshot both from desert grit and lack of sleep, covered in a layer of fine dust, they were tired, hungry and most of all thirsty. A few heads drooped from lack of sleep.

Forcing a passage through the crowded streets, the men paused briefly opposite the Hotel Victoria. No further opposition came from the Turkish barracks, but as the column neared the centre of the city, dense masses of people were seen filling the streets and squares. There were Arabs of every class in their long galabiehs, Syrians, many in European dress, armed uniformed men (later proved to be the gendarmerie), wild-looking Druses from the Hauran, with their distinctive headgear and painted cheeks, Turkish and Greek civilians, Jews, Armenians, and many others. A large proportion carried firearms, which they now discharged in the air, at the same time uttering frenzied cries and chants.

Cautiously the Australians continued along the narrow, ancient alley-like thoroughfares, slowing down to a steady trot through the tight streets, trying to avoid the holes and bumps and the gutter–canal that ran through the middle of most streets. Tension was high. They knew that the city was still crammed with arms, ammunition and explosives. Even though they were going at a slow walk, the resonance of the horse's hooves on the cobbles had a terrifying impact. It almost sounded like a long drum roll, as each hoof beat was amplified between the close-set houses. Despite the distinction of being the oldest city in the world still inhabited, Damascus seemed dirty, dull and evil smelling. The soldiers saw no sign of the orchards heavy with fruit, or fountains splashing water upon marble tiles and mosaics. Soon, though, a vision of grandeur did appear in front of them.

The riders arrived at the imposing Serai, or hall of government, with its wide stone steps guarded by sentinels with muskets. Between sentinels stood groups of officials and notables looking gloomy and unsmiling, staring into the street, apprehensively waiting to meet the victors. Olden glanced around to see if any Germans were present. He was unaware that the Turkish powers had handed control over to the Arabs. Were the men facing him Syrian Arabs? Were they Prince Feisal's supporters? Were they from the secret political groups?

Clasping a revolver in each hand, Olden, with two other officers, climbed the sweeping stairs flanked by guards and entered a vast, airy, high-ceilinged gaudy salon built to indicate the might and splendour of the Ottoman Empire. The time was 6 am. An interpreter was called for. Olden recounted the conversation in his memoirs. He enquired: 'Where is the Governor?'

'He waits for you in the Hall above.'

Glances of intelligence and appraisal passed between Olden and the men. He had no way of knowing that Damascus was no longer an enemy city and, therefore, was not really surrendering. The most important Turks had fled the previous afternoon and evening, and before they had departed, the Arab, Emir Said al-Jezairi, had been made temporary governor, aided by some of the members of the al-'Ahd.

Wearing a dark suit and a tarboosh, this small man assumed the dignity of his new position. Seated in a straight-backed gold and plush chair with carved legs, he leant slightly on the table in front of him. An exiled patriot, grandson of the Sultan of Algiers, he had decades earlier sought refuge in Syria after setting up the nationalist movement against the French. The Australians strode across the marbled floor, watched by a large group of men standing in rows, attired in the flowing robes of Eastern officialdom. Olden stopped and asked Emir Said to join them in the centre of the room. With grace Emir Said walked across the room, his hands outstretched to greet them, saying in Arabic, 'In the name of the City of Damascus, I welcome the first of the British Army'.

'Does the city surrender?'

'Yes; there will be no further opposition in the city.'

'What, then, is all the firing in the streets?'

An official replied that firing pistols into the air was an Arab form of celebration. 'It is the civil population welcoming you.'

'They [the civil population] may retain their arms for the present, prevent looting by the Arabs, and otherwise maintain order. As for the shooting in the streets, issue orders that it must cease immediately, as it may be misunderstood. You will be held responsible for this.'

'You need not fear,' replied the Emir. 'I will answer for it that the city will be quiet. We have expected the English here, and are prepared for them.'

Emir Said then began a flowery speech in Arabic, accompanied by applause from the Arabs. Olden cut him short. It seemed more prudent to avoid anyone saying too much. He told him that the British commander-in-chief, Allenby, together with Chauvel, would arrive later, adding that the speeches should wait for them. Accepting assurances that his men would not be molested, he warned that Damascus was surrounded. Refreshment was then offered by the Arabs but was declined by the Australians. This was ungracious – indeed it was a gross insult to Eastern sensibilities – but Olden thought it more important to rejoin his men, who were waiting outside in the street.

As soon as he did so, the Australian horsemen continued to make their way through the city. Their progress assumed the aspect of a triumphal procession, with huge masses of people becoming hysterical in their manifestations of joy. They clung to the horses' necks, kissed men's stirrups, showered confetti and rosewater over them, shouted, laughed, cried, sang, clapped hands and fastened flowers in the bridles. The official diary noted that 'troops were sprayed from the balconies with champagne, perfumes, rose leaves and confetti'. Weeping women waved from overhanging balconies.

Hungry horses happily nibbled at sweet cakes, grapes, peaches – and water. The men swilled it around their parched palates before swallowing, and spilled a few drops over their handkerchiefs to wipe their faces. Storekeepers bore armfuls of fruit, sweets, cigars and cigarettes. From the windows of tall buildings, Muslim women, raising their dark veils, shouted what Olden described later as sounding like 'Meit allo wesahla! 'Meit allo wesahla! ' [a hundred welcomes]. The cry was taken up and carried along the crowd in one continuous chant.

A surprise guest increased their numbers – Captain H. B. Cross, of the 38th Battalion. He had been taken prisoner by the Turks on the western bank of the Jordan on 23 September, and along with a captured Australian Flying Corps lieutenant, had been escorted to Damascus. On the Monday morning he had been packed into a train with hundreds of others for Aleppo, but by nightfall, just when they were on the point of departure, the horizon had been illuminated by a huge explosion. The Turks came to the conclusion that the earlier train had been captured and blown up. So the prisoners were hurried off into the town itself and put into 'a quite decent room for the night', as Cross later related in a letter. 'The next morning we were sitting about when one of the escorts who had been in the town came in a state of great excitement saying, "English Cavalry" – a magic word to us. The other officer and I, realising what had happened, at once bolted out of the door and up the street where, to our great joy, we saw a regiment of the Australian Light Horse [the 10th] riding in with revolvers in hands. We ran up the street and procuring spare horses, rode off with them through the town and out on the other side for about eight miles…after a meal of bully and biscuits which tasted as good as anything I've ever eaten…'

There was no time for the 10th Light Horse to visit the Street called Straight, the Long Bazaar or Darb el Mustakim, mentioned in the Bible, or the Gate of God through which the pilgrims pass, but at least, like Saint Paul, they had been on 'the road to Damascus'. Just as Venice and Marseilles are old seaports, Damascus is the ancient port in the desert, its capital. A centre of commerce and camel caravans, home of the Damask rose, a halting-place between Babylon and Baghdad, Damascus is so out of the ordinary that the previous year Lawrence had written: 'Damascus is a lodestar [a guiding star] to which Arabs are naturally drawn, and a city that will not easily be convinced that it is subject to any alien race'. And so it proved to be. The Australians rode quickly out beyond the city and on the road to Aleppo, continuing their pursuit of Mustafa Kemal. Meanwhile, as so often when secrecy is paramount, communications were sometimes ambiguous. Not only were the Australians ignorant of the political nuances determining day-to-day actions, but it seems that Chauvel was ignorant of Lawrence's full brief of installing Feisal as ruler of Syria.

Chapter Seventeen

Lawrence Arrives in Damascus

There was a gap of about an hour between the 10th Light Horse departing from the centre of the city of Damascus and further Allied troops arriving at around 9 am. Was Damascus going to fall to British or French rule? Was the city to be secure for the Arabs, that is, the Arabs alone, not as puppets of a Western power? Was almost 1,400 years of unbroken Muslim rule about to be broken? Only time would resolve the most acute of the many problems during the entry: the absence of the main player, Feisal, who, with his exhausted troops, was still somewhere between Deraa and Damascus, having being engaged in the merciless battle against the rearguard of the Turkish Fourth Army. Would the delay hinder Feisal's position? Who really would rule Damascus? Apart from any political implications, would it not have been better for Muslims to be the first to enter the city that was home to Islam's fourth-holiest shrine, the Omayyad Mosque, and the tomb of the warrior Saladin?

The sun was well up when Lawrence, wearing the dazzling white clothes of a desert sheikh, complete with a curved, ornamental dagger hanging from his waist, arrived in Damascus. He already knew much of the area well, as he had visited Syria three times over the last ten years. He had made a daring clandestine incursion there as a spy earlier that year, but had first visited the city in 1908, when he was a student at Oxford doing a backbreaking walking tour in Syria to research Crusader castles for a thesis. Four years later, having graduated from university, he had visited Syria again while working as a Hittite archaeologist.

No previous visit equalled his arrival on 1 October 1918. The revelry was such that celebrations had already been going on for two hours. At about 9 am, an impressive Allied show-of-force procession through the city began. The 14th Cavalry Brigade were in the lead, followed by the two French regiments (attached to the 4th Australian Light Horse) and parts of the 5th Indian Division, which had just arrived from Deraa. Despite his importance, Lawrence was in the rear of this convoy. Although things had not gone to plan, he acted with confidence, waving like a royal from the comfort of an open car as he was driven through the cheering streets of the ancient city.

This position was unexpected. Competent though the British-led Allied forces were, nobody understood the intricacies of the political situation in Damascus in the way that Lawrence did. He would have to act quickly if he was to save Damascus for Feisal, who still had not arrived. During the next few days, indeed the next few years, Lawrence's political influence would be enormous. Much larger than his overall military contribution to the whole Middle East campaign was his pen. It was through Lawrence that the West learnt that the Arabs – especially Prince Feisal and his father Sherif Hussein – were a force to be reckoned with.

In his writing, Lawrence made no reference to the Australian troops who had preceded him. He implies, but does not state, that he was part of the historic party that entered the city first. 'We drove down the straight-banked road through the watered fields, in which the peasants were just beginning their day's work. A galloping horseman checked at our head-cloths in the car, with a merry salutation, holding out a bunch of yellow grapes: "Good news: Damascus salutes you".'

The description went on describing his entry:

> *So in the Blue Mist we set off to show ourselves... When we came*
> *in there had been some miles of people greeting us: now there were*
> *thousands for every hundred then. Every man, woman and child*
> *in this city of a quarter-million souls seemed in the streets, waiting*
> *only the spark of our appearance to ignite their spirits. Damascus*
> *went mad with joy...*

How would the simple fact that the Arabs had not been the first to enter Damascus affect the future of Syria? As stated earlier, the Declaration of Seven, which had been made in Cairo in June that year, had clearly stated that the British would recognise the independence of the Arabs in 'areas emancipated from Turkish control by the action of the Arabs themselves during the present war...'.

Contrary to Lawrence's version, later that day Chauvel cabled Allenby to tell him of the progress:

THE AUSTRALIAN MOUNTED DIVISION ENTERED THE OUTSKIRTS OF DAMASCUS FROM THE NORTH-WEST LAST NIGHT, AT 6 A.M. TODAY THE TOWN WAS OCCUPIED BY THE DESERT MOUNTED CORPS AND THE ARAB ARMY.

But Chauvel's report on 'the capture of Damascus and the arrangements made for the Civil Administration thereof' to the War Office (95/4371) dated 2 October contradicts this. Chauvel states that the Australians entered Damascus on the 'evening of September 30th'. This is one of the differing accounts referred to by Jeremy Wilson in the Prologue, and like the other War Office documents, is now in the Public Records Office in Kew, London. Assessing the cause of the error is difficult. Was it that he was disturbed by Lawrence's exaggerated claims of the Arab irregulars entering the city the night before? Or had he meant that they were on the outskirts of the city? Whatever the reason, this deviation from the truth undermined what really happened, devaluing the authenticity of the Australian entry.

In Damascus, friction between Chauvel and Lawrence was visible. The manner in which Lawrence overstated his authority heightened the hostility between the two men. Both of Chauvel's versions contradict Lawrence. According to Lawrence, 4000-armed Arab tribesmen of the Arab irregulars had entered the city the preceding night. Unofficial though their entry was, there does appear to be a grain of truth in this claim. But it is unlikely that there was anything like such a large number, and they did not go to the Serai or make themselves obvious. Certainly a number of Ruwalla horsemen arrived in the city to look for Ali Rida al-Rikabi and ask him to form a new government. This would be confirmed when the Arab army entered the city the next day. Hunt though they did, they did not find Ali Rida al-Rikabi – he had already slipped out of the city and found General Barrow in his camp.

Chauvel was outraged by the claims. He believed that as he had placed troops at each exit and entrance to form a cordon around the city to prevent the departure of the Turks, these troops would have seen the horsemen enter and Ali Rida al-Rikabi depart. But it must be remembered that the soldiers were not all in place until the following morning. Jeremy Wilson, in the notes at the back of his massive biography of Lawrence, explains that 'Irritation over this matter helps to explain his bad relationship with Chauvel and his disparaging treatment of the Australians...'.

Lawrence James, in *The Golden Warrior* (1990), mocked some of the assertions by Lawrence over Damascus, calling them 'a mixture of fudge and fabrication concocted to give the impression that the Arabs and not the Australians liberated Damascus. According to him, 4,000 Bedouin infiltrated the city during the night, but, overcome by an inexplicable shyness, they did not reveal themselves to al Qadir, the Australian horsemen or the remnants of the Turkish garrison'.

Professor Stephen Tabachnick, though, came to Lawrence's defence, saying that the priority of the Australians could not be proved 'given the facts that the Sherifian forces always had sympathetic people inside the city'. He added that in conditions of war 'it becomes difficult to say just who actually set foot where first'. But if this were the case, why did the officials in the Serai make the formal welcoming party to the Australians?

If the Arabs had not been first into the city, they were soon made to appear as if they had been. Fulfilling Lawrence's pro-Arab dreams was also a way of blocking the French out of the Middle Eastern dominion that had been so clearly allocated to them in the Sykes–Picot agreement.

Professor Eliezer Tauber, in his book *Arab Movements in World War I*, traced how, in a series of telegrams, the arrival of the Australians was distorted until it was made to appear that the Arabs had been first past the post. He explains how at 1400, a telegram was sent from Allenby to the War Office stating: 'We took Damascus at 06:00 today. Details follow'.

The promised telegram, sent on the same day, altered the facts:

> *Last night the Australian Mounted Division entered the outskirts*
> *of Damascus from the north-west. The town was occupied by the*
> *Desert Mounted Corp and the Arab Army at 6 am today.*

The result of this was that the War Office communiqué of 3 October announced that at 6.00 am on 1 October, Damascus 'was occupied by a British force and by a portion of the Arab army of King Hussein'.

After a month had passed, the entry of the Arabs with the Australians had become well established in government records. The myth that the Arabs had taken Damascus had begun. One entry in *A Brief Record of the Advance of the Egyptian Expeditionary Force* – 'Compiled from Official Sources', from despatches sent by Allenby to the Secretary of State for War and earlier published in the *London Gazette* – states:

> *At 0600 on Oct. 1 the Desert Mounted Corps and the Arab Army*
> *entered Damascus amidst scenes of great enthusiasm. After the*
> *German and Turkish troops in the town had been collected, and*
> *guards had been posted, our troops were withdrawn...*

As stated earlier, views of who was first into Damascus were slanted in the hope of influencing not only who would rule Syria but also the carve-up of lands and cities. Lawrence's effacement of the role of the Australians, according to George Lloyd (later Lord Lloyd), was not because of any desire for fame, but designed to further the Arab cause for self-rule. His scribbled notes say 'L. not working for H[is] M[ajesty's] G[overnment] but for Sherif'.

When he arrived in Damascus, Lawrence, like Olden before him, went immediately to the Serai. He rejected the men in authority, and appointed Shukri Al Ayyubi, a local pro-Hashemite nationalist. Despite this, when Chauvel later asked Lawrence who was governor, Lawrence put him in touch with the 'wrong man'. Lawrence, at that point, omitted to say that the Algerian leader had been deposed and Shukri al Ayyubi was now governor of the city. Nor did he admit that one of the causes of spreading riots in the city was competing power factions jostling to take over.

The rivalry between the Australians and Lawrence found its way into the draft of Lawrence's book: 'These sporting Australians saw the campaign as a point-to-point with Damascus as the post, which the best horse would pass first. We saw it as a serious military operation, in which any unordered priority would be a meaningless or discreditable distinction. We were all under Allenby, and Damascus was the fruit of his genius'.

On the other hand, Lawrence was strongly criticised by the Australians for the callous and bloody massacre of Turkish soldiers by his Arab forces at Deraa. Summing up the situation, Phillip Knightley said: 'Lawrence hated Chauvel (who stood up to him) and was mortified that the Australians had beaten his beloved Arabs to Damascus without really appreciating the historical significance (hence the point-to-point dig) and thought of the Light Horse as Colonial troops'. It could be argued that the greatness of the achievement of the Australians lay not in the act of being first, but in their non-stop role in the tough campaign preceding it.

In neither his newspaper articles nor his books did Lawrence make any mention of the horsemen, the role of the horses or their entry into Damascus. Nor did he mention how afterwards the presence of both men and horses was necessary to maintain order. Neither does he acknowledge their courage and effort. At one stage the Desert Mounted Corps rode fifty-eight miles in thirty-four hours without unsaddling. The only references in his book to British horses in the twelve days prior to 1 October were brief. The first was when he wrote that General Barrow told him 'to ride beside him, but his horses hated my camel, so the General Staff bucked along the ditch, while I soberly paced the crown of the road…We had lit the furnaces and hoped to begin watering his horses in an hour'. The second was when writing about the period after the taking of Damascus, when he put in a few grumbled words in the middle of a chapter: '…no forage and he had forty thousand horses to feed'.

Eventually Feisal and the Arab army arrived – on 3 October from Deraa by a special train. Quickly, though, they mounted horses. Chauvel described Feisal's arrival, coming 'at a hard gallop followed by some forty of fifty Bedouin horsemen'. By chance Allenby arrived around the same time. He had been driven in an armoured Rolls Royce from Tiberias to Damascus, a journey that took eight hours.

When Lawrence announced that Feisal and several hundred followers were outside Damascus and wanted to stage a triumphal entry into the city, Chauvel, who was at first reluctant, decided in the end to let it go ahead. He later wrote in his notes: 'As Feisal had had very little to do with the "conquest" of Damascus, the suggested triumphal entry did not appeal to me very much but I thought it would not do harm and gave permission accordingly'.

Writing home in a letter on 3 October, Chauvel gave a surprisingly cheerful gloss to the events: '…We've marched about 120 miles and I am now writing this on Jemal Pasha's desk in his own house at Damascus. We have had a great and glorious time, and the Chief [Allenby], who motored from Tiberias today to see us, has just told me that our performance is the greatest cavalry feat the world has ever known…'.

The mood of these letters contrasted vividly with Chauvel's earlier despair among the disorder and disease and 'Lawrence's preoccupation with Arab politics'. He added that 'he should have been providing an efficient link between myself and the Arab government'.

Chauvel's notes are stored in archives in the Allenby papers in the Middle East Centre at St Antony's College, Oxford. Included in them also is a discussion that took place in Damascus with Allenby, in which Lawrence, contrary to what he wrote later, denied that Feisal had any knowledge of the Sykes–Picot agreement:

> *The Chief turned to Lawrence and said: 'But did you not tell him that the French were to have the Protectorate over Syria?'*
> *Lawrence said: 'No, Sir, I know nothing about it'. The Chief [Allenby] then said: 'But you knew definitely that he, Feisal, was to have nothing to do with the Lebanon.' Lawrence said: 'No, Sir, I did not.'*

This is a clear example of just how contradictory Lawrence could be. In Chapter 101 of *Seven Pillars of Wisdom*, Lawrence, discussing the effect of criticism by those who thought that Feisal was 'misled by British promises', wrote: 'Fortunately, I had early betrayed the treaty's existence to Feisal…to help the British so much that after peace they would not be able, for shame, to shoot him down in its fulfilment…I begged him to trust not in our promises…but in his own strong performance'.

Lawrence's stance of not admitting that he had previously told Feisal about the British agreements was in keeping with what he had revealed in conversations a year earlier with his friend George Lloyd. According to Lloyd, Lawrence had earlier implied that his attitude would be 'non-negotiatory'.

A week after arriving in Damascus Lawrence issued a press release and an unsigned article in the *Palestine News*, which appeared on 10 October. These both stated that the fall of Damascus was due to the Arabs who had been 'first in'. In protest, Chauvel wrote: 'In order to avoid the risk of any such misrepresentation being handed down to history, I, as General Officer commanding the troops that captured Damascus from the Turko-German forces, hereby definitely state that no Arab troops entered the city of

Damascus until after Australian, British and Indian troops had moved right through it and all organised enemy forces had either been killed, captured or dispersed'.

A similar article by Lawrence, but unsigned, was in *The Times* on 17 October under the title 'The Arab March on Damascus': '...the Arab Camel Corps formed the far right of the Allied advance upon Damascus, which was entered on the night of the 30th, Arabs being the first troops in'. This was expanded in *Seven Pillars of Wisdom*. Lawrence also gave the impression that the generals were asking his advice and that he was in a position to make decisions about appointees in the new administration. More importantly, he implied that Chauvel was subordinate to him. Lawrence was working for the British and so should have made their interests paramount, but he appeared to be more sympathetic to Feisal. He added that Chauvel refused to salute Feisal's black, white and green Sherifian flag and that he had reluctantly approved Lawrence's claim for Feisal to rule Syria. Chauvel unwillingly followed Lawrence's lead.

Feisal's entry culminated in his formally taking over the city, emphasising the Arab claim. Allenby tried to deflect French anger by putting in a French liaison officer so as to make it appear that Feisal was under French protection. Views of what happened were so slanted that published accounts appear to be about separate events. As with most battles, differing versions appeared in the brigade histories, the personal memoirs, the general histories, the official histories and the newspaper articles written soon afterwards. Sometimes in war, some adjustment and orchestration is needed to ensure that more than one nation is seen to be successful, but the distortion went well beyond this in the case of Damascus.

The French and the Arabs both continued to argue their claims with passion and hostility. Friction was increasing. Wavell, in his biography *Allenby in Egypt*, described how the French, furious at the British encouragement of the Arab cause, 'complained that British officers were openly supporting the Arab claim to control the whole of Syria and accused Allenby himself of partiality'. Colonel Brémond (of the French army) pointed out that the British government had confirmed the French claim in the

Sykes–Picot agreement, yet now the British were acting against this. Lawrence's partiality towards the Arabs and hostility towards the French was easily seen.

Allenby himself wrote at the time: 'All nations and would-be nations and all shades of religions and politics are up against each other and trying to get me to commit myself on their side'.

As well as the dispute between the French and the British, there were heated arguments between the different Arab factions. The Arab army was causing a commotion in Damascus. There were killings in the streets and also serious looting. On the second day of the occupation, as a further show of strength, Chauvel escorted a squadron of the 2nd Light Horse, guns and armoured cars through the streets and up Pilgrims' Road. He awed the turbulent city into silence. Shops opened again and order reigned.

The Official History of Australia in the War of 1914–1918, Volume VII *Sinai and Palestine,* by Henry Gullet, published in 1923, proves how ambiguous Lawrence's claims about his procession were. Gullet, summing up the arrival, said:

> *Lawrence rode into town with a few Arab horsemen on the heels of the advance guard of the 14th Cavalry Brigade, the Arabs believed that they shared with the Indians [troops with General Barrow] the honours of the first entry…Galloping with loud shouts about the streets, trailing their coloured silks and cottons, and firing their rifles, they made a brave display. Their melodramatic demonstration, in sharp contrast to the casual bearing of the hard-fighting Australians, who had risked all nearly two hours earlier, chilled the Christians but aroused the great Moslem crowds to frenzy…About 8.30 am Chauvel drove in from his advance headquarters at Kaukab to arrange for the civil administration of the city. He found Shukri Pasha [who had replaced the Algerian] at the Serai, agreed that he should act temporarily as military governor and then drove back to confer with his three Divisional Commanders.*

During Allenby's brief visit to Damascus, Lawrence asked him for permission to take his accumulated leave and return to England. Allenby replied, 'Yes, I think you better had'. Lawrence went directly to Cairo, then sailed from Port Said to Italy, where he caught a train. Within three weeks – a week before the armistice – Lawrence was back home with his mother in Oxford. He was still only twenty-nine and he was about to become one of the best-known military figures in World War I.

Although his daring raids against the Damascus–Medina railway never achieved the promised results – because the Turks had quickly repaired the railway whenever it was blown up – he had pinned down thousands of Turkish troops and caused unrest wherever he went. Liman von Sanders later despaired at how Lawrence and the Arabs incited the local populations to oppose the Turks and Germans. Lawrence and the Arabs had fought hard and endured terrible hardships, but they not had to bear heavy casualties when attacking unbroken Turkish formations, such as the Allies at Beersheba and Haifa. Lawrence's really great and lasting achievement still lay ahead.

Chapter Eighteen

Disturbances in Damascus After Entry

Early every night, the mosquitoes were out drawing blood. They were the enemy that came close to defeating the men. Soldiers who had gone through battles unscathed collapsed into makeshift hospitals, and then into graves. While the casualty rate during the advance was low, disease was horrific. The wave of pneumonic ('Spanish') influenza, accompanied by the extremely contagious malaria, put nearly half the Desert Mounted Corps out of action. This, added to the increasing number of sick and wounded Turks, was creating an insurmountable problem. Patients were distributed among six hospitals, each one deficient in equipment, medical and surgical staff. Patients lay in deplorable conditions.

From the week ending 5 October to the end of the following week, admissions to hospital from the Desert Mounted Corps more than doubled, from 1246, to 3,109. Nearly four times the number of horsemen died in the cramped, unhealthy dormitories of Damascus as had been killed on the advance (Officers: 16 killed, 48 wounded, one missing. Other ranks: 109 killed, 317 wounded, 32 missing). Coffins were made quickly out of whatever planking could be found. Autumn flowers to scatter on them were scarce.

Before the war, culverts in the streets had been built, and the water supply and sanitation modernised. Now the water supply was choked with foul-smelling corpses and the streets were littered with uncollected debris. Sanitation was lacking in the hospitals; rats gorged on corpses putrefying alongside the living. Blood was a common sight. So was hunger; the railways were still not working and no transport was available to bring in food. Instead it came in camel caravans.

Short rations, scarcity of water, lack of rest and disease had taken a heavy toll on the men's morale, but rumour had it that the advance would not be halted until Aleppo was taken – and that was a risky 120 miles into Turkish enemy territory. Indeed the capture of Damascus was not the end of the journey for the horsemen. Allenby had insisted earlier that without a naval landing north of Beirut at Alexandretta to bring in supplies, he could only advance in stages, as before. The men sharpened their swords and, with no way of knowing where Germans and Turks were hiding, rode into uncertainty.

Liman von Sanders had gone north to Baalbek. Allenby's visit to Damascus was brief, as he wanted to remain in headquarters at Tiberias, where he could assess the overall situation in Lebanon as well as Syria. He was monitoring the northward progress of Kemal and Liman von Sanders. Speed would force the Turks to an early armistice, before Germany capitulated. Allenby had already given instructions for the men to advance further north and capture Riyaq, thirty miles north-west of Damascus. Riyaq was the railway town at the terminus of the standard-gauge railway, which now came all the way from Constantinople.

Kemal had reassembled his troops, set fire to Riyaq railway station and demolished installations, including the town's waterworks. He then rode 200 miles north to Aleppo. As he went, he gave orders to set fire to ammunition stockpiles, much to the horror of the locals. Thousands of Turkish troops remained behind to become prisoners of war; many, in the confusion, deserted to Feisal. At last the remaining troops of the 4th army were moved under the command of the 7th army and Kemal took complete control.

Arriving at Aleppo, Kemal moved into a suite with a balcony in the impressively grand Baron's Hotel, where he had stayed in August. The ancient city of Aleppo was suffering from a late heatwave. Clouds of dust choked the streets, the men and the horses.

On the morning of 15 October, Kemal, hearing an uproar, went out onto his balcony to see the streets below filled with angry crowds. The Desert Mountain Corps had arrived and was occupying the city. Hardly bothering to pack his bags, Kemal left the hotel and took up headquarters nearby, preparing to meet the Australians and the British. On the night of 25/26 October, north of Aleppo, Kemal directed the fire. The British and Arab forces were defeated and pushed back. This, the last successful resistance of Turkish forces on the Palestine Front, gave new energy to Kemal's striking force. Not admitting defeat, Mustafa Kemal limited combat to keeping foreign troops out of Turkey itself. This was the end of the great Ottoman Empire, but now Kemal would fight to the last for the mother country; he would concentrate all on the defence of the homeland and form a new frontier in the mountain ranges of Asia Minor. In his memoirs, Liman von Sanders relates how he had earlier taken leave of Kemal, saying, 'We have disagreed with each sometimes but I believe we part as friends. I am proud to leave my command in your hands...'.

Kemal might well have driven the British and Arab forces out of the northern tip of Syria. But while the Turks were fighting, Allenby's triumph, along with the Allied breakthrough on the Salonika Front in Greece in mid-September, was bearing the fruit of victory. Turkey was now impotent. The Anglo–Turkish Armistice was about to be signed – and decades of warfare and more bloodshed were to follow.

On 30 October 1918, the representative of the new Sultan, Mehmed VI Vahideddin, who had succeeded to the throne on the death of his elder brother in July the previous year, signed an armistice on board the British cruiser *Agamemnon*, which had earlier taken part in the naval bombardment on the Dardanelles. The terms were not dictated by Allenby, but by the commander-in-chief of the Mediterranean fleet, Sir Somerset Gough-Calthorpe. Austria and Bulgaria had already signed separate armistices with the Allies.

The first clause of the twenty-four articles of the Turkish Armistice was for the 'Opening of the Dardanelles and Bosphorus and access to the Black Sea. The Allied occupation of the Dardanelles and Bosphorus forts'. The conditions imposed amounted to complete surrender. The Turks had not only lost their Arab-speaking territories in the war; they were losing control of Turkey itself. The long struggle that had begun at Gallipoli had come to an end. Or so it then seemed.

Within a fortnight of the signing of the armistice, a month before the third anniversary of the departure of the Anzacs from those beachheads, two British regiments sailed west. The British sailed through the Narrows towards the Golden Horn at the gateway of Constantinople. Instead of taking one week, as originally predicted in 1915, to fight their way through to Constantinople, they had taken 300 weeks. But as explained earlier, the Russian government, with whom Britain had made the agreement in 1915, had disappeared. Unlike the Tsars, the Bolsheviks had no desire to take Constantinople. Turkey-in-Europe thus survived.

The Turkish Armistice hastened Germany into signing its own with France, America and Britain. On 11 November 1918, peace was declared: 'Hostilities will cease at 11:00 hours today, November 11th'. But the end of fighting did not bring freedom from strife. Syria, Lebanon and Palestine, like so many other countries, were suffering from problems caused by inflation, the collapse of law and order, refugees and borders. Palestine was OETA South (Occupied Enemy Territory Administration) under the British; the coastal portion of Syria from Alexandretta to Acre, including Beirut and Lebanon, was OETA North (later West) under the French; and the area from Aleppo to Damascus, to the east of the French zone, OETA East, was under Arab administration. All three administrations were under the direct authority of Allenby as commander-in-chief.

Another outcome of the armistice was that the vanquished were back again on the ridges of Gallipoli. The flowers and shrubs there had started to recover. Skulls sprouted with wild flowers and tendrils twined around bones whitened by the sun and the rain. Soldiers walked silently over and around the tens of thousands of incomplete skeletons and scattered bones. Shovels began digging graves. On the Nek, the remains of around 300 Australians were found in a strip of scrub no larger than three tennis courts. The sanctification of the site began.

The 7th Light Horse at last got to The Narrows. They arrived on 5 December with the Canterbury Mounted Rifles, just as the weather turned extremely cold. Emotions ran strong. Bean organised a small 'Australian Historical Mission', including veterans and the artist George Lambert, to visit the site and gather historical evidence and relics for an Australian memorial collection. Lambert was moved by the horrible sight of the trenches littered with bones that 'showed up white even in the faint dawn'.

The friendly negotiations during the armistice had given false impressions and over-optimistic hopes to the Turks. Verbal promises and reassurances had been made by Gough-Calthorpe; he could not – and did not have to – fulfil them. After the signing, Turkish newspapers reported that the terms were lenient. Journalists had seen through the ambiguity of the wording, which indirectly gave the Allies an excuse to enter Constantinople. This was because the seventh point gave them the right to occupy any strategic part of the Ottoman Empire if any situation arose that threatened security. When 3626 British, Italian and French troops disembarked and moved into the city, the Sultan protested, but he could make no move to stop them. By then a stooped and feeble old man, described as having 'considerable dignity, amiable disposition and unaffected manners', the Sultan seemed willing to agree to any terms imposed by the Allies so long as he kept his throne, his palace – and his latest young wife. He watched as the representatives of Britain, France, Italy and Greece divided the city into four zones. The British, as well as controlling the Galata and Pera zone, filled the Bosphorus with battleships. Vickers, the British armaments firm, recovered control of the docks and the arsenal.

Kemal claimed that the treaty had destroyed the Turkish nation. But he bided his time before taking any action. On exactly the same day as the British anchored in the Bosphorus, 13 November, Kemal arrived by train in Constantinople. With great style he moved into a spacious suite on the first floor of the grand Pera Palas Hotel, still the social centre of foreign life in the capital, and, much to his annoyance, about to become the home of many British officers. He found the occupation of the city by the British insufferable. Once, when some British officers invited him for a drink at his hotel, he said, 'We are the hosts here. They are the guests. It is fitting for them to come to my table'.

When the cost of living in the hotel became too much for an unpaid soldier, Kemal moved into a nearby house (in the Sisli district) belonging to friends from Aleppo. Kemal was plotting. In the last two months of 1918 he had two audiences with the Sultan. By trying to appease the wrath of the occupying forces, the Sultan hoped to salvage something out of the wreckage and reduce British support for the Greeks.

Rumour has it that these meetings between the Sultan and Kemal were not just to talk about the future of Turkey, but also to discuss marriage between Kemal and the Sultan's daughter, Sabiha Sultan. Whether Kemal rejected the idea or whether the Sultan discouraged it because of Kemal's reputation for womanising has always been a matter of conjecture. According to some rumours, during his trip to Germany in 1917 Kemal had gone to Marienbad for treatment for syphilis. When he was younger he was said to be too arrogant to catch the fancy of the women he lusted for, but his attractiveness to women increased with his age and status. This was later confirmed in the memoirs of Zsa Zsa Gabor, who visited Kemal in the last years leading up to his death in 1938. She wrote candidly about her many secret afternoon rendezvous with him. By then Kemal was the most powerful man in the country – and the most ruthless. He had evicted the Sultan from his golden throne, and become the president of Turkey and an international politician. But we are jumping ahead...

It took only four years from the signing of the armistice for Turkey to become a republic, and for Mustafa Kemal to disestablish Islam. Two years later the Caliphate itself was abolished. Since the fall of the Caliphate, Islam has been fragmented; there has been no Islamic Pope, as it were. Hussein in the Hejaz, as keeper of the Holy Places – Mecca and Medina – claimed some rights as spiritual leader of the Muslim world and briefly tried to fill the void by proclaiming himself Caliph. But this was short-lived. Within a few months he was forced to abdicate – before the Wahhabis entered Mecca. The position of Caliph has been vacant ever since. But it could be said that its power had proved to be illusory anyway. One of the seldom referred to failures of the Turks during World War I was the *jihad* declared by the Sultan in 1914.

Indeed, Turkey's religious effort, in contrast to its sturdy military effort, which had included memorable triumphs over the Allies at both Gallipoli and Kut, was completely ineffective everywhere. Even the Emir of Afghanistan had refused to co-operate with the *jihad*, despite continual urgings by the Turks and the Germans. The *jihad* never became a rallying war cry or had its desired effect – unifying all Muslims during World War I. Muslims did fight Muslims. The response to the *jihad* in India, Egypt, Russia and other countries was meagre and insignificant. There had been no Muslim units in the British or Russian armies who had refused to fight against the Turks. In Allied countries Muslims had failed to form a resistance or join their brothers-in-arms to rise up against their British or French colonisers.

In India, then the most populous Muslim country on earth, with about 60 million Muslims, the lack of impact had been particularly noticeable. The British had conscripted thousands into the regular Indian army and despatched them to fight the Muslims of the Ottoman Empire. The response had been similar in other countries. Although there was resistance to conscription in Russia in 1916, most Russian Muslims were indifferent. It was the same story in the Hejaz in western Arabia. The *jihad* failed to stop Arab tribes under Sherif Hussein and Prince Feisal launching the Arab Revolt from the Holy City of Mecca itself. Indeed, the failure of the 1914 *jihad* was so complete that it devalued the word, showing that such religious symbols no longer inspired the Muslim masses. Nationality had been a greater unifying force than religious faith. As well as failing as a call to rise up, it underlined the disunity among the followers of Islam.

Now, though, Britain not only had the custody of the Holy Places in Palestine, but the navy was back in the Black Sea and Constantinople, not as an ally but as a conqueror. Only four years had passed since Rear-Admiral Arthur Limpus and his seventy-two naval advisers and staff who had been helping Turkey modernise her navy, had left Constantinople. But at the end of 1918 nobody knew what the final outcome of the peace settlements would be. One thing, though, was very clear. Britain, by reversing her role of supporting the Ottoman Empire, now exercised a real power in the Middle East.

Chapter Nineteen

The Men Lose Their Horses and The Horses Lose Their Lives

The slowness of demobilisation, controlled in London by Winston Churchill, who had been appointed as Secretary of State for War and for Air, made troops restless. Most were impatient to get out of khaki uniform and back to civilian life. All available transport, from railway carriages to donkey carts, trucks and ships, was packed to the bulkheads. At least a million British troops, including over 270,000 Australian troops in Europe, Britain and the Middle East, waited to board boats to take them back to their wives and families. Although new merchant-service vessels had been made in British shipyards, thousands of vessels, sunk by the Germans, were now at the bottom of the sea.

But not all troops could be demobbed yet. Thousands were stationed everywhere, from Berlin to Jerusalem, to enforce the terms of the often unpopular peace treaties, and to maintain order. They occupied Germany to ensure that she honoured the terms of the armistice; Ireland was, yet again, about to erupt into revolt; fighting had flared up again on the Afghan and north-western frontier of India; civil war was so fierce in Russia that Britain, along with other nations, sent troops to intervene and aid the White Russians in their fight against the Bolshevik Red armies; and troops were needed to police the newly created mandate in Palestine, as well as in Egypt and Iraq.

One of the best roads in Syria ran from Tripoli, on the coast of Lebanon, to Homs, the town halfway between Aleppo and Damascus, so Tripoli was chosen as a camp for many of the regiments of the Light Horse. Others were stationed further south, at Surafend. Here the Australian and New Zealand soldiers soon grew weary of being ambushed by the Arabs and seeing their comrades killed while the authorities 'did nothing'. After a New Zealand sergeant was disturbed one night and jumped to his feet only to be shot dead by an Egyptian, the New Zealanders decided to deal with the village themselves. A party, armed with sticks and chains, segregated old men, women and children and proceeded to exact revenge on the able-bodied men. There are dozens of versions of what happened that night. One fact is certain, though. The next morning revealed a tragic picture. Men had been hurled into a well over which a large grindstone had been placed.

For some unexplained reason Allenby blamed the Australian Light Horse, even though it is usually said that the New Zealanders had been the wrongdoers. He ordered a mass parade. Addressing the men in fiery terms, he called the Australians, among other things, murderers. Only a few men took part in the punitive raid, yet Allenby punished all the Light Horse. Allenby ordered that all leave be stopped, and that those on leave be recalled, and informed Chauvel that recommendations for honours and awards would be withdrawn. Rex Hall stated in his memoirs, *The Desert Hath Pearls*, that other soldiers from other regiments who were involved were not blamed. He added that this resulted in the commanders and staff responsible for the victory in Palestine and Syria, with two exceptions, remaining 'victimised, left without honours or medals, unhonoured, unsung'. With some bitterness, he continued his attack with the strong words: 'history should, in my opinion, record this drastic action as being to Allenby's lasting shame'. Further snubs against the Australian officers are contained in his memoirs:

> *When on leave in London, I was acting as ADC to Lieutenant General Chauvel…At his dictation I wrote several letters on the subject to the War Office, to authorities in Cairo and to certain senior Officers. One…was a plea for a knighthood for Brigadier-General Granville Ryrie, one of his Brigade Commanders. This was successful, but the other Commanders and Staff Officers of the Desert Mounted Corps (perhaps with one other exception), many of whom had been submitted on the 'deferred' list, missed their awards.*
>
> *…some year or two previously, an order had been issued that no Staff Officers were to be recommended for 'immediate' awards, as they should not, by their duties, take part in front-line action, and that they were to be included only in the 'deferred' list. Correspondence ensued over the next two years…On 5 April 1921, General Godley finally wrote: 'I have looked into the question of Honours and Awards…and can find no trace of any of your supplementary recommendations having been turned down by the Army Council.' The only conclusion is that General Allenby's supplementary list got lost between Cairo and the War Office.*

The men of the 10th Light Horse, then stationed at Tripoli, were told that they were to be shipped from Port Said. They assumed that this would be soon. But the issue of Turkish prisoners-of-war and the resettling of Armenian refugees had to be dealt with before the troops, stores and horses.

Nothing was said about the fate of the horses. Some men and horses had been together all through the war; others who had shipped their own horses from Australia, longer. Having suffered the same privations, and having daily companionship from each other, soldiers and horses were unusually close.

Scant recognition was given to the four-legged heroes who had suffered so much. Yet the overthrow of the enemy owed a great deal to these animals. This was the first major war in which the Army Veterinary Services had an efficient organisation to care for injured animals, but the welfare of the animals was not a post-victory consideration. During the long months of fighting, many a man had dreamt of going home with his horse and being cheered while riding it in a triumphal march either up Collins Street in Melbourne or Pitt Street in Sydney.

But with the battles won, the horses were no longer needed. The unit of man and horse would be split; the animals that had escaped slaughter by the enemy were prepared for sale to the highest bidder. Directions came from London from the Horse Demobilisation Committee at the War Office. Reasons given for the sale of the horses were the shortage of ships, the price of transportation and the draconian Australian quarantine regulations. The expense of bringing horses home was not warranted. No official figures exist, but it has been calculated that 22,000 English, Indian and Australian horses were sold to Egyptians. In treatment that was as callous as it was unfair, these devoted animals were just cast aside. Banjo Paterson was extremely distressed by the decision to dispose of the horses in this way. On 25 February he was given fourteen days' sick leave and was one of the first officers to get a place on a homeward-bound ship, departing for Sydney on the *Kildonan Castle* on 1 April.

Thousands of Allied horses were sold. No exception was made, even to the beautiful thoroughbreds and Walers like Olden's Yaboo and Orchardor, which had been donated, or for those that had been the personal horses of the Light Horsemen in Australia. My father's horse, though, was not among them. The harshness general meted out to animals by Arabs forced him to make the heartbreaking decision to shoot the companion he loved and trusted. This deed was enormously painful for him – he clearly killed part of himself in the process. He rode his horse out on a last gallop into the unforgiving desert, dismounted and tied a handkerchief onto the horse's bridle to shield its eyes. The eyes of a horse are set in the sides of the head, so it is unable to see objects in front of it nearer than about six feet. Robbie aimed his gun and shot the horse in the middle of the forehead.

Shooting a horse was a serious offence. The number of 'lost' horses caused a notice in the Regimental Routine Orders on 24 February:

> *Lost Animals. Animals that are lost will be reported to BHQ, also to Aus. Mtd Div. immediately. After a period of seven days from date of loss has elapsed, a Court of Inquiry will be held and proceedings forwarded to BHQ for Brigadier's concurrence.*

But it seems that this notice was only issued as a deterrent. In the army records I could find no details of the proposed Court of Inquiry. It was obviously realised why these horses were being 'lost'.

Many a man buried his spurs and saddlery. A poem, *The Horses Stay Behind*, by Oliver Hogue, who died of influenza in 1919, writing under the pseudonym 'Trooper Bluegum', expresses their sadness:

> *I don't think I could stand the thought of my old fancy hack*
> *Just crawling round old Cairo with a 'Gypo on his back,*
> *Perhaps some English tourist out in Palestine may find*
> *My broken-hearter Waler with a wooden plough behind.*
>
> *I think I'd better shoot him and tell a little lie:-*
> *'He floundered in a wombat hole and then lay down to die.'*
> *May be I'll get court-martialled; but I'm damned if I'm inclined*
> *To go back to Australia and leave my horse behind.*

Public anger led to a little leniency being introduced to the horse disposal policy. Half the remaining animals would be sent to the Indian cavalry units; the rest would be shot. Regimental Routine Orders in army archives are official, and do not record personal reactions. Item 7 is simply:

Classification of Horses – the BVO will classify the horses of this Regt. Tomorrow 23rd.inst. RFQMS and Farrier Sergeants will parade RHQ at 0900. As many horses as is possible will be left on the lines. Horses classified by BVO will be scissor clipped under his instructions. These identification marks will not be interfered with in any way and Os/C sqdns will be responsible that the marks are maintained.

A last race meeting was held and photos taken. Then the horses were led to the olive groves outside Tripoli. While tethered in their picket lines, enjoying their last nosebag, bullets flew towards them, aimed at their heads by special squads of marksmen.

They still paid their way. Their hides, manes and tails were sold, along with their recyclable horseshoes. The official diary entry for the 10th Light Horse just says: '24/2/19 183 horses were destroyed belonging to the 9th and 10th Reg'ts. A commercial English class under Chaplain Riley was commenced. Bishop Price delivered a lecture in the YMCA the subject being "Chinese & Japanese life and ideals".'

The horses were not given a burial. Each skin was allocated a ration of seven pounds of salt to turn it into saleable leather; each tail and mane were bundled into bags for the profitable horsehair market. The soldiers were angry and bewildered and their grieving was acute. Such was the reward for a job well done.

What happened to the flesh of the horses is not recorded. Horseflesh is considered 'unclean' by Jews as well as Muslims. To qualify as a 'clean beast' and be part of the diet in Mosaic Law, an animal had to eat grass, chew the cud and have cloven hoofs. Neither the camel, the horse nor the ass fitted into this category, as their hooves were not cloven.

Only one horse came back to Australia between 1914 and 1919. He was Sandy, the charger of General Sir William Bridges, the first commander-in-chief of the Australian Imperial Forces, who was killed at Gallipoli. Sandy was shipped back to Melbourne to walk in the State funeral procession down Collins Street. He carried nothing but Bridge's empty saddle. In the traditional manner of a funeral parade, his riding boots had been turned in the stirrups. Emotions ran so high that when Sandy died his head was preserved and put on show in the Australian War Memorial in Canberra.

Over a decade later, Lawrence, who had showed indifference to the horses in the Damascus campaign by failing to mention them in *Seven Pillars of Wisdom*, showed empathy with the grief caused by the slaughter of the horses. After reading *Red Dust* by John Lyons Gray ('Donald Black'), a book that told of an Australian trooper's disillusionment about both the war and way the army dealt with the horses, Lawrence wrote: 'The one outstanding element in him seemed to be his sensibility. He is more moved by death and pain than were most soldiers. That comes out powerfully in the last few pages, when he sorrows for his dead horse'.

The surviving horses in the Middle East did not thrive. My father's pitiful shooting, in my view, was vindicated when Dorothy Brooke, the wife of a former commander of the cavalry in Egypt, visited Cairo in 1930. The broken-down old horses with the arrow-shaped British brands still visible on their mangy flanks being forced by the lash to haul heavy loads, slowly being worked to death, shocked her. She started the Old War Horse Fund and raised enough money to buy 5000 horses 'sold to bondage in a foreign land'. Her descriptions were harrowing: 'You could hang a coat on their projecting bones…they looked like hat stands…their hooves curled upwards…'. But as the average horse dies at eighteen years of age, most of them would have been on their last legs anyway.

Each worn-out and weary animal was given a day or two of rest and loving care by the Fund before being humanely put out of its misery. Today the Brooke Hospital for Horses (Cairo) purchases suffering horses, donkeys and mules, and provides education programmes and free veterinary services. Among the thousands of horses that the charity helps may be a descendant of those animals that bravely fought in that forgotten cavalry feat on the long road to Damascus.

Nearly three months had passed since the armistice had been signed when, on 3 March 1919, my father bade farewell to Syria and Palestine. Taken by lorries to a pier near Tripoli, the men embarked on the SS *Ellenga*, and arrived at Port Said two days later. Then a train took them to an old haunt they would rather have not revisited, the British base at Moascar. Here rifles, bayonets and other equipment were handed in and the war-weary men waited to march to a ship. But they were kept hanging around. Nine days later, they heard that they were not going home. Nor were they going to war. They were to help the British garrisons control the rioting population clamouring for self-rule. The men were reissued with equipment, rearmed and remounted. A photograph of my father's new horse shows that he was black in colour and larger than his old horse. Like other men disappointed not to be going back to their families, my father was sullen and resentful. War was what they had enlisted for, not to be policemen enforcing order in civil disputes.

During the war the Egyptians had been relatively quiet, even though life had been excessively difficult for the local people, as increased trade and traffic was countered by inflation and gross shortages. And, as stated in Chapter Six, tens of thousands of Egyptians had been conscripted against their will into the Labour Corps to build the railway and pipeline across the Sinai Desert into Palestine.

When the war was over, contrary to what the Egyptians had been told during the negotiations to set up the British Protectorate in 1914, concessions to self-rule were forgotten. Egypt, unlike Syria, Mesopotamia (modern-day Iraq) and the Hejaz, was not to be represented at the Peace Conference. It had no seat, no place, and no voice. A deaf ear was turned to the calls of 'Egypt for the Egyptians'. The Egyptians rebelled. Britain, unwilling to give up Egypt because of the canal, refused to negotiate. The leader, a much-loved lawyer, white-haired and dignified Saad Zaghloul, who had earlier been a minister of education and justice, was exiled to Malta.

Soon the British authorities in Egypt became aware of a restless dissatisfaction among their own troops. Nervous that they, like others round the world, might be about to rebel, the authorities introduced incessant drill: energetic physical exercises before breakfast, followed by a day of route marches and squad drill of such pitiless intensity that the Australians took action. One morning they went on strike. Things improved a little.

Feelings between the British and the Egyptian insurgents intensified after eight British officers and nurses on a holiday trip to see the ruins in Luxor were clubbed to death or killed with swords by Egyptian rebels.

On Sunday 6 July, a telegram came to Brigade Headquarters: the men were to embark on the SS *Oxfordshire* on Thursday 10 July. First, all gear (such as ground sheets and knives and forks) had to be returned to store. Eventually, eleven months and three weeks after he had first set foot on Egyptian soil, my father departed from the Moascar camp – and within hours he was walking up the gangway. The men crowded together, jammed up against the railing, watching as they made their way through the canal and the Bitter Lakes area. At dusk the following day, the ship sailed into the Red Sea. It seemed nearly as hot as it had been in the Jordan Valley. Their quarters in the hold of the ship were so sweltering and airless that my father was one of the many who hung a hammock on deck near the lifeboats, even enjoying the risk of the heavy salt spray turning into waves when seas broke over the side.

A sense of freedom and fun grew, especially when a few of the fare-paying passengers with cabins and portholes travelling to India via Colombo hung hammocks near the soldiers at night. They swapped novels, old newspapers, chatted and sang. For Robbie, who for six years had experienced only the all-male existence of either the station or army, this was his initiation into happy-go-lucky mixed society. His skill at cards, chiefly bridge, was his entrée into a new world. Much to everyone's surprise he won the bridge tournament. Five photographs of his new friends were among the treasured contents of the suitcase under my parents' bed.

The ship spent two days in Colombo. Shore leave was granted and six of them hired a car and went to Mount Livinia and had a slap-up dinner at the Hotel Bristol. Night after night, leaning over the deck rail, the men searched the skies, hoping to be the first to see the Southern Cross among the stars. It was sighted on 5 August.

By Christmas 1919, a quarter of a million Australian troops had travelled home on 137 ships. Soldiers were greeted with cries of 'our gallant boys' and promised a 'world fit for heroes'. Reminders of the cost of victory included the new young widows, fatherless children, a tragic number of limbless and blinded men, cripples and those with permanent disabilities.

Despite the relief that the fighting was over, 1919 was not a year of joy. Families were faced with different sorts of problems, and with death closer to home. Worldwide, more people died in the influenza epidemic than had been killed in the war. The move back to civilian life was far from easy. People in Britain, Australia and elsewhere spoke of the Lost Generation and began to question the point of war, and of the sacrifices made. Fuelled by the poignant verses of Siegfried Sassoon and Wilfred Owen, a general disillusionment spread worldwide.

Chapter Twenty

The Peace Conference
in Paris

L ike a veiled woman in its tight, ancient streets, a mystery still floats over the face of Damascus, obscuring the truth. More than eighty years later, public perceptions are still imprecise. Because of omissions, the foreshortening of events and ambiguities in both Lawrence's version and subsequent publications, as well as the film *Lawrence of Arabia*, many people are under the impression that Lawrence was first to enter Damascus. When voices rose up criticising him, few listened. Of all the stories arising out of the war, the exploits of Lawrence with the Arabs gripped the British the most.

The huge British-led victory against the Turks gave Britain immense bargaining power when the Paris Peace Conference negotiations over the Middle East began. Lloyd George certainly did not see why Britain, having conquered Syria, should hand it over, with increased frontiers, to the French. Many politicians considered France rapacious in her ambitions to control Syria and Lebanon, believing that an expansion of French authority in the area, especially in the form of a protectorate, would unbalance British control of the Middle East.

Lawrence, who since the fall of Damascus had been promoting the cause of Arab independence in the press, was officially in Paris as a technical adviser to the British delegation; he also acted as Feisal's interpreter. Pleading the Arab cause, Lawrence fought for them at the council table as vigorously as he had done in the desert. He did not find being on French soil, surrounded by Frenchmen and officials from the British Foreign Office who had been party to the Sykes–Picot agreement, an inhibiting factor. On 20 March he rightly predicted that if French rule were imposed on an unwilling Syria, 'there would be trouble and even war' between the French and the Arabs.

Britain insisted on being the power that placed advisers in any new Arab governments, but so did the French. The Syrians were reluctant to have a French mandate over them, even with the doctrine of self-determination. France argued passionately, reminding all present of the much referred to Sykes–Picot agreement.

On 6 February, Feisal, wearing flowing robes of dazzling white, accompanied by Lawrence, presented his case. Already some of the British delegation were exasperated by Lawrence, agreeable and popular though he was. On the whole, his uncritical pro-Arab stance and his abrasive language threatened to drive a wedge between the British and the French. Lord Curzon, then the foreign secretary, suspected that he was fuelling Feisal's stubbornness.

When Lawrence returned to Oxford, exhausted and disappointed, he continued his campaign to help the Arabs. Article after unsigned article appeared in *The Times* and he took up a research fellowship at All Souls College to continue writing the classic that would immortalise the role of the Arabs in the war: *The Seven Pillars of Wisdom*.

Lawrence's father had died earlier in the year. Few, apart from his father's earlier family in Ireland and the College of Heralds, noticed that owing to a lack of heirs the baronetcy was now extinct. If he had been legitimate, Lawrence might have become Sir Thomas Chapman, especially as two of his brothers had been killed in the war.

The diminutive figure of Lawrence began to dominate all aspects of the war in the Middle East. He had influential friends and contacts everywhere, from the government to the literary and theatrical worlds, as well as the new emerging world of the cinema. Lowell Thomas was unceasing in his promotion of Lawrence and the most 'romantic campaign in modern history'. Thomas travelled the English-speaking world with his lecture and slides show of 'The War in the Land of the Arabian Nights'. More than a million people in London alone paid to see the enthralling 'Lawrence of Arabia' lecture and lantern show. Along with clichés about the mysterious East, it depicted Lawrence leading the Bedouin tribes in a bid for freedom against their Turkish oppressors. Silhouettes of palm trees and camels in the desert sunset highlighted the romantic character of his desert guerrilla campaign. It all had an irresistible appeal – and, at the same time, animated the places that the Bible had, at some stage, made so familiar to most in the audience. Sixteen posed photographs of Lawrence in almost as many costumes and outfits presented a face of the war that people could bear to watch. The horrors in France, with its morass of blood and mud, and monotonously slaughter, did not make good cinema.

Queues for tickets to the show were so long that it was moved from the Royal Opera House to the even larger Royal Albert Hall. Seeing Lawrence as the face of a new, benevolent British imperialism, the English-Speaking Union, at the prompting of Churchill, encouraged the British impresario Percy Burton to take the show worldwide. Huge sums – somewhere between a million dollars and a million pounds – are quoted as estimates of the profits.

Myths and illusions about the campaign were developing fast. Nothing demonstrates the inconsistency in the descriptions of the whole Middle East campaign more than *The Times History of the War*, Volume XVIII, page 252, which states:

> *During the night of 30 September, troops of the Australian*
> *Mounted Division and the vanguard of the Emir Faisal's force*
> *both penetrated the city, and both claimed to be the first to enter*
> *Damascus… The formal entry of the Allied troops was made at six*

o'clock in the morning of October 1, a British force and a part of the Arab army marching through the streets.

This contradicts page 202 of Volume XIX, which states:

The entry of the Desert Mounted Column was made at 6 am on October 1, and at 6.30 am a detachment of the 10th Australian L.H. Brigade (Brig.-General Wilson) under Major Olden reached the Serail, being the first Allied troops to enter Damascus. The Sherifian Camel Corps was only about half an hour behind them.

To confuse readers even more, a footnote refers to Volume XVIII without saying that the information there is contradictory. It quotes *The Times* and says that the articles were 'written by a correspondent who was with the Arabs and shared in their campaigns'. As journalists writing for *The Times* were at that time always anonymous, the book fails to say that the writer was none other than Lawrence himself.

Meanwhile, the ferment in the Middle East came to a head. In 1920 Syria was still in turmoil as Syrians strengthened their stand against the French. Even the validity of the declaration by an elected assembly proclaiming Feisal to be king of an independent Syria was soon disputed by the French. The peace conference moved from Paris to San Remo, where the mandates for Syria and the Lebanon were allotted to France, and Britain was given Palestine and Mesopotamia. The Lloyd George coalition committed Britain to being a Jewish National Home, a new colony in the British Empire that would be as Jewish as England was English.

Opposition to French rule in Syria meant that France needed 90,000 troops – mostly North African Arabs and black Senegalese – to take Damascus on 20 July. Syria was just one part of the former Ottoman Empire which was now seething with unrest. As predicted by Lawrence, in Mesopotamia, millions of British pounds were being spent on repressing rebellion caused by the unpopularity of the British administration.

In March 1921, Churchill, who was now Secretary of State for the Colonies, accompanied by his temporary official adviser on Arab Affairs for the Colonies – none other than Lawrence – flew to Egypt to chair the Cairo Conference to settle the Arab lands. They were about to fulfil Sherif Hussein's wish and thrust two of his sons into prominence in the Arab world.

It had not occurred to Churchill until then that a son of Hussein could be a ruler of an entirely new state. But by chance, Abdullah was in Amman during the conference after his earlier failed attempt in southern Syria to stir up trouble against the French. As Britain held the mandate for both the eastern and western banks of the River Jordan, at the suggestion of Lawrence, Churchill made Abdullah the emir of a completely new area, Transjordan (later the kingdom of Jordan) which would have Amman as its capital. In exchange for Abdullah's undertaking to do his utmost to check any hostile local movements against the French, Britain paid him generous aid and a large sum annually to maintain a police force. Philip Mansel, in *Sultans in Splendour*, said that Abdullah 'divided his leisure between his two wives, a favourite black slave and writing Arabic poetry. He was a charmer with laughing eyes…However, he ruled Transjordan as an autocrat, and until his assassination in 1951 never abandoned hope of becoming King of Syria'.

Lawrence's backing at the conference was certainly one reason why Feisal became the king of Iraq. Although still under British protection, Iraq, like Transjordan, enjoyed a degree of self-government, but because Feisal was forced upon the country as part of British policy, local people harboured resentment against him to such a degree that over the years the Royal Air Force frequently had to enforce order with bombing raids. Feisal had excellent advisers, including Nuri Bey, his former chief-of-staff, soon to be Iraq's first prime minister. Despite good intentions, however, Feisal was never a great success as a ruler. Nor was his son, Ghazi, who took over when he died in 1933.

In a draft preface to *Seven Pillars of Wisdom*, which was not included in the book, Lawrence wrote 'He [Churchill] executed the whole of the MacMahon undertaking for Palestine, for Transjordan, and for Arabia. In Mesopotamia he went far beyond its provisions, giving the Arabs more, and reserving for us much less, than Sir Henry MacMahon thought fit. In the affairs of French Syria he was not able to interfere…I do not wish to publish secret documents nor to make long explanations, but must put on record my convictions that England is out of the Arab affair with clean hands'.

For the two decades before World War II, Lawrence's theories on guerrilla warfare and 'the indirect approach' were much studied by military theorists, including Basil Liddell Hart. He wrote that Lawrence was a strategist 'of genius who had the vision to anticipate the guerrilla trend of civilised warfare that arises from the growing dependence of nations on industrial resources'.

By the summer of 1922, Lawrence felt that as far as it lay within Britain's power, Churchill had made a just settlement. However, in 1926, in Arabia, Hussein's rival, Ibn Sa'ud, the fighting prince of the Nejd, supported by a strict Muslim sect, the Wahhabi, overthrew Hussein. Saud consolidated Arabia and his family rule there to this day. Hussein spent his last days as a refugee in one of his son's palaces in Jordan.

Epilogue

L awrence himself was later ambivalent about some of his book – as can be seen by yet another letter published in *T. E. Lawrence to his Biographer Robert Graves*, in which he admitted, '…don't give too much importance to what I did in Arabia during the war. I feel that the Middle Eastern settlement put through by Winston Churchill and Young and me in 1921…should weigh more than the fighting…'.

In his letters to the Australian-born author, Frederic Manning, Lawrence hints that he might have exaggerated the military achievements of the Arabs in 1930. These were published by Edward Garnett in his comprehensive collection of Lawrence's letters in 1938, and were brought to my attention by the former librarian of the Mitchell Library, Sydney, who located the original in the archives in Sydney:

> *I was a rather clumsy novice at writing, facing what I felt to be a huge subject, with hanging over me the political uncertainty of the future of the Arab Movement. We had promised them so much, and at the end wanted to give them so little. So for two years there was a dog-fight up and down the dirty passages of Downing St. and then all came out right – only the book was finished. It might*

have been happier, had I foreseen the clean ending. I wrote it in
some stress and misery of mind.

The second complexity was my own moral standing. I had been
so much of a free agent, repeatedly deciding what I (and the
others) should do: and I wasn't sure if my opportunism (or reality,
as I called it) was really justified. Not morally justifiable. I could
see it wasn't, but justified by the standard of Lombard St. and Pall
Mall. By putting all the troubles and dilemmas on paper, I hoped
to work out my path again, and satisfy myself how wrong, or how
right I had been.

So the book is the self-argument of a man who couldn't then see
straight and who now thinks that perhaps it did not matter: that
seeing straight is only an illusion. We do these things in sheer
vapidity of mind, not deliberately, not consciously even.

I wake up now, often, in Arabia: the place has stayed with me
much more than the men and the deeds...It was tremendous
country, and I cared for it far more than I admired my role as
man of action. More acting than action, I fancy, there...I did not
believe finally in the Arab Movement: but thought it necessary, in
its time and place. It has justified itself, hugely, since the war, too.
...Yet: as I hinted, much of the dramatic action was very
reluctantly put in. It felt cheap, then, and looks cheap now. I
preferred Arabia when I wasn't in it, so to speak!

The precise style of this letter contrasts with the imprecise style and the
vagueness of his earlier descriptions, which had unwittingly – or, perhaps,
wittingly – blurred the facts. It throws a fresh light on what he had written
earlier; indeed it could almost be said that with a few strokes of his skilful
pen, Lawrence altered the popular concept of the Arab Revolt and the final
weeks of the Palestinian/Syrian campaign. With neither the equipment and
expertise, nor the numbers and cohesion, the Arabs, masters of guerrilla
tactics and raids, could not have achieved so much. Lawrence's extraordinary
endurance – not to mention his ability to extract gold and ammunition from

the British – helped give the Arabs, and the British, not just military success but also a political triumph.

Five weeks after the above letter, Lawrence was once more writing to Manning. 'For me to write of the dog-fight in Downing Street would hardly be possible. I kept no notes, and the days used to flicker and change continually. Politics are matters of fine shades, and all I cared about was getting my own way, by one means or another. So I never got a detached view. Only I did get my own way'.

After resigning from the Colonial Office, he swapped both his city suit and the glamorous flowing robes of the desert for the grey-blue uniform of the RAF. Seeking anonymity, like his father, he resorted to using an assumed surname, calling himself 'John Hume Ross'. Despite only being in the ranks, Lawrence corresponded with some of the leading artistic, literary and political figures of his time, including Mr and Mrs George Bernard Shaw, Mr and Mrs Thomas Hardy, E. M. Forster, Lord and Lady Astor, and James Elroy Flecker. He rode his motorbike down the aisle of Lady Chapel at Siegfried Sasson's wedding, and Churchill was a friend who never lost an opportunity to sing his praises. Lawrence was a man, according to Churchill, whose pace of life was faster than normal. Only during the fury of war did he find himself in perfect relationship to men and events.

After four months, the press discovered Lawrence. Again he was discharged. With the help of well-placed friends, he re-enlisted almost immediately in the Tank Corps as 'Thomas Edward Shaw'; he served until mid-1925 at Bovington Camp in Dorset, during which time he rented a nearby cottage called Clouds Hill. Two years later he rejoined the RAF, where, as a skilled mechanic, he helped develop a ramjet speedboat. In his spare time, he translated Homer's *Odyssey* for an American publisher for a penny a word and wrote *The Mint*, about life in the RAF, passing harsh judgement on its regime. Publication would have damaged the reputation of the service which Lawrence had come to love, so he stipulated that it should not appear before 1950.

In March 1935, Lawrence's twelve-year term of enlistment came to an end. He retired to Clouds Hill, planning to start a private press and produce a small edition of *The Mint*. Living alone, he was oppressed by gloomy forebodings. Thomas Hardy's widow said he had been nervous and worried of late. The tapping of a bird on his window had especially unsettled him. Robert Graves told her that Lawrence considered this an omen of death. In April Lawrence wrote to a friend: 'Bother that bird: he taps too regularly, and distracts me'. On the morning of 13 May, Lawrence rode to nearby Bovington Camp on his powerful motorbike to post a parcel of books to a friend and send a telegram to another, Henry Williamson, to arrange for his visit the next day. While travelling back home, his bike swerved to avoid two young cyclists. In the course of the accident Lawrence was propelled over the handlebars of his bike and fatally injured. He was brain-dead instantly.

Within hours of it being known that T. E. Lawrence was in hospital after a crash, a 24-hour guard was put around his bed and the military authorities said that from that moment on, they would post any bulletins regarding Lawrence's progress. They did not do such a thing when General Montgomery died. Why should a ministry be in control? Had Lawrence had another secret role? By chance, while writing this chapter, the Special Operations Executive (SOE) adviser gave me some embargoed papers from 1940 and 1941, in advance of their release in the Public Records Office in Kew, London. One paper revealed that when Churchill had set up this top-secret service organisation in 1940, one of the first men he had recruited was Lawrence's brother Arnold, another archaeologist. Churchill had sent him to Jerusalem in April 1940 as SOE liaison officer between the British and members of the Haganah, the underground Jewish army. Arnold's job was to recruit members, mostly young European-born Jews, to undertake guerrilla activities against the Vichy French and Germans in Syria. Although many of the Haganah soldiers feared prison sentences being imposed on them by the British authorities because of their past guerrilla activities against Arabs, they were willing to enlist in the British army. Arnold, though, like his late brother, turned out to be pro-Arab, and he was not popular with the Jews; his time in Jerusalem only lasted six months. The fact that Arnold was recruited by the top clandestine intelligence organisation increases the possibility that Lawrence may have had a role with security. Perhaps after giving up his role as Aircraftsman Ross, Lawrence, always enigmatic and mysterious, had continued contact with intelligence, but this is only conjecture but it must be remembered that he had played in intelligence in World War I. One of Lawrence's special needs as an intelligence officer, as a go-between between the British and the Arabs, was secrecy.

Viscount Halifax, a former Viceroy of India and Chancellor of Oxford University, summarised Lawrence's duality. When unveiling the bust of him in St Paul's Cathedral, he said: 'No-one can read his private letters…without being conscious of sharply alternating moods, almost the conflict of competing personalities'. After Lawrence died on 13 May the legend of Lawrence of Arabia flourished. Apart from the bust of him placed in the crypt of St Paul's Cathedral, another was erected at his old school in Oxford. Because of this fame, his little house Clouds Hill welcomes over 15,000 visitors during the six months of the year it is open; his *Seven Pillars of Wisdom* has sold over a million copies and is never out of print. Revenue from this bestseller, after its publication in 1935, secured the success of the company, Jonathan Cape.

Richard Aldington, the first author to discredit the Lawrence legend in England, met such opposition when he wrote his biography of Lawrence that publication was initially in France, in 1954, under the title *Lawrence L'Imposteur*. Its publication coincided with a time of escalating East–West tension preceding the 1956 Anglo-French invasion of Egypt, which nationalised the Suez Canal and caused renewed debate about the Arab boundaries. The book raised questions about Lawrence's role but it failed to destabilise his virtual icon status.

Aldington, presenting Lawrence as a romancer and self-salesman, broke with the 25-year tradition of never questioning Lawrence's role as a British war hero: 'But the most startling and disconcerting trait in Lawrence's character,' he wrote, 'is the propensity which seemed uncontrollable in him to put out highly embellished stories of himself and his doings'. He argued that Lawrence's reputation had been artificially preserved by a flock of admirers. It is often said that this book was the first to mention Lawrence's illegitimacy, but in 1946 a biography of Lawrence by Léon Boussard, *Le Secret du Colonel Lawrence*, had told the world that Lawrence's father had been an Irish baronet who lived under an assumed name in an illicit union with his mother, even though his first wife was still living. Publication of Aldington's book went ahead in England in 1955 under the title *Lawrence of Arabia: A Biographical Enquiry*. Dismissed by one Lawrence supporter as 'a shameful attack on his memory and reputation', the book was greeted with denials, counter-claims and protests by what became known disparagingly as the 'Lawrence Bureau'. Aldington told *Newsweek* that his biography had begun as 'a sympathetic study of a military hero', but he had begun to 'feel that Lawrence was only a legend, then a legend intentionally spread by him with little or no regard for the truth'.

Presenting Lawrence as a romancer, Aldington paved the way for a more balanced approach. A series of critical books followed. Various biographers suggested that Lawrence had played up the role of the Arabs in their liberation, and that their role would not have been significant without the military or financial backing of Britain. Lawrence's character also came under scrutiny. *The Secret Lives of Lawrence of Arabia*, by Phillip Knightley and Colin Simpson, published in 1969, told of Lawrence setting up situations where he would subject himself to masochistic beatings. This was published at a time when there was renewed interest in Lawrence due to the Robert Bolt–David Lean film of 1962, the 1967 Arab-Israeli war and the oncoming oil crisis.

In the notes at the back of Jeremy Wilson's authorised biography, *Lawrence of Arabia*, is what could be considered an admission that the Australians were first to Damascus. Wilson says: 'Lawrence did not mention in *Seven Pillars* that Australian troops were in Damascus before the Arabs made their triumphal entry (or that, by arrangement with Allenby, they were supposed to give the Arabs precedence). Lawrence also admitted to Robert Graves: "I was on thin ice when I wrote the Damascus chapter... SP [Seven Pillars] is full of half-truth, here'.

On the basis of these omissions, detractors such as E. Kedourie have claimed that his whole account is discredited. After visiting Clouds Hill with

Wilson, we went on to look at Thomas Hardy's house nearby. While strolling through the woods I asked Wilson why he had not included the fact that Lawrence had omitted the arrival of the Australians in *Seven Pillars*. He replied that there was not room for all the details in the text.

Although the fall of Damascus – and the chaos and quarrelling – was affected by both Lawrence's closeness to the Arabs and his romantic vision of them, there are no prominent public memorials to him in Syria. Nonetheless, he is remembered. The proprietor of a hotel bookshop in Damascus said he was awaiting copies of Lawrence's thesis on Crusader castles written when he developed his passion for Syria and the Middle East as a student. 'It always sells well,' he said. In contrast, at the once luxurious and grand Baron's Hotel, Aleppo, one can see his hotel bill from 8 June 1914 in a prominent glass display case. William Dalrymple, in his prize-winning book *From a Holy Mountain*, describes it as an 'unpaid hotel bill'. The Lawrence Society, though, says that such a remark was inaccurate and unfair; the original had been stolen.

Peter Mansfield, in his book *The Arabs*, took the view that Lawrence had exaggerated both his role within the Arab Revolt and the revolt itself. He said that 'the Arab irregulars made an important contribution to the defeat of the Turks, but there was little they could do on their own…Although there can be no doubt about the devotion and admiration of his Bedouin followers for "al-Orens" as they called him, they were relatively few in number and are now dead'. Leon Uris, in his novel *The Haj*, continued the theme: 'This Arab "revolt" of a few thousand men was led and later glorified by the British officer T. E. Lawrence'.

Lawrence's status was boosted by David Lean's prize-winning 1962 film *Lawrence of Arabia*, starring Peter O'Toole. This brilliant production gave the impression that Lawrence had had the major role in the defeat of the Turks. It reflects what was written in the months and years soon after the war, when the British and Allied forces were relegated to the shadows and the role of the Arabs was brought to the fore. Audiences do not even get a glimpse of the Australian Light Horse in the entire film, which continues to blot out the truth about who got to Damascus first.

Phillip Knightley, who has written extensively on Lawrence, went as far as writing a letter in 1980 to Professor Stephen Tabachnick. The letter was later published in *The T. E. Lawrence Puzzle* (University of Georgia Press, 1984):

> *I think much of the unhappiness in the Middle East over the past 50 years can be directly attributed to British policies that Lawrence had a hand in implementing. I think his fame was largely due to one man, Lowell Thomas, and all Lawrence's later difficulties were due to an overwhelming sense of guilt at the double game he played – not an uncommon problem for spies and double agents, I'm told.*

Knightley enlarged his theories on the consequences of Lawrence's action in his book *Australia, the Biography of a Nation*:

> *The Anzac legend was not created as a celebration of his [the Australian soldier's] fighting qualities or because Gallipoli was a great victory, which it clearly was not. If this had been the intention then the taking of Damascus by the Australian Light Horse ahead of both Allenby's British troops and T. E. Lawrence's Arabs – a triumph that made Lawrence hate the Australians for the rest of his troubled life – would have been much better material with which to work to create a legend.*

Regardless of the reason why Lawrence overlooked the Australians, his powerful prose stood the test of time and overshadowed the thousands of men and horses involved. Thus everyone knows Lawrence of Arabia but the horses and the Australian Light Horse who took part in that historic ride are unfairly forgotten. Apart from letters such as those written by Lawrence to Robert Graves and Frederic Manning, correcting the earlier mistakes and misconceptions would have been difficult as, apart from anything else, it would have undermined the positions of Abdullah and Feisal in Transjordan and Iraq.

As *Lawrence of Arabia* continues to be screened, and as *The Seven Pillars of Wisdom* continues to be read, so the myth continues to be perpetuated. But, for all that, it is a myth – and a very powerful myth – not history. The Australians, not Lawrence and the Arabs, were first to Damascus; their claim was diminished because their commander, Harry Chauvel, excellent though he was, over-iced the cake by saying that they actually arrived at least six hours earlier than they did.

Like a guilty secret worried by the ravages of time, the quiet redbrick house at 2 Polstead Road in Oxford still conveys a veneer of respectability that is somehow at odds with the unspoken memories of its former occupants. The once highly polished front door is faded, the brass knocker is tarnished, the front garden is levelled with tarmac and the sandstone in the front bay has been eroded by the weather, as has the paint around the windows.

Inside the house the presence of Lawrence can still be felt. Closeted behind a thin, pale green cupboard door in the corner of the old dining room, the pencil markings used by the children to pinpoint their heights when they measured themselves each year, are still visible. Upstairs, Lawrence's tiny attic bedroom looks out onto the same layout of the back garden and the same old apple tree. Across the landing, if one listens carefully, the sound of Lawrence and his brothers, Frank, Arnold, Bob and Will, having pillow fights still echoes. But it is all pretence. The pretence that shielded the Lawrence family from social stigma and scorn may be gone, but there are still traces of memories from a bygone age where outward appearances, such as bell-pulls for servants, grace before meals and church on Sundays, were important. Anything that rocked this foundation was to be shunned. Lawrence's parents tiptoed on a tightrope for fear of shattering their brittle shell, which was built on a lie and a false name. Their very being would have been destroyed if the illegitimacy of their five sons and the fact that the self-styled Mr and Mrs Lawrence were living 'in sin' and had never married became known.

Terrence Phillips, a retired lecturer, who has lived in Lawrence's old house since his mother bought it in 1966, says he gets few enquiries about Lawrence now, even though his former college put up a blue plaque saying that

Lawrence lived there. Like all idols, Lawrence has suffered the ebb and flow of acceptance over the years; his many biographers agree that certain episodes, stories and anecdotes are contradictory. Aspects of his reputation have become tarnished, but his tenacity has earned him a permanent place as a British hero.

Whether it is his involvement in the Arab Revolt, his days in Oxford (centred on Polstead Road), or his time in the armed forces, the same words always occur: 'mysterious', 'secretive', 'enigmatic' and 'elusive'. Clouds Hill is no exception. Like Polstead Road, this small, out-of-the-way cottage reflects Lawrence's spartan nature; unlike his old family home, though, it also echoes and vibrates with the spirit of the man.

The place is as Lawrence arranged it. There are his rows of books and gramophone records; outside the garage which housed his motorbike still stands; and above the door, in the carved lintel, one can still read the Greek inscription: 'Why Worry? Why indeed? To the casual visitor, a visit to Clouds Hill, meticulously organised though it is, is a salutary experience. There is no electricity, no kitchen. As there was no sanitation either indoors or outside, guests, including Lady Nancy Astor, were obliged to crouch and hide behind a tree. The temporary privy Lawrence had built for his mother when she stayed at Clouds Hill during his absence in India with the RAF was demolished on his return. He also removed the flowers she had planted around the house. Ronald Storrs said: 'He would provide bread, honey and cheese for visitors but he could not put them up' unless, he continued, 'it was a sleeping bag on the floor'. Just as the Lawrence myth is full of contradictions, so is Clouds Hill. Apart from his motorbike, books and music, the water heated in a paraffin boiler was arguably Lawrence's one luxury. While there was no kitchen, there was a bath with a complicated plumbing system that pumped water from a spring in the valley. But this aside, Clouds Hill ends a story that began with a man entering a foreign country, taking in its culture and trying to shape its future. It is paradoxical that Lawrence is not publicly commemorated in the Arab lands on which his fame rests. But Lawrence was a minimalist who sought isolation and obscurity. Clouds Hill complemented that nature very well.

By the time I experienced war for myself – for three months as a journalist in Vietnam – nearly fifty years after the victory in 1918, tanks and trucks had replaced horses. I saw bloodstained stretchers shouldered out of helicopters as the sergeant called 'KIA' (killed in action), and Vietcong prisoners on their way to be interrogated, roped together, being led through a clearing, their eyes blindfolded with black rags.

I understood my father's unspoken revulsion for war. As I write this I realise that, like him, apart from my newspaper reports at the time, I, too, have suppressed my memories of the horrors of war.

My experience as a war correspondent inspired me to set up a shrine to fallen soldiers. As no public memorial devoted exclusively to the thousands of Australian troops killed in Europe, Egypt and the Middle East in World War I and World War II had been built in England, I organised an Australian War Memorial at Battersea Park, London, and a dawn service on Anzac Day. This has grown each year and is now a significant event. It is due to be moved to Hyde Park Corner in 2003.

Two months after Anzac Day, 1997, the Prime Minister of Australia, John Howard, came to Battersea to lay a wreath and make a speech. He thanked me for bringing the custom of the dawn service to England. But I could hear my father saying, 'But what about the horses? It was the horses that did it'.

This book is dedicated to those heroic animals on the Great Ride, whose bones now lie in Syria. As I write this I hear their gallop, crushing the earth under their hooves, going on and on to win a bloody and dramatic war that still has not resulted in peace. The tragic long-term results, stretching to the present day, could not then have been foreseen.

While writing this book, the Arab-Jewish conflict in the Middle East once more exploded into large-scale border disputes, and it drew my attention to the politics and hidden motives of the 1918 campaign. There is sometimes a general misconception that today's clashes between Israel and Palestine stem from the Six-Day War, but, as I hope can be seen by this book, the schism goes back forty years before that, to World War I. Back to the final peace settlements with Winston Churchill in 1922. Back to the horses. Back to the

British policy to keep the Arabs on their side. Back to Lawrence's promotion of guerrilla warfare.

I had hoped that somehow the writing of this book would bring my father back to life, but he is still an opaque figure, always seen vaguely. But through my exploration of the Great Ride I have, at last, come to understand better the forces and times, the events that shaped the Middle East and helped shape him, as well as a generation of other Australian men – indeed, twentieth-century Australia.

A rare memorial to these horses is a plaque outside the Royal Botanic Gardens in Sydney – a long, bronze relief of three horses, heads hanging low, ammunition pouches around their necks, being led over sand dunes.

ERECTED BY MEMBERS OF THE DESERT MOUNTED
CORPS AND FRIENDS OF THE GALLANT HORSES
WHO CARRIED THEM OVER THE SINAI DESERT
INTO PALESTINE 1915–1918.
THEY SUFFERED WOUNDS, THIRST, HUNGER
AND WEARINESS ALMOST BEYOND ENDURANCE
BUT NEVER FAILED. THEY DID NOT COME HOME.
WE WILL NEVER FORGET THEM.

Today it is often forgotten that the fall of Damascus was also the beginning of the 'Jewish State' versus the 'Arab Awakening' and the states and mandates from which later emerged Iraq, Syria, Lebanon, Jordan and Israel. It is also usually overlooked that it was neither the Jews nor the Arabs that conquered these countries from the Turks, but the British Army, aided as may be tragically seen, from a visit to any of the war cemeteries there, by the Australian Light Horse.

Acknowledgments

I am extremely grateful to the many people in Britain and Australia who have made this book possible and I commence my long list of thanks with my late aunt, Paula Kynaston-Reeves and my sister, Margaret Morrissey, who gave me both information and encouragement in piecing together Robbie Robertson's war experience. My special thanks go to my mentor Dame Miriam Rothschild, in whose house much of this book was written, and to the present Lord Allenby, who gave me such valuable feedback on the book. I could never have pulled all the strands together without the patient help of George Haynes, Joelle Fleming, Jane Dorrell in Chelsea, Maureen and Alan Sherriff, Miriam Cosic, Carolyn Lockhart, Donald and Myfanwy Horne, the late Dr Eric Andrews, Alan Ventress, Anthony Mockler, Phillip Knightley, Jeremy Wilson, Dr Yigal Sheffy, Professor Eliezer Tauber, John Lee, Ed Erickson, Peter Davies, Stephen Tabachnick, St John Armitage, Penny Hart, Colonel Don Murray, Rick Parker, Robert Bowring, Blane Hogue, Don Gallagher, Professor Stephen Grabbard, Paddy O'Brien, Justice Kemeri Murray, Barry Tobin and Terrence Phillips.

The happiest times have been in libraries or in bookshops, and I especially thank Guy Penman at the London Library; John Montgomery of the Royal United Services Institute; Geoff Brewster at the Australian War Memorial Library; St Antony's College and the Bodleian Library, Oxford; the Imperial War Museum; the Public Records Office, Kew; the Library of James Cook University, Townsville; the State Library of New South Wales; the Mitchell Library; the Townsville General Library; the Chelsea Library; the British Library and Tonnoir's Bookshop.

There is, alas, not room to list all the people who helped and guided me on this long trail, but I would like to extend a special word of thanks to Clare Wallis of Simon & Schuster, and to proofreader Sarah Shrubb. And I would like to thank all those who have given me permission to reproduce quotes especially Phillip Knightley, Jeremy Wilson, Stephen Tabachnick, the trustees of the Seven Pillars of Wisdom Trust for permission to quote from the works of T. E. Lawrence, and George Sassoon for permission to quote from the works of his father, Siegfried Sassoon. I am especially grateful to the research done by many authors whose descendants I have not been able to track down: Harry Bostock and Arthur Olden in Western Australia and Rex Hall in Melbourne.

PICTURE CREDITS: Apart from the three by Frank Hurley which are from the State Library of New South Wales, all illustrations are either from the Australian War Memorial or my late father.

Bibliography

A Brief Record of the Advance of the Egyptian Expeditionary Force, July 1917 – October 1918, HMSO, London 1919.

Adam-Smith, Patsy, *The Anzacs*, Thomas Nelson, Melbourne, 1982.

Aldington, Richard, *Lawrence of Arabia. A Biographical Enquiry*, Collins, London, 1955.

Amery, L. S., *The Leo Amery Diaries*, J. Barnes & D. Nicholson, Hutchinson, London, 1980-1988.

Armstrong, H. C, *Grey Wolfe – Mustafa Kemal*, Arthur Barker, London, 1932.

Baker, Randall, *King Hussain & the Kingdom of Hejaz*, Oleander Press, New York, 1979.

Barrow, G, *The Fire of Life*, Hutchinson, London, 1948.

Beadon, R.H, *Some Memories of the Peace Conference*, Temple Bar Publishing, London, 1933.

Bean,C.E.W., *Official History of Australia in the War of 1914-1918*, Angus & Robertson, Sydney,1921.

Beaumont, Joan (ed), *Australia's War 1914-18*, Allen & Unwin, 1995.

Beckett, Francis, *Clem Attlee, Politicos*, London, 2000.

Bodleian Library – family papers

Bodleian Library, *T E Lawrence: The Legend and the Man*. Cat. of Exhibition, Oxford, 1988.

Bostock, Henry, *The Great Ride*, Artlook Books, Perth, 1982.

Boussard, L., *Le Secret du Colonel Lawrence*. Editions Mont Louis, 1941.

Brereton, J. M., *The Horse in War*, David & Charles, Newton Abbott, 1976.

Broadbent, Harvey, *The Boys Who Came Home*, ABC, Sydney, 1990.

Brookes, Dame Mabel, *Memoirs*, Macmillan, Melbourne, 1974.

Brown, M & Cave, J., *A Touch of Genius. The Life of T.E. Lawrence*.

Brown, Malcolm, *The Letters of T. E. Lawrence*, J. M. Dent & Sons Ltd, London, 1988.

Bullock, David L., *Allenby's War*, Blandford Press, London, 1988.

Burg, David & Purcell, E., *Almanac of World War I*, University Press of Kentucky, 1998.

Carlyon, Les, *Gallipoli*, MacMillan, Melbourne, 2001.

Carter, Jan, *Nothing to Spare*, Penguin, Melbourne, 1981.

Cocker, Mark, *Richard Meinertzhagen*, Martin, Secker & Warburg, London, 1989.

Cutlack, F.M., *War Letters of General Monash*, Angus & Robertson, Sydney, 1934.

Dalrymple, William, *From the Holy Mountain*, Harper Collins, London, 1997.

Dalrymple William, *In Xanadu*, Harper Collins, London, 1989.

Davison, Frank Dalby, *The Wells of Beersheba*, Angus & Robertson, Sydney, 1947.

Denton, Kit, *Gallipoli, One Long Grave*, Time Life Books Australia, 1986.

Erickson, Edward J., *Ordered to Die*, Greenwood Press, Westport, Connecticut, 2001.

Facey, A. B., *A Fortunate Life*, Freemantle Arts Centre Press, 1981.

Falls, C., *Armageddon: 1918*, Nautical & Aviation Publ. Co. of America, 1964.

Falls, C. & MacMunn, G., *Military operations, Egypt & Palestine*, HMSO, London, 1928-30.

Fewster, Kevin & Basarin, *A Turkish View of Gallipoli*, Hodja Educ. Co-op, Richmond, Vic.

Firkins, P, *The Australians in Nine Wars*, Rigby, Adelaide, 1971.

Fromkin, David, *A Peace to End all Peace*, Andre Deutsch, London, 1989.

Garnett, David, *The Letters of T. E. Lawrence*, Jonathan Cape, London, 1938.

Graves, R.P., *Lawrence of Arabia and His World*, Thames & Hudson, London, 1976.

Graves, Robert, *Lawrence and the Arabs*, Jonathan Cape, London 1927.

Graves, Robert & Liddell Hart, *T.E. Lawrence to his Biographers*, Cassell, London, 1976.

Gullett, H. S., Barrett, Chas, Barker, David, *Australia in Palestine*, Angus & Robertson, Sydney, 1919.

Gullett, H. S., *The Official History of Australia in the War of 1914-18*, Angus & Robertson, 1923.

Hall, Rex, *The Desert Hath Pearls*, Hawthorn Press, Melbourne, 1975.

Hill, A. J., *Chauvel and the Light Horse*, Melbourne University Press, Australia, 1978.

Howarth, David, *The Desert King*, McGraw Hill, New York, 1964.

Hughes, Matthew, *Allenby and British Strategy in the Middle East*, Frank Cass, London, 1999.

Hutchinson, Garrie, *An Australian Odyssey from Giza to Gallipoli*, Hodder & Stoughton, Sydney, 1997.

Idriess, Ion, *The Desert Column*, Angus & Robertson, Sydney, 1932.

Israeli-Turkish International Colloquy, The First World War: Middle Eastern Perspective. Tel Aviv, 2000.

Jabotinsky, Vladimir, *The Story of the Jewish Legion*, Bernard Ackerman, New York, 1945.

James, Lawrence, *The Golden Warrior*, Weidenfeld & Nicholson, London, 1990.

Jarvis, Major C.S, *The Back Garden of Allah*, John Murray, London, 1939.

Jones, Ian, *The Australian Light Horse*, Time Life Books, Sydney, 1987.

Kedourie, E., "The Real T.E. Lawrence" in Commentary Vol. 64 No.1, July 1977. 8pp article.

Kedourie, E., *In the Anglo-Arab Labyrinth*, Frank Cass, London, 2000.

Kinross, Patrick, *Atatürk*, Weidenfeld, London, 1993.

Knightley, P. & Simpson, C., *The Secret Lives of Lawrence of Arabia*, Thomas Nelson, Ln, 1969

Laffin, J, *British Butchers and Bunglers*, Sutton, Gloucestershire, 1988.

Lawrence T.E., *Seven Pillars of Wisdom*, Jonathan Cape, London, 1935.

Lee, John, *A Soldier's Life*, Macmillan, London, 2000.

Liddell Hart, B., *The War in Outline 1914–18*, Faber & Faber, London, 1936.

Liman von Sanders, Otto, *Five Years in Turkey*, US Naval Institute, 1927.

Mack, J.E., *A Prince of Our Disorder*, Weidenfeld & Nicolson, London, 1976.

Macfie, A.L., *Atatürk*, Pearson Education Ltd., Essex, England, 1994.

Mango, Andrew, *Atatürk*, John Murray, London, 1999.

Mansel, Philip, *Constantinople, City of the World's Desire*, John Murray, London, 1995.

Mansel, Philip, *Sultans in Splendour*, Parkway Publishing, London, 1998.

Mansfield, Peter, *The Arabs*, Penguin, London, 1976.

Mitchell, E, *Light Horse to Damascus*, Macmillan, Melbourne, 1987.

Nicolson, Harold, *King George V*, Constable, London, 1952.

Olden, A.C.N, *Westralian Cavalry in the War*, McCubbin, Melbourne, 1921.

Orga, Irfan & Margarete, *Atatürk*, Michael Joseph, London, 1962.Ovendale, Ritchie, *The Origins of Arab Israeli Wars*, Longman, London, 1984.

Oxford Companion to Australian Literature, Oxford University Press, Melbourne, 1985.

Palmer, Alan, *Victory 1918*, Weidenfeld & Nicholson, London, 1998.

Paterson, A.B., *Collected Verse*, Angus & Robertson, Sydney, 1933.

Paterson, A.B., *Happy Dispatches*, Angus & Robertson, Sydney, 1934.

Perrett, Bryan, *Megiddo 1918, The Last Great Cavalry Victory*, Osprey Military, Oxford, 1999.

Powles, Guy, *The New Zealanders in Sinai & Palestine*, Whitcombe & Tombs, Auckland, 1922.

Rattigan, Terence, Ross, *The Collected Plays of Terrence Rattigan*, Hamish Hamilton, London, 1964.

Reeves, N. & Taylor, J.Howard Carter, *Before Tutankhamun*, British Museum, London, 1992.

Rhodes James, Robert, *Gallipoli*, Pimlico, London, 1999.

Roberts, John Stuart, *Siegfried Sassoon*, Richard Cohen Books, London, 1999.

Salibi, Kamal, *The Modern History of Jordan*, I.B. Tauris, London, 1993.

Semmler, Clement, *The Banjo of the Bush*, Angus & Robertson, London, 1967.

Sheffy,Yigal, *British Military Intelligence. in the Palestine Campaign 1914-1918*, Frank Cass, London, 1998.

Stafford, David, *Churchill and Secret Service*, John Murray, London, 1997.

Storrs, Sir R., *Lawrence of Arabia. Zionism and Palestine*, Penguin, London, 1941.

Tabachnick, Stephen E., *The T.E.Lawrence Puzzle*, The University of Georgia Press, USA, 1984.

Tauber, E, *The Emergence of the Arab Movements*, Frank Cass, London, 1993.

Taylor, A.J.P., *The First World War*, Hamilton, London, 1963.

The Times History of the War, The Times, 1915–1921, 22 volumes.

Sassoon, Siegfried, (ed.Rupert Hart-Davis), *The War Poems of Siegfried Sassoon*, Faber, 1983.

Sassoon, Siegfired, (ed.Rupert Hart-Davis), *Siegfried Sassoon War Diaries 1915–18*, Faber, 1983.

Sykes, Christopher, *Crossroad to Israel 1917–48*, Bloomington, London, 1973.

Ward, Russell, *The Australian Legend*, Oxford University Press, Melbourne, 1958.

Wavell, Sir Archibald, *Allenby: A Study in Greatness*, George G. Harrap, London, 1940.

Wavell, Sir Archibald, *Allenby in Egypt*, George G. Harrap, London, 1944.

Wavell, Colonel A. P., *The Palestine Campaigns*, Constable, London, 1928.

Wilson, Sir Arnold, *Journal of Central Asian Society*, p. 111.

Wilson, Jeremy, *Lawrence of Arabia*, Heineman, London, 1980.

Wilson, R. H., *Palestine 1917*, D.J.Costello, Tunbridge Wells, England, 1987.

Wingate, Sir Ronald, *Wingate of the Sudan*, John Murray, London, 1955.

Zwar, Desmond, *In Search of Keith Murdoch*, MacMillan, Melbourne, 1980.

Index